Women in America

FROM COLONIAL TIMES TO THE 20TH CENTURY

Women in America

FROM COLONIAL TIMES TO THE 20TH CENTURY

A Note About This Volume

Mrs. J.W. Stow was in Europe when her husband, an honorable and wealthy San Francisco gentleman, was suddenly stricken. In her absence, he approved a death-bed will that disposed of their community property in a spirit directly contrary to the love and mutual respect that had marked their married life. The widow hurried home and found herself penniless, her affairs in the hands of a Probate Court being administered by hostile executors. Of vigorous mind and spirit, she undertook a crusade against the legalized injustice by which she was being victimized. She did platform readings, lectured and wrote. In this book, she describes her ordeal, presenting the bills she introduced in state legislatures along with lists of the notable Americans who helped sponsor them. It reviews with eloquent anger that never violates good sense, taste or logic, the history of her marriage, the economics of marriage, the legal status of marital relations and the unjust law that deprives the widow of treatment accorded a widower and callously degrades memories of respect and love.

PROBATE CONFISCATION

UNJUST LAWS WHICH GOVERN WOMAN

MRS. J. W. STOW

ARNO PRESS
A New York Times Company
NEW YORK – 1974

Reprint Edition 1974 by Arno Press Inc.

WOMEN IN AMERICA
From Colonial Times to the 20th Century
ISBN for complete set: 0-405-06070-X
See last pages of this volume for titles.

Manufactured in the United States of America

Library of Congress Cataloging in Publication Data

Stow, Marietta Lois Beers, d. 1902.
Probate confiscation.

(Women in America: from colonial times to the 20th century)
Reprint of the 1878 ed. published and sold by the author; printed by Rand, Avery, Boston.
1. Probate law and practice--California. 2. Widows --California. I. Title. II. Series.
KFC205.S76 1974 345'.794'077 74-3974
ISBN 0-405-06123-4

PROBATE CONFISCATION

Mrs. J. W. Stow

UNJUST LAWS WHICH GOVERN WOMAN.

PROBATE CONFISCATION.

BY

MRS. J. W. STOW,

AUTHOR AND LECTURER.

" I've had wrongs
To stir a fever in the blood of age,
Or make the infant's sinews strong as steel."

Third Edition.

REVISED AND ENLARGED.

PUBLISHED AND SOLD BY THE AUTHOR.

1878.

Stereotyped and Printed by
Rand, Avery, and Company,
117 Franklin Street,
Boston.

TO

MY FATHER

(Eighty-one years of age),

This Book

IS AFFECTIONATELY DEDICATED.

"Long life implies virtuous habits: it is a real honor."

FIRST PREFACE.

Casus belli.

WHY do I write this book? Why do I not do a purely womanly deed, and suffer in silence? Why do I refuse to turn the other cheek when one is smitten to a red-hot flame with injustice and inhuman oppression? Why? My answer is, "If I did not speak, the very stones would cry out against such a state of things as is still tolerated in this confiscation prize-tribunal, misnamed a court of justice; tolerated in the white light of the nineteenth century; tolerated with the spread-eagle glorification about the *justness* of the laws." I cry out because I am hurt, wronged, outraged, insulted.

> "I've had wrongs
> To stir a fever in the blood of age,
> Or make the infant's sinews strong as steel."

I have been plundered of my fortune, time, and good feelings. I have been reduced to a state of beggary, because I could not handle my private property — property which the estate owns not a farthing in. The estate, I believe, has been held undistributed — when there was no just cause for delay — for months, with a percentage accumulating on debts at the rate of many hundreds of dollars per month. In over a year and a half, there never has been a published account of the condition of the estate rendered by the executors, who are acting without bonds. This is legal *justice*, approved of by the autocrat of the Probate Court.

I would strike at the vitals of this hydra-headed monstrosity — this thieving court — which sequesters, for the benefit of itself and its unscrupulous accomplices, the substance of the widow and the fatherless, and the babes out of the mother's bosom, even claiming them while they are yet in embryo beneath her heart.

Call ye this justice? Accursed be such justice, and the framers of such diabolical justice! Bury it and them out of sight, in the lowest Gehenna and the deepest sea of Sodom!

Some of these chapters have been written in bitterness, some in mirth. The ludicrous will blossom out, oftentimes, through the sables of grief and the hot shot of injustice. The gloomiest sky cannot always weep. The maddest tempest cannot always rage. The sun will shine, the flowers will bloom, the birds will sing, and the south wind will blow.

Portions of them have appeared from time to time in the "Woman's Journal." If the perusal of them will beget thought — if thought will beget action — if action will beget reformation — then they have not been written in vain.

I make no apologies for errors committed. I have taken my texts from authority. If I am strong in my prejudices, I am honest in my convictions.

SAN FRANCISCO, March 15, 1876.

SECOND PREFACE.

Meo periculo.

Do I write these pages because I have no love, admiration, and respect for noble manhood? Nay, verily! There is not a creature living that bends the knee and bares the brow in loyal homage to the nobility of manhood more deferentially than I do. Purity of character, genius, ability, and high attainments, are held by me in the highest reverence. When I skim over mountains, or plunge through them, after the tireless iron horse; when I look down upon Rome in miniature, from the dome of St. Peter's; when I see the airy thread that unites Brooklyn and New York, inwrought in every fibre with brain-power and masterly skill; when I see the beautiful ship upon the wave, and remember the strong cable beneath it that brings the Old World within speaking distance, — I exclaim, "How godlike is man! How wonderful his daring! How marvellous the result! How the whole world would lapse into its primitive state, without his firm hand and steady brain brought to bear upon the Archimedean lever!"

Do I descend into the depths with drag-net and muck-rake, and bring hidden things of a disagreeable nature to light, with the expectation that I shall win admiration by so doing? Ah, no! I am not so blind as that. But some one must bear the cross, the flame, the opprobrium; some one must enter the fiery furnace with bare uncovered feet; some one must use "strong language" (it is the only suitable and appropriate drapery for a reformer to clothe thought in), to rouse the careless, the indifferent, the supine. I should be traitor to truth, were I to suppress the utterance of it, and to allow error to go unrebuked. I dare stand firm for right, firm for truth, and firm for duty. Evil must be combated with unfaltering firmness. The want of moral courage to resist wrong, injustice, and tyranny, at all hazard, is fatal to all reform.

My tongue shall be palsied by no fear to offend, no desire to please, no dependence upon the judgment of others. I walk by my own God-given light, not by the reflected ray of any one else's lantern. I shall call things by their right names. I shall not veneer a lie into a falsehood, nor a theft into a trifling peccadillo. I shall press forward with a firm step, never faltering, never turning to the right nor to the left; never sheathing my sword of truth, but sharpening it upon every rock of injustice that obstructs my path, with all the fervor with which Shylock whetted his knife to sever the pound of flesh. Wrong and injustice have brought me to this: therefore I have set my face against wrong and injustice in a perpetual and never-ending warfare — so long as I am able to take the field and do battle. This is my mission.

I have made an unqualified attack upon this leprous-livered Probate Court, and I never intend to abandon the siege so long as I am able to wield a pen or utter a word.

To the great cardinal principles of right against might, I have pledged my undying fealty — a fealty to which I am rendering the best effort of my life. I shall stereotype the cause I represent with action, and clothe that action in heroic habiliments. Against this solid masculine barrier which obstructs the highway of woman, made solid by subjugation, by legal ostracism, by coercion, by personal outrage, led on by the Hotspur of absolutism, I will hurl the javelin of ridicule, the logic of truth, the broadsword of relentless warfare, the arrows of conviction, barbed with untiring zeal and persistent energy, until the withes of man's tyranny are bent and broken asunder, and woman's deliverance fully accomplished.

I am ruled by despots, in spite of protest, resistance, and defiance; and the only weapon I have to hurl at the usurpers is free speech.

Readers of the first edition of "Probate Confiscation" have urged me to modify the general tone of the subjects treated in this revised edition. That I cannot do conscientiously, for I have not written to tickle the fancy, or lull the guilty, steeped in luxury and selfishness, into a Lethean sleep, whose waking is death. Let them, the would-be modifiers, be scourged for nearly three years by a corrupt system, as I have been, and then let them say whether it should be qualified or not. For, until they have trodden the wine-press of this probate abomination, they wot not of its horrors. The opinions herein expressed I stand ready to prove, if proof is called for, by facts, stubborn facts; and these facts cannot be explained away. Every reformer must fortify the position taken, by showing examples of the original attitude from which society has gradually emerged, as a comparison with its present condition, if he would provoke inquiry and discussion, without which reformation is impossible. This I have done, regardless of fear or favor.

This volume is prefaced by present and former conviction in which I have earnestly sought to make the whole subject of probate practice broader than personal grievances. It contains a record of truths, such as I am willing to meet at the bar of final judgment, and such as will place the present condition of the Probate Court, where it deserves to be placed, on a level with the plagues of Egypt.

In every chapter I have endeavored to show the bastard power of moneyed might and sex-might over right, and the unjust and cruel laws made by man for the subjugation of woman. If I have failed to do so, I am in the same deplorable condition that the boy was, who, after his first attempt at drawing, felt it necessary to write under the nondescript effort, "*This is a man!*" However *I* am not as obliging as the boy was.

BOSTON, March 19, 1877.

CONTENTS.

PROBATE CONFISCATION.

CHAPTER I.

A BILL FOR THE PROTECTION OF WIDOWS AND ORPHANS.

Jus divinum.

"UPON the death of the husband or wife, one half of the entire community property, without administration, belongs to the surviving husband or wife, together with the home and all pertaining thereto, and the other half to their children, the issue of their marriage; and, if they have no children the issue of their marriage, then the entire community property belongs to the surviving husband or wife, without administration; and no executor appointed in the will of said husband or wife shall have the management, control, or disposition of the community property, or any portion thereof. The surviving husband or wife shall have the sole management, care, control, and disposition of said community property, as a surviving partner has the sole power to settle the affairs of a copartnership at the death of one of the partners. The surviving husband or wife may sell and dispose of so much of the community property as he or she may deem for the best interest of all parties concerned, or as may be necessary to pay and satisfy all debts and demands against such deceased husband or wife.

After the settlement of said debts and demands against said deceased, and the collection of all debts due to the deceased, the residue of said community property, aside from the homestead, or home and its belongings, shall be distributed and apportioned as herein provided; and, further, that no guardian appointed by the deceased husband or wife shall be recognized in law without the consent of the living husband or wife.

"This Act shall take effect, and be in force, from and after its passage.

"SAN FRANCISCO, Jan. 3, 1876."

MR. SPEAKER AND MEMBERS OF THE SENATE ASSEMBLED.

Gentlemen, — In urging the passage of this bill, I am but pleading the cause — the common cause — of humanity, as well as of all widows and orphans. The existing Probate Court, when brought to its extreme test of legal power, has more of the character of a prize tribunal than a court of justice. The widow's estate and the persons of her children are at once seized by the court, — the estate, should it be insolvent, for the sole benefit of creditors; and the orphans to be placed under other guardianship than that of the mother. It matters not how capable the mother may be, she is only a woman; and, therefore, some fossilized grandfather on the paternal side may be created sole dictator and controller of the children, thus setting aside the power of the widow as parent. Every mother should be able to call her child her own by absolute management and control, without legal interference.

Dumas, *fils*, in speaking to the husband of the wife, says, "Initiate her loyally in your destiny, human and divine, in order that, if you should die before your children be capable of directing themselves, she may not need another *man* to direct them, but may constitute herself father and mother, the loftiest grade to which woman, brought out and developed in her full value, can arrive."

The Probate Court takes from its victim the hard-earned fruits of her toil. She can bring no bill against the estate for services well and efficiently rendered as wife, mother, nurse, and housekeeper. All persons should be protected in their industry. It denies justice to the widow by cruelly rejecting her testimony, even though she be the sole evidence of value in the case. Every person should enter the courts freely, as witness or party. Until this is done in every particular, and beyond possibility of question, it is vain to say there is justice or humanity for widows and orphans in the courts of the land; and it is vain to say that all mankind are free and equal in this nation, or that this is a republican form of government in any true sense. No one should be despoiled of any of their rights; but all should be free and equal before the law. Every citizen in the country should feel secure in individual rights, by being secured the full panoply of citizenship. In vain you accord to them the right of sovereignty, if you despoil them of other rights, without which, sovereignty is only a name. The law, under probate administration, fixes the stigma of dishonesty upon the brow of every widow. It assumes that she will only pay the debts of the marriage-firm by compulsion; and in the enforcement of this monstrous supposition she loses a large portion of her property through the manipulations of the Probate Court, besides the loss of time, and the wear and tear of clothing and good feeling. She walks the earth with the ever-conscious weight of a dead hand upon her, if the husband has appointed executors and and guardians over herself and children, which is stronger and more potent than her living will.

It is for the living that I plead. The dead are among the things of the past. We cannot foretell to-day the events of to-morrow. We are not omniscient: then why cling to the old superstitious fallacy of carrying out every whimsical wish of the departed, whose horoscope was dimmed by the gathering shadows of dissolution? How many valuable lives have been wrecked through this slavish adherence to perfecting and completing the plans of the deceased! Every day and hour brings its monitors. The things of yesterday are old to-day: they are among the events of the past. Life is the present and the future. The past is dead: it can only live in history.

The wresting from the widow any portion of the entire management and control of her half of the community property is contrary to the genius of all our laws and institutions, and sets at nought the true relation of husband and wife as business partners. To concentrate in the body of half the people, the power to make and administer the laws without the consent of the other half, is utterly irreconcilable with every principle of free government. It is the very definition of tyranny itself; and I trust that this honorable House will ere long banish it forever, as unworthy of longer sufferance.

"The victory of blood, which was so painfully won a hundred years ago, must be confirmed by a greater victory of ideas: *then* the renowned words of Abraham Lincoln may be fulfilled, and 'this nation, under God, shall have a new birth of freedom, and government of the people, by the people, and for the people, the *whole* people.' To this end I seek no merely formal recognition of woman, seething with smothered wrongs, but a practical, moral, and political recognition, founded on common rights, knit together by common interests, and inspired by common faith; where our Constitution, interpreted anew, shall be a covenant with life and a league with heaven, and liberty for all shall be everywhere not only a right but a duty. Then will equality, long postponed, become the master-principle of our system, and the very frontispiece of our Constitution. Indemnity for past wrongs we renounce; but security for the present and future we pray. This is the one thing needful. This is the charity which embraces all other charities. This is the pivot of the future. This is at once the corner-stone and the key-stone of the structure of our government, the palladium of our hopes, the crown of our aspirations."

Adult humanity should have but one law to govern it; then no one would be despoiled of any rights, but all would be equal before the law. "Are men in this stronghold of freedom less patriotic and noble than the emperor of Russia has shown himself to be in our day, when he by proclamation, fulfilling the aspirations of his predecessors, set free twenty-three millions of serfs, and then completed his work by investing the freedmen with civil and political rights, including the right to testify in courts, the right of suffrage, and the right to hold office, thus giving them untrammelled sovereignty over their own persons?"

Would it not be an auspicious moment, during this centennial year, to deal as honorably by nearly the same number of political serfs, that dwell in the land of the free and the home of the brave? Put this boasted bravery into practice, by proclaiming a new freedom, and carry it out by word and letter.

In conclusion, I ask that the widow may be protected in all her rights, as a member of the marriage-firm, as mother and guardian of her own children, and as an honest person until she proves herself otherwise, at which time legal interference can overtake her, and have redress, the same as in the case of a widower; and that she be in no way molested or interfered with by the Probate Court.

What member of this House would like to be deprived, at the death of his wife, of the management of his property for months and years? How could he sit silent while witnessing daily the depletion of his accumulated wealth, that which had been gathered through years of toil and privation? How could he be patient while his children were being beggared and himself unhoused by the unrelenting justness of the laws? O man! all-powerful man! you must put yourself in a widow's place ere you can judge righteously. You will have to be plundered, robbed, and sent forth naked, ere you can feel the sting of the Probate Court in your flesh, its hot iron in your heart, its scorpion barb in your soul.

The law should be so amended that there could be no possibility for the surviving partner to be held in mortmain a day or an hour; that the homestead or home should be held sacred and inviolable for the sole benefit of the surviving partner, and the children during their minority; that the property of the children should remain undistributed until the youngest had arrived at majority, when distribution should take place with a full recognition of the claims of each — share and share alike. If it is right to divide the property for the benefit of the children at the father's death, then it is equally important to make a division after the death of the mother. Half-orphans are more likely to suffer wrong at the hands of stepmothers than stepfathers. They are oftener turned out of doors penniless by fathers than by mothers. Protect the home and fireside from sacrilegious invasion, and protect the rights of the children.

Oh for an arrow, barbed with conviction, to pierce the hearts of my auditors! when feeling its smart, its power, its justness, they might, yea, they *would*, banish from this land this curse to widows, this relic of barbarism, this Probate Court.

How shall I rouse, how startle you, into a comprehension of the unjustness of the Probate Court in its unqualified, untempered power over widows and orphans? I entreat you to abolish it at once and forever, as far as community estate is concerned. It is a hideous excrescence upon the face of our boasted civilization, — an agonizing cancer in the heart of affliction. Banish it from our midst. It has outlived its usefulness. Its breath is putrid, its body leprous. Put it away! It contaminates the touch. The dust of the ages is upon it. Thus I make my last plea, my last prayer, before the highest tribunal in the State, beseeching it to remove this crying evil. I appeal to its members — to their patriotism, manhood, gallantry, honor, love, and compassion — to annihilate at one fell blow this indefensible and cruel law, which calls for prompt redress. Show yourselves men in noble deeds, and gods in lofty thought. Amen and amen!

CHAPTER II.

A PROTEST.

De profundis.

I COME before this people and this nation with a protest that will tingle the cheek with shame twenty-five years hence, if not now, to think that in the last quarter of the nineteenth century there should have been a possibility of such a need, — a protest against the untempered cruelty to widows and orphans, in our courts of justice. *Courts of justice!* rather let me say courts of *injustice* and *confiscation!*

The Probate Court fattens upon the widow's mite and the orphan's substance. If a man is spared the slow torture and depletion of grinding through this court, then a woman should be spared also. Why this invidious distinction? The Probate Court arrays itself in warlike attitude toward all widows and orphans. It was declared by Mr. Marcy, the Secretary of War during the Mexican campaign, that an invading army had the unquestionable right to draw its supplies from the enemy without paying for them, and to require contributions for its support, and to make the enemy feel the weight of the war.

Every widow is made to feel the weight of this probate war, as it drags its interminable and consuming weight along; and to feel, too, that the arsenal and magazines are all on the side of the invader.

What can she do? She is but chaff, caught in an ill wind, before its power. Yet she should protest and rebel, and urge every other widow to protest and rebel, until the warfare became general, and known as the War of the *Weeds*, in contradistinction to the War of the Roses, — a mixed and unjust warfare, strong and officially public on one side, weak and individually private on the other. On the side of the Probate Court it is under the authority of the laws of government, and is therefore public; but on the other side it is without the sanction of any recognized law made by God or man, and is therefore private.

Many of the most intelligent women, aided and abetted by many of the most intelligent men, are in active rebellion against the established governments of the civilized world, which are so oppressive to the best interests and condition of women, the legally disabled half of the great family of Adam. Rebellion is defined as the crime of treason, which is usually called the greatest crime known to the law, containing all other crimes as the greater contains the less. But neither the magnitude of the crime, nor the detestation which it inspires in some unregenerate minds, shall hinder our pressing forward to the final *victory* which is inevitable. "The finger of prophecy points to this movement as the most magnificent reform that has ever been launched upon the world ;" and no bugle shall sing truce till the beacon lights of victory, nobly won, are kindled on every mountain-top, from ocean to ocean, and from sea to sea.

The *just* law makes it a crime for a husband to die insolvent while broken up housekeeping, particularly if he owns no real estate ; for then the widow is stripped bare, and stranded indeed upon the bitter and inhospitable shoals of ancient and modern law. Without real estate, she is robbed of her five thousand dollars in a homestead, and no money, stocks, dry goods, or any thing else, is given her as an equivalent. She is mulcted of the value of her household furniture, simply because she had none, and of the month's supply of provisions for the family and for the out-of-door animals, if she had possessed the latter. The law allows her a span of horses, a cow, pigs, and poultry, but she has none of these ; and it pursues its unswerving course, and the reputed rich man's widow finds herself a pauper whom nobody owns. Such a heinous law pivots upon injustice and refined barbarism, and not upon any principle of honor or humanity.

A man who happens to have a home and landed property leaves his wife at his death, when the estate is insolvent, in possession of something tangible to keep the wolf from the door. A homestead valued at five thousand dollars is set aside for the benefit of the family, and at least nine hundred dollars' worth of furniture if he was keeping house, and a month's supply of provisions for in doors and out, also the horses and carriage if he owned any,— which may be very valuable,— a cow, and other live stock; and the widow finds herself comparatively comfortable. But not so with her less fortunate sister, whose husband has been overtaken by the grim messenger in the gilded saloons of a palace hotel. He owned no real estate. He was a merchant, lawyer, stock-broker, or sporting-man, and had no foot of land to call his own, outside of Lone Mountain, and perhaps not there. He left his widow no homestead, no furniture, no live stock, no month's supply of provisions for herself and babes, and none for the horses and cow which she has not got, and never had perhaps; but then, she would like to have their value in money. But no! The wise Legislature cuts *her* off without so much as the proverbial *shilling*.

What a sublime law!— that gives to one widow the value of several thousand dollars, solely because it happens to be in special property, instead of money in the bank, stocks in the hands of speculators, dry goods in the Custom House, or drugs in the apothecary's shop; and says to another widow, "Go, woman, and starve in peace. Why vex our sensitive ears with your complaints?" Such a grief-stricken and law-stricken mourner cannot resort to the widow's last ditch,— a boarding-house or a lodging-house,—

for where can she get the money to buy furniture? She cannot take in plain sewing; for a sewing-machine costs money. She might be qualified to teach in the public school department; but then, again, she would have to purchase her position, most likely, — judging from the history of the past in San Francisco, — and that would also take money. And so with every thing else; it takes money to win a position, however humble. The probate judge gets out of his disagreeable position by saying to such widows, "I'm not to blame; I don't make the laws: I only enforce them. You must go to the Legislature for redress." As well might he advise them to make a journey to the moon, or the antipodes, for redress. The Legislature is an august and arrogant body, that has small sympathy with widows' tears and orphans' moans, else it never would have framed such savage laws to govern them. "Hasty, reckless, ignorant legislation is the true cause of much of the evil. The blame is traceable to men who seek to handle subjects which they do not understand, and who are called legislators." Not until women are absolute, and make laws to govern men, will they (men) fully comprehend the inconsistent and anomalous situation.

It is said, "A person attainted of treason forfeits all his personal estate, of every name and nature" (the same as a widow does with an insolvent estate, without landed property), "no matter what its amount, even if he does not forfeit his real estate."

A community estate in fee-simple belongs absolutely to the man-owner, and is in all respects subject to his disposition, unless it has been declared a homestead. There would seem to be no reason for its exemption from seizure by creditors, which is not equally applicable to personal property. The claims of the family are as strong in the one case as in the other. Besides, personal estate, in the present days of commerce, is usually much larger than the real estate.

Thus a widow is treated precisely the same way that a traitor or felon is, who is convicted of the highest crimes upon the calendar excepting murder. She forfeits all, if her husband leaves an insolvent estate at his death, — if there be none of the special conditions which the law provides for. All her substance is confiscated to pay *honest* debts. In the name of highest heaven, has she no individual claim against the estate, to be admitted? Is it just or honorable that she should be debarred from putting in a claim against the estate, for services well and efficiently rendered as wife, domestic, nurse, and housekeeper?

Again, "a traitor forfeits all personal estate, and a felon all personal and real estate." This works a great hardship to the wives of this class of criminals. They — the wives — are punished almost as severely as the real offenders, by being stripped of all their possessions. Why not leave at least half of all the substance to the innocent family? It surely belongs to it.

If the wife becomes a traitor or a felon, the husband is not thus scourged for her crimes. She alone is punished; he is left in full possession of all the property, community or otherwise. Sex is thus branded with the stigma of infamy; the crimes of the husband and father are stamped upon the brows of his wards — the wife and children — by the open and shameless confiscation of all their goods. Can such an act be termed just? No! It savors of barbarism and the dark ages, and not of enlightenment and Christianity. In this case the scales of justice are apparently in the hands of the harlequin with cap and bells, instead of the blind goddess whose delicate touch is capable of so fine an adjustment that not a hair's weight can escape her notice. Ah! how long must she wait ere she will be permitted to assume her place, and mete out justice to women?

Equality must commence at the hearthstone. I shall ever maintain, in spite of all august laws, that the two adult heads of the household are equal in position, and, as such, should thus be held in law, — turn and turn about. Intrinsic justice demands it.

CHAPTER III.

CONFISCATION.

Caput mortuum.

It is maintained, that confiscation is no more unjust toward the property of offenders than fine, from which, of course, it only differs in degree. Thus a fine could be laid upon the family of a felon, that would take away every thing but their persons; the same as the probate law does in the case of the special class of widows under discussion.

Again: "Every adult citizen, in a community having the form and character of sovereignty, has a right to individual life; and in defence of such life they should be allowed to put forth all their energies. In vain you accord to them the right of sovereignty, if you deprive them of other rights without which sovereignty is only a name. 'I *think*, therefore I am,' was the sententious utterance by which the first of modern philosophers demonstrated personal existence. 'I *am*, therefore I have rights,' may be the declaration of every individual when his or *her* legal existence is assailed. The disparity between the laws which are made to govern men and women is as marked in its character as that between a judge and a general, between the blade of the guillotine and the sword of the soldier, between the open palm and the clinched fist. They are different in origin, different in extent, and different in object. They are made by rulers for the benefit of rulers, and to coerce a subject class."

A prominent statesmen of Massachusetts has recently declared that "the sovereign people of America are *gentlemen*." Never was there a more pertinent and truthful declaration made in the Old Bay State; and the truth, with its applied principles, extends to the Golden State of the Pacific, without one jot or tittle of abatement. These masculine laws are arrayed in hostile attitude against *all* women, but more particularly toward such as are widowed without real estate, who are living, at the time of the death of their husbands, in rented houses with rented furniture, or in hotels.

The principle of war is a denial of the right of private property to a belligerent enemy. A widow is not a belligerent enemy, she has broken no faith; and yet she is denied all rights in her property if the husband dies insolvent. Even its careful management is refused her, should there be an all-powerful creditor who objected. The executor is paid for manipulating the estate, but even this much is not allowed her out of her own substance. The property of such widows is all seized by creditors as enemy property; and there is no law, tempered by humanity, to stay the hand of the spoiler.

In ancient Rome property thus plundered from a foe became military prepossessions; and the title to an estate thus acquired was considered the best to be obtained, and its symbol was a spear. I would most respectfully suggest a symbolic death's-head and cross-bones as an appropriate emblem for the title of widow-prepossessions in the nineteenth century.

Again: "During the progress of a rebellion, every rebel's individual property is liable to seizure, upon the land or upon the high seas." Houseless and landless widows, if the estate is insolvent, are treated just as rigorously as rebels in arms are treated. No tender compassion takes off the edge from the teeth of the law toward them. It exacts its *just* pound, and has a keen knife to execute the demand. The warfare waged against widows adopts the old Napoleonic code, that war should support itself. Thus the grand headquarters, the Probate Court, is supported by the confiscated substance of the widow and the fatherless, the bereaved slaves that pine under these cruel and oppressive laws.

But this ignoble bondage to barbarous customs and inhuman laws ought to engender active rebellion in the breast of every wife and mother; for she knoweth not what a day may bring forth, nor how soon she will be caught in the unrelenting jaws of the Probate Court.

The man, the law, and its active engine the court, are the legal masters of all women; and the woman is the slave. This is not the best condition of things for either party. The ancient Scythians said to Alexander, "Between the master and the slave no friendship exists: even in times of peace, the rights of war are still preserved."

What women are demanding is, that these galling chains may be broken asunder, that the law-shackled and law-oppressed may go free. Vattel says, "To deliver an oppressed people is a noble fruit of victory: it is a valuable advantage gained, thus to acquire a faithful friend." Men will find, in the good time coming, that they have been fighting against their best interests in thus debarring woman from much that makes life sweet to man. All that is asked is, that women may be governed by the same laws which govern men. Is this an unreasonable request?

It matters not how rich a creditor may be: the law permits and requires the Probate Court to confiscate all the substance of the widow, for his benefit, if the estate is insolvent. She can retain nothing of value. Even her presents, made many months prior to the death of her husband, if they chance to be valuable, are taken from her to satisfy the greed of the creditor. He is permitted to exercise his belligerent rights to the fullest extent. Nothing is sacred in probate law. It is impossible for her to claim the immunity usually conceded to the land of an enemy within our territorial jurisdiction. For the widow in her grief there can be no just exemption;

under certain conditions, all her property is confiscated.

The Probate Court constitutes itself a PRIZE TRIBUNAL, and enjoys a fixed place in the judicial system of the United States. It seizes upon the persons and estates of the widow and orphans, the moment the husband and father has the ashes of earth strewn over his inanimate form. The hearing is by the court alone, without a jury, excepting in one single case, — the contesting of a will, substantially according to the forms derived from the old Roman code; and the judgment is against the property captured, pronouncing its condemnation and distribution for the sole benefit of creditors. In this hostile and inhuman seizure it little recks what becomes of the despoiled sufferers, — the widows and orphans. To deprive this legally oppressed class of all resources, ought to be alike repugnant to reason, equity, and humanity.

Confiscation, it is true, is as old as history itself. But in early times it was exercised toward enemies only. The innocent were not scourged. King David confiscated the goods of Absalom's confederates. Widows with insolvent estates are not recognized confederates; but, under certain conditions, they do not escape the punishment nevertheless.

Cæsar caused the confiscation of all the property of the Catalinian conspirators, for the enrichment of the public treasury. Widows whose estates are insolvent are not conspirators; and yet their substance goes to enrich the Probate Court treasury, and the real or imaginary claims of creditors.

Justinian, in his immortal revision of the law, abolished confiscation excepting in the cases of high treason. Widows with insolvent estates, and no land, and no homes, and no furniture, and no month's provisions, are not all traitors; and yet all their substance is confiscated. In the worst days of the Roman Republic, when confiscation was at its height, there were some humane rulers, like Antoninus Pius, under whom all the goods of a convict were left to his family. Nineteenth-century lawgivers had better take a lesson in and follow out these humane principles, which they now, in certain cases, wholly ignore.

Throughout Roman history, confiscation was inseparable from war. Houseless widows with insolvent estates are not warriors, and they are not all imbued with a military spirit. Why, then, treat them as such?

Confiscation was a devastating engine of vengeance and robbery during the feudal system, which spared neither genius nor numbers. The Protestants, during the theological conflict in Germany, were stripped of their possessions to punish them for heresy. Widows with insolvent estates are not necessarily heretics, and yet they share the same fate. Spain exercised like intolerance towards the Moors and Jews. They were robbed of all their possessions, and sent forth naked wanderers, without the wherewithal to be clothed, housed, or fed — *à la* nineteenth-century widows.

Confiscation, by the laws of Great Britain, was the inseparable incident of treason. It was a punishment to rebels, the same as their blood was corrupted, or as the estates of the victims of the scaffold were confiscated for the enrichment of the government. Henry VIII., after abdicating his religion and repudiating his queen, filled his coffers with the confiscated treasure of the monasteries.

During the Revolution, the property of tories, loyalists, and refugees, was confiscated for the benefit of the rebels in arms. In thus tracing the law of confiscation, from early times down to the present epoch, we do not find a single precedent that will equal in cruelty this probate confiscation of the nineteenth century.

Our forefathers rebelled against oppression a century ago; and why should not their brave spirit infuse itself into the vital being of their daughters to-day, who are yet under the ban, in spite of the blood-bought victory?

As the centennial birthday of one-half of their children draws nigh, I recognize the old spirit of rebellion, which animated them to do and die on many a well-won field, rousing within me; and I can hear the steady tramp of thousands who share the same feelings. We are coming, Mother Freedom, ten hundred thousand strong! There will be no pausing, no turning back; for there are no insurmountable difficulties to such as are determined to win. The will to do and dare is a mighty argument of success in all undertakings. Freedom is never secured as a gift, but only as a reward, bravely earned by one's own exertions, one's own sacrifices, and one's own toil.

CHAPTER IV.

MARY JONES'S PROBATE EXPERIENCE.

Instar Omnium.

To better illustrate this useless, expensive, and time-wasting operation, I will state, — with some digressions, — in as brief a manner as possible, the tedious process of probating one woman, who owed but two debts, all told, besides the expenses of the last sickness and burial. I think, when I have finished the recital, that you will agree with me, that the mills of the probate-law gods grind exceedingly *fine* and exceedingly *slow*. I have taken the record from Belknap's "Probate Law."

Thomas Jones died intestate, in the city and county of San Francisco, leaving an estate of community property valued at $14,137; and Mary Jones his widow, being of lawful age and sound and disposing mind and body, prayed to the probate judge to be allowed to manage and control the property belonging to herself and her three minor children. This prayer was most graciously granted, because there were no objections made, after having passed through the usual forms and delays of advertising.

posting, binding, and swearing, which consumed several weeks.

Twenty days after her letters of administration were granted, she had a statement of affairs ready for publishing. This should have been *prima facie* evidence for the judge, that he had not misplaced his confidence. Still he rested secure, for he had compelled her to give bonds to the State of California, for the sum of $10,700, that she would not cheat the widow and orphans of the late Thomas Jones, deceased; and, as though that were not absurd and cruel enough, she was obliged to have John Smith and James Brown bound with her. A trinity of unusual and remarkable names, — Jones, Smith, and Brown! *What a dreadful bond!* almost as bad as Shylock's, and quite as cruel. A widow's substance is the life-blood of herself and babes.

In the second form of this lightning process, the appraisers come in due order, with great flourish of trumpets, having been cried through the press, and posted in three prominent places, for ten days. What an heroic and ennobling act, that compels a widow, in her should-be sacred grief, to submit to the outrage of having three strange men rummaging through the house, pasting tickets of valuation upon every thing from a skillet to a piano, from a gridiron to a sofa! poking their inquisitive noses into closets and bedrooms, leering into cabinets and mirrors, if they could but catch a momentary glance of their asinine faces — for, if any thing would impart an ancestral expression to a man's face, it would be just such unholy sacrilege as this within a house of mourning.

Every thing that has garnished and beautified the home, and much that the wife has scrimped and saved to obtain, is coolly appraised; and, should she chance to be absent, unclean hands are laid upon her private personal property, and every thing of value which was her husband's personal property is scraped into the vortex of ruin and wreck. In the name of all humanity, — I cannot smirch the name of Christianity in this unholy, unsavory connection, — is not the house desolate enough without having pictures stripped from the walls, bureau-drawers ransacked, and the home, which should be sacred to grief, overrun with executors, appraisers, sheriffs, clerks, and reporters?

Can this be a Christian land, and such legalized robbery, disgraceful to our civilization, be permitted to be? Why not make one huge funereal pyre, and vivicremate the wife and babes along with the father and husband? It is but a step removed from the present shameless barbarism of the Probate Court; and I repeat and reiterate the statement that it is a confiscation court, created by men lawgivers to rob widows and orphans; a court which cries, "Peace, peace, and be ye clothed and fed!" should the case be a contested one; for then it must hear the objections on the other side, ere it will issue an order for the payment of a family allowance which it has previously granted.

A court of justice! It is a court of *in*justice and confiscation, and a disgrace to the age in which we live. I know whereof I speak. I am a widow, and am passing through this probate crucible for the refinement and subjugation of *relicts*. I have no more knowledge or voice in the management of my estate than the governor of this State has. Hundreds of shares (if Mr. Stow's word was of any value) of valuable stocks have disappeared altogether; and promissory notes due the estate from sleek-looking men, whose dress and bearing would suggest their ability to pay their honest debts, are put down in the inventory at "*no value*."

Why are not widowers probated? Surely, what is such sublime sauce for the goose ought to be fine garnish for the gander. Why these one-sided laws, which refuse their vulture protection to men? Would that they might be protected for one little year, and be obliged to plead daily, sick or well, as I have done, for the small pittance — the allowance money — taken out of their hard earnings, and be refused even that! I think this charming probate business would sink down low, lower, lowest, into the seething, boiling caldron beneath this crust of earth where it belongs, never to rear its hydra head again.

But to return to Mary Jones's probate experience. After the furniture had been appraised, it was set aside to her. Why this needless expense of thirty dollars, and the annoyance? Her next prayer was for an allowance in money to keep the souls and bodies of the heirs of the late Thomas Jones together; or, in other words, to prevent the family from *starving* during the administration. And then again she prayed that the roof that sheltered her, and under which her babes were born and her husband had died, might be set aside for a homestead; that, together with the four walls that supported it, and the ground upon which they stood. Now, this same lot with the house thereupon had been legally declared a homestead many years prior to the death of the said Thomas Jones; therefore this second declaration would appear to the veriest dullard a superfluity at least, if *nothing* stronger. Both prayers were granted, after rehearsing for the fiftieth time the fact that Mary Jones was the duly appointed administratrix of the estate of Thomas Jones, deceased (as though a living man's wife could be administratrix of any man's or woman's estate during wifehood), and that Mary Jones was his lawful wedded wife, and therefore his lawful widow, and the lawful mother of the aforementioned *lawful* minor Joneses.

In the seventh prayer is found the petition of the executrix to the probate judge, praying "*His Honor*" to accept her annual account, with all the vouchers, &c. And also she further prayed that the Court might appoint some person to represent the minor heirs of the late Thomas Jones, who had no legally appointed guardian. *No legally appointed guardian!*

Did not the forming hand of the Almighty appoint Mary Jones their legal guardian, before a higher tribunal than man has dared to create for the shackling of one-half of God's great human family? *O motherhood! where is thy crown of glory?*

Prayer number eight. Order had come out of chaos. Mary had every thing brought to a head, and ready to be closed up. Therefore the executrix of the late Thomas Jones, deceased, prayed and petitioned that the judge would *permit* her to close the affairs of the estate of said deceased, and retire from the heat, turmoil, and strife of public life, to the more congenial atmosphere of private life. After the incidents to the delay of six forms, it was "ordered, adjudged, and decreed, that the said Mary Jones, administratrix as aforesaid, having brought the said administration to a close, her letters of administration be vacated."

Although honorably discharged from her position of trust, Mary Jones was still a beggar at this confiscation court of injustice. And for what, pray, was the ninth prayer? Freedom, put sackcloth upon thy loins, and ashes upon thy head, and bow thy face in the dust while I name it. A mother in the free Republic of the United States of America is forced by law to pray to a strange man to be permitted to have the guardianship of her own flesh; for the legal right to protect and care for her own babes, the fruit of her womb, blood of her blood, bone of her bone, flesh of her flesh; that which germinated within her body, and whose growth and development, each day and hour, a portion of her own life was given to perfect. For this she had passed through the modern tragedy of childbed, and bit back the pain when a man-child was born; for this she had sat out the stars, in sickness, when no eye but God's was upon her; for this she would have given her life as a ransom, if need be; for this she would have toiled till the back broke and the sinews cracked.

And this was the ninth prayer!

Only once after this was Mary Jones brought to her knees by an earthly judge; and that was to be allowed to sell some real estate belonging to her children, to pay for their education. This was the tenth and last-named petition in this sickening record of prayers to a mundane potentate. The serf-like degradation of the free-born daughters of America to-day is well illustrated in this probate proceeding.

Ten times did this woman pray, during the one year, eight months, and twenty-eight days (the actual time that it took to settle the estate and pay the two debts owed by the husband); and each time the prayer was granted, because there was nothing to hinder. It cost her two thousand dollars in gold, as nearly as I could estimate; it did not give the cost of all the proceedings. She was sworn fifteen times, and bound four different times, with four different men, for the added sum of $19,200, which was $5,063 more than the valuation of the entire estate.

It passed through eighty-five different forms, and had fifty-one additional oaths, to give sufficient strength and due legal sublimity to the transactions. It took six men to appraise her property, to fix the mete and bounds of the valuation of all her possessions; one judge, fifteen different lawyers and notaries, three clerks and deputy clerks, and forty-seven other men, auctioneers, witnesses, referees, reporters, posters, two uncles, and two guardians, besides two newspapers, and the last-named *actual* and legally appointed guardian, Mary Jones. The fact that Thomas Jones was dead was confirmed one hundred and fifty-nine times, by actual statement; enough to convince the most sceptical that he had handed in his last account.

What necessity was there for probating Mary Jones? She was an honest woman, as all her acts in this nefarious proceeding prove, — willing and anxious to pay all her debts. Not a large all, — two thousand dollars and the expenses of the last sickness and burial, four hundred and fifty dollars, being all that she owed. For this trivial sum of money, — which would have been paid in one month's time, at a cost of probably twenty-five dollars for advertising, if she had been let alone, and not brought up to face the Probate Court *mélange* of uncertain fruition and public exposure, — she lost two thousand dollars and nearly two years' valuable time, besides the wear and tear of gowns and good feelings.

Talk of the sacred retirement and sanctity of

home! Put such precepts into practice with widows. Precept is not worth a straw without the practice. Mary Jones was harassed and tormented for twenty months and twenty-eight days, pestered by lawyers' delays, exasperated by probate clerks (who are not over-civil to widows), harried by appraisers, distracted by reporters, set on edge by the condescending *urbanity* of the judge, and more or less ruffled by the hundred and one other men who had their fingers in her individual pie.

There is no more call for such a court for women than there is for men. It puts, in all its acts, the brand of dishonesty upon the brow of every widow. A widower is trusted with the entire estate which consists of community property. He is not probated. The law does not lay violent hands upon his substance, and the bodies of himself and children, as soon as his wife ceases to breathe. His time and money are not filched from him by any court of *in*justice. He is left in undisturbed possession of what years of toil have brought to him and his.

This is a free country. Free indeed where such things are permitted to be! Shame upon such freedom! It is a criminal proceeding against the innocent without cause, — a corroding ulcer upon the face of our boasted civilization; and it should be branded with the anathemas of the oppressed and downtrodden throughout Christendom. Not until the criminal proceedings of the Probate Court abominations are fully ventilated, will people rouse themselves to the necessity of abolishing it as far as it relates to community property. Who will claim that the outrage perpetrated upon Mary Jones, under the cover of law, was not open and shameless robbery of valuable time and hard-earned money? or deny that it was a criminal act which should put all men called legislators to the blush?

What would Thomas Jones have said to those minions of the law, called appraisers and guardians, if Mary Jones had just been covered with the ashes of earth, instead of himself? Standing beneath his roof-tree, with a rifle charged to the lips, he would have exclaimed, "Cross my threshold at your peril! You are trespassers, and the first one that braves my warning *is* a *dead man!* If I don't pay my two debts, then let loose your legal blood-hounds, but not before!" And, if Thomas Jones had put his threat into execution, it would have been in defence of his paternal rights and his financial life, — and no one would have blamed him.

Under similar circumstances, *I* would carry out *my principles*, and defend my children and my property with my life. If I had been in San Francisco, those executors would not have found it such a pleasant pastime to pillage the abode of the dead. They would have encountered a very serious obstacle, and their full-fledged executive powers would have been called into active exercise in *executing* a very lively retreat, if they valued limb and muscle.

CHAPTER V.

THE SCIENCE OF GOVERNMENT.

Præmonitus, præmunitus.

WE hear a great deal nowadays about the science of government being included in our popular system of education; that every boy should be made familiar with the general outlines, at least, of a government in which he will have an active voice at majority. I say, "Yes, by *all means*, give every boy and girl a chance, especially the latter." I would have the girl-baby nourished at the mother's breast on probate pap; at the knee, with the nutritious lessons that the law could wrest her from her mother's arms, and consign her to the tender mercy of strangers; at the dawn of womanhood, that she was to be a servant in her future husband's house, in all save *salary;* and that, at her death, she could not will away a dollar of the united earnings of herself and husband, but that he could convey it all away from her on his death-bed, leaving her entirely destitute, that is, if it were not in real estate; that he could appoint her most implacable foe master of her substance, and the legal guardian of her children and her unborn babe, giving the dead father more legal power over the unborn child than the living mother; and that she could be held in mortmain until that child became of age. These are some of the pertinent lessons in the science of government which should be early inculcated in the minds of "little women." They should be bred in the bone, infused into the blood, so that they may remain long in the flesh, of every female child.

I know that every loving and trusting wife thinks, "Oh! my husband could never be guilty of such an outrage toward me as to appoint an enemy of mine to have power and control over property which we — my husband and I — have earned together." I thought so too; and there is not a husband in the United States that could by any possibility express more love and tenderness towards his wife than mine did towards me. But you must bear in mind that wordy expressions are but the leaves and blossoms: beautiful, fragrant, and charming as they make this life, yet they are not the golden fruition, the fruit. Only the ripe fruit of DEEDS makes these things secure and of genuine value after the lips are cold which have uttered them.

Your husband may be stricken down without a will (the majority of men usually put off the making of their wills and their souls' salvation till the last moment), and then the Probate Court at once takes possession of your estate and the persons of yourself and children; or some mercenary villain may catch your husband's ear at the last moment, when he has no power left for any thing excepting to die, and you may be robbed of all your possessions; and the *just* law protects this noble transaction.

Less than a week before my husband died, he received a letter from me — I was in Europe — in which I requested him to send me two thousand dollars, saying, "I shall have used all the face of the letter of credit by the time the money arrives." He received and read my letter three days before he signed the will, which was brought to him ready-made when he was in a dying condition, for the sole purpose of getting control of the estate. At the same time I believe that he conveyed away a large part of our community property; not for just debts, for the law protects all such — except the wife's. He did not (so they say) pay for the letter of credit which I had used; and he made no provision for my longer stay abroad, nor for my return home. And yet he had said to my sister, but a few moments before this inhuman transaction, "Tell Lizzie that my love for her has known no diminution during these years of wedlock. I love her now the same as I did the day that we clasped hands at the altar." Nevertheless "they say" that in a few brief moments this dying husband had forgotten that love ever takes a palpable expression; that the object of affection requires food and raiment, is chilled by the hoar frost, and scorched by the fierce sunlight. If Jack, his dog, had been seven thousand miles away and destitute, *he* would not have been forgotten.

Once, when we were at Santa Rosa, Jack was stolen from the office in the city; and Mr. Stow sat at the telegraph-operator's desk for three consecutive hours, and sent and received twelve despatches, and was in a state of the greatest anxiety until the wires flashed the welcome news that a large reward had safely returned the missing dog. Now this — apparently — kind-hearted man is branded, after death, by his professed best friends, with the stigma of hypocrisy and dishonesty toward his absent wife; a wife whom he had sent away a few months before, with so many prayers for her safety, and so much care for her every want, and whose letters to her had breathed such deathless affection. In the last letter I received from him he said, "Darling, I am so lonely without you! To think of the leagues, the cruel leagues, that separate us! And yet —

> 'The widest land
> Doom takes to part us leaves thy heart in mine,
> With pulses that beat double. What I do
> And what I dream include thee, as the wine
> Must taste of its own grapes. And, when I sue
> God for myself, he hears that name of thine,
> And sees within my eyes the tears of two.'

During the day I do not mind it so much; but when I face homeward (*home!* there is no home where you are not) such a sense of desolation sweeps over my soul as I cannot well express to you. Gertie — the dear child — does all that she can for me; but she cannot take the place of her sister who is so far away, dying, perhaps, without my ministering hand upon her brow. O God! When I think of the dangers, by land and sea, which you are daily exposed to, my poor brain reels. When night folds down her sable wings, shutting out all the light, a vague, indefinable feeling of inexpressible sadness comes over me, that we shall never see each other again. I came across this little sentiment from the graceful pen of Miss Muloch the other day. It touched a vibrating cord in my own bosom; and I enclose it to you, thinking perhaps that it will awaken a responsive thrill in yours.

'Oh the happy meeting from over the sea!
When I love my friend, and my friend loves me,
And we stand face to face, and for letters read
There are endless words to be heard and said,
With an anxious glance, half shy, half strange,
That asks, "After all, is there any change?"
Till we settle down as we used to be —
For I love my friend, and my friend loves me.
Oh the blessed meeting of lovers true!
'Gainst whom Fate has done all that Fate could do,
And then sunk, vanquished, while over these slain
Dead weeks, months, years, of parting and pain,
Hope's rosy banner waves gallant afar,
Untainted, untorn, from the cruel war;
And the heaven of the future, wide, cloudless, and bright,
Arches above them — God guards the right!
But oh for the meeting to come one day!
When the spirit slips out of the tired clay;
When the standers-by, with a tender sign,
Shall mutely cover this face of mine,

And I leap forward, — whither none know, —
But outward, onward, as spirits go ;
And eye to eye, without fear, I see
God and my lost as they see me.'

"I sometimes feel that this depression is a premonition of my coming dissolution. Forgive me for saying it. I do not do it to alarm you, but only to let you know, that, should the 'call' come in your absence, I should, if permitted, come to you in my outward and onward flight, and you should feel 'my spirit's wing upon your cheek.'"

Perhaps his "spirit's wing" did touch my cheek; for, the night following the day that he died, I dreamed that he was dead. These things are as mysterious as death itself, and recall what he said to me upon this subject when I first knew him: "We think we know each other, and see clearly; but we do not, and never shall till this shadowy veil of life is rent asunder."

And this is the man who was perfectly lucid (so they say) in his last moments; who made presents, and put all the property into the hands of his wife's most implacable foe, but forgot to make his sister-in-law any present, — she who had taken such tender care of him, and to whom he turned in the agonies of death, and breathed forth his last sigh within her arms. How very reasonable it looks!

Why was not the two thousand dollars that I had asked for by letter despatched to me from the Bank of California, which issued the letter of credit?

That bank was owing Mr. Stow, at the time, several thousand dollars. And, if the letter was not all paid for, why was not the balance subtracted from the sum owed my husband, instead of robbing me of any portion of it? The Probate Court awarded me seven hundred and fifty dollars to pay my bills and return home, and one hundred dollars a month, for my support during one year. The widow of J. W. Stow is to be housed, clothed, fed, doctored, and nursed, — if sick, — on a hundred dollars a month, besides paying a lawyer an unknown sum for getting it! I never, since I arrived at woman's estate, have been compelled to live upon so small a sum — until now. Why, I think that Mr. Stow gave away more than that amount, directly and indirectly, every month during our eight years of married life.

I say it, and I say it fearlessly, that such a sum offered to J. W. Stow's widow, as a sufficient amount to keep her in her usual style of living previous to his death, — even though it were not contested, — is an outrage upon his memory, and a flagrant insult upon his mode of life and his provision for his family. It says in the California probate law, that the widow is to have a support for one year at least, when the estate is insolvent, equal to her former style of living.

Does the probate judge suppose that J. W. Stow lived in an unfurnished domicile which cost less than a hundred dollars a month, let alone every thing else? He gave the rent of one of our houses for two years and a half to one of his employees, and paid the water-rent. The house rented for a hundred dollars a month, and the water was four dollars extra; making a hundred and four dollars a month that he gave to one individual.

For seven years previous to my marrying Mr. Stow, I was actively engaged much of the time in humanitarian work, and thousands of dollars in public funds have passed through my hands. But now a person who has been an employee of my husband is administering upon the estate without bonds, — a person who has never risen to first principles, and whose judgment I would not defer to in the most trivial concerns of life. Besides, he is my bitter enemy. I feel, and justly, that I am far more competent than he to adjust my financial affairs, as I have had large experience, and as I have all my time, and every one — it is a most human law — works best for his own interest. Had I been by the bedside of my husband during his last illness, this enemy would never had power over my effects. At one time, when we were at Sacramento, Mr. Stow was taken very ill, and thought he was dying. He said to me, " Darling, I leave every thing to you. I have unlimited confidence in your executive ability." No other name was so much as mentioned. In the semblance of death he thought only of me and my future well-being, while in the reality (they say) I was entirely forgotten. *I don't believe it;* and there is not strength enough in the English language to make me believe it, either. I believe that I was abundantly provided for, and that the facts have been suppressed.

Every person acquainted with J. W. Stow knew the pride of the man, let alone his honor as a gentleman, his benevolence as a humanitarian, and his social position in the community. Now, taking the most extreme case: suppose that he had sent abroad an enemy, with a thorough business understanding that the enemy should depend upon him financially; and, in the face of all this, that he should die, with all his mental faculties unimpaired, and leave this person destitute and unprovided for, thousands of miles from home and friends: what would be thought of such a transaction? It would be monstrous to to treat an enemy thus; but what can be said when such a course is pursued towards a wife? I can add no stronger evidence in regard to the character of the man than the following expression of the Chamber of Commerce: —

Be it resolved by the Chamber of Commerce of San Francisco, That in Joseph W. Stow we recognize a rare combination of those qualities of head and heart that mark the able man of business, the true friend, and the public-spirited citizen. His quick perception, sound judgment of men and affairs, ready tact, indomitable energy, and unflagging industry, gave him a permanent place in the front ranks of mercantile life, and enabled him frequently to carry on at once, and successfully, several operations, each one of which might have overtasked the faculties of an ordinary man. Of fluent tongue and facile pen, he was able to exercise a high degree of influence upon

public opinion; yet that influence was always exerted in promoting the highest good of the community. Combining rare versatility of talent with never-failing brightness and geniality of temper, he attracted men towards him from all classes of society; and so kind and genial was his disposition, that of all the thousands who came in contact with him, —

> 'None knew him but to love him;
> None named him but to praise.'

"Yet it was in his character of *philanthropist* that he most endeared himself to the hearts of all who sympathize with misery and destitution. In the organization and administration of public charities, none of his contemporaries have exceeded his sacrifices. His advice, his means, his priceless labor, and his time, were always at the service of the unfortunate. His memory will ever be green in the hearts of hundreds who, but for him, would have endured untold aggravations of the sufferings he so kindly and promptly relieved.

"*Resolved*, That this Chamber will ever recall with grateful affection the virtues and accomplishments of our late friend and former vice-president, so influential in its counsels, and so bright an ornament of society.

"*Resolved*, That we tender to the widow and relatives of the deceased our heartfelt sympathy in this season of their bereavement, and that the secretary be instructed to furnish them a copy of these resolutions, suitably engrossed, under the seal of the Chamber, and to spread the same upon the minutes."

CHAPTER VI.

LETTER OF CREDIT.

Inest clementia forti.

I WAS sick unto death for six weeks; made so by the annoyance and vexatious delays of this probate confiscation business. During that time I wrote the probate judge, the executor's lawyer, and the non-executive executor, and begged them to grant me a sufficient amount of money to pay my board-bill, to hire a nurse, and to buy some medicine. A most dignified and manly reticence was maintained on all sides. When I was able to go out, I went to the judge, and asked him for an order for my money. He replied, "It is a contested case. I cannot grant an order without a hearing on the other side." — "But why," I urged, "must I abide this delay? I have been very ill, and am not able to be out to-day; but I am threatened with a lien on my house" (private property), "and must have some money. What right has this court to listen to any contestation which takes the bread out of the mouths of widows and orphans? Why has this rich bank a right to withhold my allowance money to pay for my letter of credit, when at the present moment it is owing the estate several thousand dollars? Why am I thus persecuted?" The judge vouchsafed no reply to my pertinent questions, but turned with a bland smile to a lawyer who had a fresh widow for the probate frying-pan.

Who makes it their business to create such heinous laws, that oblige me or any other widow to plead as suppliant paupers for our own earnings? — money which has been earned as a wife; for, if a wife does not earn money as a wife, then let all women look to it in future, so that they may not take a leap into the darkness, to have time to repent at leisure in the sad light of dawning truth.

I said to Mr. Pringle, the executor's lawyer, "Do you think that Mr. Stow could have been in his right mind when he made presents, and gave nothing to my sister, who cared for him so tenderly, and with whom he lived, and would live with no other person, during my absence? Do you think it probable that he could have forgotten us both, while he remembered others, and gave away every thing of value that he possessed, even to his dog? Do you think, if Jack had been in France, that Mr. Stow would have forgotten to provide for his return?" The lawyer made answer: "Mr. Stow paid a $3,000 mortgage on your place after he was taken sick." — "What of that?" I continued: "that was money that I had placed in his hands to be held in sacred trust, before I married him; and you are perfectly familiar with all the details of that transaction. That money would have been paid years ago, and the mortgage raised, only for the advice of the lawyer, who made an egregious blunder at the time of the purchase. Supposing that money had been community money instead of all mine: what then? What had that to do with the case? Would that have provided me with bread in Europe, or paid my passage home? That argument has not the weight or substance of a straw."

I returned to San Francisco on the first day of November, 1874, with only half a dollar in my purse. I went the next day to the Bank of California, and said to the president, "There are $150 yet due on my letter of credit; and, as I have been informed that the entire face was paid before my husband's death, it will much oblige me if you will give me the balance." He looked at the letter, and said, "No: you have overdrawn, as to time of payment, already." — "But," I continued, "I greatly need the money; and if it has not all been paid, as you affirm, you can take the balance out of the money which this bank is owing the estate for services rendered it by my late husband. The letter was a free gift to me from Mr. Stow many months before his death, for a specific purpose — to travel in Europe with, — and for that I have used it. This rich bank, whose officers, many of them, were Mr. Stow's intimate friends and co-laborers in the marts of business, surely would not wrong his widow by withholding any portion of a gift to her from him, even though the law is so cruel that it would protect it in so doing."

No, it would do nothing of the kind; and it further demonstrated its power as a creditor by throttling the Probate Court for months, so that I could not get my allowance money. I had to go to the expense of employing a lawyer to get it, which took seven weeks ere I obtained one dollar of what the court had allowed. I was driven to such an extremity that I was obliged to sell my silver and a portion of my library to get the money to pay my taxes (without representation). This set of silver was the first present that my husband made me after our marriage. One lovely morning, soon after we commenced housekeeping, it arrived from New York, and was sent up to our beautiful home on Rincon Hill. He was delighted to think it pleased me so much. I think if he could have cast a horoscope of the horrible future, and seen me plodding round the streets of San Francisco, and begging acquaintances to take five or ten dollars' worth of tickets for the raffle, he would have felt somewhat differently.

I said to the probate judge, "Do you suppose that my husband made no provision for my coming home? Would you have left your wife thus beggared?" — "No," he replied, "I should not have left *my* wife thus; but Mr. Stow had a perfect right to leave *you* thus. The law protects his acts in so doing. No one can divine his motives." — "But," I pleaded, "I have a prior claim as a wife to administer upon my estate; and for that I should be paid money, which I greatly need." — "No, you have not," he made reply, "if he appointed some one else over your estate." — "But this person had Mr. Stow perfectly under his control for ten days before he died; and, besides, I will not outrage my womanhood by speaking to this executor; he is my enemy, and that of itself should be a sufficient reason for his removal. I have all my time; and he takes such scraps of time as he pleases from his legitimate business, to attend to mine. If he were an honorable man, he would relinquish his trust thus questionably obtained." The judge replied, "I will answer your questions in order. First, Mr. Stow had undisputed right to appoint whomsoever he chose over *your* estate, — as you are pleased to call it, — and you can remove the appointee only by proving that he is squandering the property, or that he used duress and undue influence to get the position. Second, his being your enemy has nothing to do in the matter. When a husband dies, the law gives over the wife to the tender mercies of her bitterest enemy, if he has been shrewd enough to manipulate the sufferer into granting the boon. Third, your having all your time, and he having his business to attend to as well as yours, does not alter the case at all. The law supposes that he will be faithful to the trust."

I would advise every *fiancée* to require an antenuptial contract that no executors should be placed over her, should she survive the prospective husband. In Hungary the widow remains the head of the family as the father was. As long as she lives, she is the mistress of the property of the deceased husband. The family is in no way broken up, and its household gods scattered to the four winds, as in our nation.

When people say to me, "The laws of California are excellent: they could not be improved," I reply, "He jests at scars who never felt a wound." I understand probate law in this State by its practical workings in my own case. My pictures were stripped from the walls by executors, my writing-desk taken, Mr. Stow's gold watch and chain, his sleeve-buttons, canes, and every vestige of his handwriting, sermons of Dr. Wadsworth's, his own written speeches, private correspondence, &c. When I asked the judge for an order for the return of these things, he said, "Are the pictures valuable paintings? If they are, I cannot issue an order for them. Should the estate prove insolvent, they would have to be sold to pay honest debts." It is supposable, with the probate judge, that all estates are insolvent until they are proved otherwise; so that nothing of value is left to the plucked widow in this high court of injustice, inquisition, and confiscation.

Mr. Stow owned no real estate: therefore I have no homestead which belonged to him and me; no horses and carriage, or other live stock and valuables that the law allows to such as have them. I had no month's supply of provisions, because I was not keeping house. No money was given me as an equivalent. A housed widow is fed for a month by the Christian Probate Court, while it lets the unhoused starve or beg, or prostitute herself, if the allowance is contested. Who stood godfather at the birth of this kind of justice?

On the Saturday before Mr. Stow's death, (he died on Tuesday) they thought he was dying, and great was the rush of the moths to this flickering and waning light. These honorable men waited till the last moment to adjust all so closely that the absent could find no joint which had not been doubly clinched against her efforts to obtain her own. A law which protects such vile proceedings is a criminal law. A law that withholds a widow's property from her own supervision, when she is in every way competent to attend to its management, is a heinous and barbarous law. No man has any just right, excepting by my choosing, to sit in judgment over my substance after the death of my husband.

What man in this Republic would like to have his fortune taken out of his hands, and placed where it would be manipulated by his bitterest enemy, — a person full of schemes for enriching himself? Are men so honest nowadays that they can observe the Golden Rule without some kind of surveillance? *I think not!* The sublime history of municipal affairs in the city in the East by the sea, and one in the West by the sea, does not warrant any such conclusion. Here is a man acting without bonds, having every thing his own way, giving such scraps of time to this matter — from his own legitimate business — as please him. He has no more right in its true sense to sit in judgment over my affairs, than he has to preside over the affairs of the supreme judge of the United States.

A dying man, at the last gasp almost, permits an employee, a subordinate, to become arbitrator over the widow's financial destinies; a person who has never risen to first principles. To set such an inferior personage over a capable woman is a gross insult to womanhood, wifehood, motherhood, and widowhood.

My husband was not to blame. For ten days before his death he was not a responsible agent. He was under perfect psychological control. Another's mind swayed his. No free volition of J. W. Stow's guided the hand which signed away our community property, making his wife a pauper as far as he was concerned. It is a most vile and unjust law that permits such a flagrant outrage upon any freeborn daughter of America. Why call us freeborn, if we are not to live in freedom, and do whatever seemeth good unto us with that which is our own? Why tantalize us with the semblance while the substance is withheld?

CHAPTER VII.

THE JUST LAWS OF CALIFORNIA.

Latet anguis in herbâ.

THERE is any amount of vainglorious boasting in California, about the just laws which men have made to govern women. Ignorance of the real facts in the matter covers a multitude of failings in these *just* laws.

A widow has half of the joint property if the husband does not convey it away before his death, and even two-thirds and three-fourths in certain cases where there are no children. But we must begin at the root of the evil, and trace this property question through all its various ramifications; then we can weigh the sands of gold, ingots of silver, and kernels of wheat, as we find them, washed clean of the sands of uncertainty, and blown clear of the chaff of doubt.

A writer says, "Law is comparatively a sealed book to women; and most women practically say, 'Where ignorance is bliss, 'tis folly to be wise.' The saddest part is, that in this they are at least half right; for a knowledge of *some* of the laws which govern women is any thing but blissful."

The California Civil Code says, "The property of the community is not liable for the contracts of the wife made after marriage, unless secured by a pledge or mortgage thereof, executed by the husband." The husband may be a confirmed invalid, supported by the pen of his wife; a gentleman of leisure, supported by the wife's genius upon the lyric or histrionic stage; an inveterate drunkard, supported by a wife's manual labor at the sewing-machine, wash-tub, and scrub-brush, — and yet this worthless and expensive appendage the just law makes all-powerful, while the real useful member of society is trodden under foot and spit upon, as far as any legal right is concerned.

Again: "The husband has the management and control of the community property, with like absolute power of disposition (other than testamentary) as he has of his separate estate;" and even then, with almost his last breath, he can convey away the community property so deftly that no known law can reach it. The wife has no legal power to restrain the husband from indorsing notes for Tom, Dick, and Harry, his dear friends, — good fellows enough, no doubt, but always out at the fingers and toes as far as money is concerned, — and thus be ruined; or by plunging into all sorts of reckless speculation, simply because another best friend grows rich upon one per cent, and he — the husband — must add his quota to the accumulating pile of such unconscionable money-graspers.

To cope with such odds, is like wrestling with a malaria, or battling with windmills. The silent reserved force of the wife, that we hear so much about, remains a silent reserved force still, until utter ruin befalls her and hers. And then, if the husband is not an unregenerate fool, he may wake up to find that Wisdom points out a new departure in the future, and that he will take counsel upon the conservative hearthstone of home, rather than at the Club, Stock Exchange, Chamber of Commerce, or the Bankers' Board.

A woman at marriage forfeits all legal freedom, unless she has property in her own right. Her individuality is confiscated upon the rose-wreathed altar of Hymen. She may have sold herself for a home, or she may have married for love; it is all the same: her place and her duties are made very plain by inexorable laws. She is a most silent partner.

A great statesman has said, "No person shall be deprived of life, liberty, or property, without due process of law; which means, without presentment or other judicial proceedings. These words, borrowed from Magna Charta, constitute a safeguard for all, nor can they be invoked by the criminal more than by the slave; for in our Constitution they are applicable to every '*person*,' without distinction of color or condition. The criminal is entitled to their protection."

The criminal's property — in certain cases — is protected, but not the wife's. She has no protection against the squandering proclivities of her husband. He can waste every thing, and the law grants her no redress. Besides, a criminal is a "*person;*" while a wife is not recognized as such in law, excepting to be taxed without representation, and hung without a trial by a jury of her peers. The sovereign people of America — it is claimed — are gentlemen. We women, it seems, are neither persons nor people; in other words, we are neither root, trunk, nor branch, but a kind of nondescript fungus, lichen, or perhaps, more appropriately speaking, a mistletoe-bough, — drawing our life and very existence from some man.

Again: "No person, whether a parent or otherwise, has any power as a guardian of property, except by appointment. In all cases, the court making the appointment of a guardian has exclusive jurisdiction to control him." A father never forfeits the control of his offspring or property, only by crime, insanity, and idiocy; therefore this provision is exclusively for the benefit of the mother.

During the husband's life he is the legal guardian and dictator of the wife, children, and property; and at his death the Probate Court steps into his shoes, and becomes the guardian and dictator of all the outgoings and incomings of the widow, taking charge of her substance and her children. And if she marries again it still retains its power over the latter. She ceases to be a free agent the moment she is caught in the matrimonial noose. The silken bonds too often prove bonds of steel and links of iron, until merciful death relaxes their unyielding power, and they fall from the crucified body, stained and corroded with the blood that has been wrung, drop by drop, from the torn heart of the sufferer. I am not surprised to hear a prominent speaker call this state of society a "savage civilization, and an infidel Christianity." It is false to every principle of freedom in this connection; a traitor to justice, and a foe to humanity.

Again: "Between parents adversely claiming the custody or guardianship, neither parent is entitled to it by right; but, other things being equal, if the child be of tender years, it should be given to the mother; if it be of an age to require education and preparation for labor or business, then to the father." In other words, if the child is still mewling and puking in the nurse's arms, the father has no stomach for it; but if it has passed the period of mumps, chicken-pox, and measles, then it is to be handed over to the father, whatever his vices may be, — as regards morality, — for of course the mother is incapable of directing its education and future pursuits in life. A person whom the law compels to have a guardian the moment she is married certainly should not have the audacity to aspire to that position herself while under the ban; for should she marry again, after a divorce from her first lord and master, there would be guardian upon guardian, precept upon precept, example upon example, — a most demoralizing and unhealthful precedent.

Again: "A guardian appointed by the Court has power over the person and property of the ward, unless otherwise ordained." This is an abominable law, and has been productive of a vast amount of sin, shame, and suffering. A dying man chooses a brother, or bosom friend, for the guardian of his young daughter — more from custom, probably, than from any lack of confidence in the ability of his wife. The child in a few brief years has arrived at woman's estate, and is very much attached to her guardian; an attachment which may end in ruin, as it has in hundreds of cases, thus wrecking the happiness of two, and perhaps three families, should the ward have married. If a husband, son, or brother of mine were to be chosen guardian of a little girl, I should use all my influence to have them decline to serve. "Lead us not into temptation."

Such laws are against nature. A mother is the only proper guardian for a daughter; and if she — the mother — be dead, then the daughter should have immediately appointed over her a woman guardian, but never a man. But, if I am rightly informed, a wife cannot act as guardian of the orphan daughter of her own sister, even. Wifehood incapacitates her for the trust, by the legal disabilities which hedge her in. Her husband can assume the responsibility, but not she. Comment is unnecessary!

I may be in error — I hope I am — in regard to this last-named outrage; for I do not quite understand some portions of the Civil Code of California although I have read them over more than once. This is one of them: "When a married woman is named as executrix, she may be appointed and serve in every respect as a *femme sole*" (Art. I. Sect. 1352, Civil Code Probate Proceedings). This is another of them, over the leaf: "A married woman must not be appointed administrator." It says that she can serve *if* appointed, but she *must not* be appointed. Those legislative Solons at Sacramento evidently hadn't the jewel of consistency anywhere about them when these lucid laws were framed. This is promising bread, but giving a stone.

Again: "The interest of a wife is a mere expectancy, like the interest which an heir may possess in the property of his ancestor. The law, in vesting in the husband the absolute power of disposition of community property, as of his separate estate, designed to facilitate its *bona fide* alienation, and to prevent clogs upon its transfer by claims of the wife. The husband has no power to dispose of the community property by devise defeating the rights of the wife." I do not understand this. It looks upon the surface like a flat contradiction. The husband is armed with full power to use the common property as though it were entirely his separate estate, and yet he cannot defraud the wife of her rights. This is a mixed problem. I pray for light, for I grope my way in Plutonian darkness on this subject.

My brother-in-law (brothers-in-law are almost as

bad, if they chance to be of the legal cloth, as mothers-in-law), who is a lawyer, says that it is because I cannot rise to the true dignity and understanding of the law. What a pity!

If the interest of a wife is a mere expectancy, what then? I may expect a full-freighted Indiaman to come sailing through the Golden Gate some fine morning, freighted with boundless wealth for my enrichment; yet this vague expectancy may never fructify. Or I may have a rich uncle or aunt old enough to die, and believe that I should not be forgotten among the legatees; and this hope too may vanish in thin air some day when I learn that my ancestor is dead, and the coveted gold has all gone to educate pious young men, of a serious turn of mind, for missionaries to the Navigator Islands. Expectancy is intangible. It is like the sparkling bubbles upon the beach, which the next wave laps up, and they are seen no more.

The homestead is a joint tenancy (unless it is made over to the wife when the husband is free from debt, or unless it was purchased with her money obtained before marriage), and subject, at his death, to be sold for his debts, — minus the $5,000 reserved from it for her benefit, — although such debts had been recklessly contracted without her consent, and against her most vehement protest.

What kind of inducement is this for a wife to be prudent and economical? The husband may plunge into every mad folly of speculation, if he can borrow money at one per cent, for which he coins his brains, manhood's strength, and heart's blood; running life's engine at high pressure, fed with brain pitch and blood turpentine, until he drops dead in the harness in the prime of manhood,—dead of high-pressure and the inflexible demands of one per cent; wrecked, stranded, in the frantic endeavor to grasp the *ignis fatuus* bubble, wealth. A man with the alluring bait of an open till before him, and once fairly launched upon the giddy maelstrom of speculation, is as thoroughly intoxicated in the uncertain game as ever the votaries of Baden-Baden were, the Bourse, or Stock Exchange.

If two men enter partnership together, one does not ruin the other financially, and kill himself by so doing, without the knowledge of the other, unless that other is a fool. A true partnership has no secrets.

If a husband made it a rule, on coming home at night, to talk over the business of the day with his wife, he would soon find an eager listener as well as an able adviser. He would not feel so stupid and sleepy after dinner either, and wish (as I heard a most intelligent lawyer in this city say) that he had a fool to talk to. A thorough knowledge of the financial condition of the marriage-firm is quite as important to the wife as to the husband.

CHAPTER VIII.

DISABILITIES OF WIVES AND WIDOWS.

Proh pudor!

"A WIFE cannot make a contract for the payment of money. The promissory note of a married woman is void." Who wants to transact business with a person thus law-crippled? She can manage her separate property, — oh, yes! how magnanimous! — but she cannot execute a promissory note which will stand the test of the crucible of law.

This is done solely to prevent a wife from entering into any business that would make her as independent as the husband. Men don't like financially independent wives. A woman can become *sole trader* only through an expensive legal process, and by proving that the husband's income is not sufficient for the support of the family.

The Civil Code says: "The court shall proceed to examine the applicant, upon oath, as to the reason which induces her to make the application; and, if it appears to the court that a proper case exists, it shall make an order, which shall be entered on the minutes, that the applicant be authorized and empowered to carry on in her own name, and on her own account, the business, trade, or profession, or art *named* in the notice; but the insufficiency of the husband, apart from other causes tending to prevent his supporting his family, shall not be deemed to be sufficient cause for granting this application." How considerate! "The applicant must publish a notice of her intention of becoming sole trader in the town and county where she has resided for the term of six months, for four weeks. The notice must specify the business, and the day upon which application will be made, the nature and place of business proposed to be commenced by her, and the name of the husband. Ten days previous to the day named in notice, the applicant must file a written petition setting forth, —

"First, That the application is made in good faith" (what a playful way to spend money, time, and good feeling!), "to enable the applicant to support herself, or herself and husband, and other claimants upon her, giving the names and relations.

"Second, The fact of the insufficient support from her husband, and the cause therefor if known.

"Third, Any other grounds of applicant which are good cause for divorce, with a reason why divorce is not sought." (The extra costs of a divorce would pay better.)

"Fourth, The nature of the business proposed to be commenced, and the capital to be invested therein, if any, and the source from which it is drawn. If the application is granted, she becomes responsible for the support of her minor children and all debts of her contracting;" and, I think, of the husband's also, for this virtually puts her in his place at the head of the household, and thus she becomes his *guardian.*

O double-refined extract of the quintessence of all masculine wisdom! How magnanimous thou art! Wherein lies the justice of compelling a poor woman to pay the (to her) exorbitant sum of fifty dollars to enable her to protect her earnings from a drunken brute of a husband? She cannot change her occupation without going through the same Christian process all over again. All this wasteful jugglery of courts and costs, and the delay of weeks and months, is humane in the extreme; for, "while the grass grows, the steed starves." The cost of court and advertising is twenty-five dollars; and no San Francisco lawyer takes a fee of less than twenty-five dollars. Under the heading of "A Noble Woman," "The San Francisco Daily Call" says, "Mrs. Minna Hartman applied to the county court yesterday, for permission to act as sole trader. She alleges in her petition that she is the mother of six children, the eldest thirteen years of age; that her husband is in feeble health and unable to labor; that he has no capital with which to establish himself in business, and is therefore unable to support his wife and family. She says she has no cause for divorce, nor does she desire one; and that she is better able to support the children than her husband is. She asks to be permitted to establish a trading-house on a cash capital of $400, loaned to her by her husband's brother."

Is not this a lovely free country, where Minna Hartman cannot safely earn money without paying tribute to a court of justice? What business has the county court, or any other court, to pry into her family history, publishing it to the world? or to dictate to her whether she shall cultivate pullets or potatoes, or occupy herself with dry-goods or drudgery, for a livelihood? This equitable court is truly *pons asinorum.*

A drunken reprobate of a protector, in Ohio, sold two cows which his industrious wife and children had earned. The sale of the milk of these cows largely supported the family of little ones. Judge and jury — for the wife tried to protect her own property — knew that the money obtained for the sale went for whiskey, and that the poor hard-working mother's babes might go hungry and cold on account of the legal robbery; yet they protected their peer, and plundered the disfranchised creature of chivalric protection.

O man, man! the flaming sword that hung at Eden's gate will yet cleave with its terrible edge woman's oppressor.

Thousands of dollars jointly banked in a savings institution, in the names of husband and wife, can be entirely drawn out by either party during the husband's life. But at his death the widow can only draw out three hundred dollars of it. For the want of these precious thousands she may lose all her mortgaged private property, while the banked money is being slowly dragged through this green-baize, red-tape probate mire of rotting hopes and the skeletons of dead men's estates.

Why is not a widower bound to this wheel within a wheel of invisible motion? Why is he not chained to this Promethean rock, JUSTICE, while the black vulture Probate fattens upon his vitals? Why, O lordly law-makers, why?

A man in Oregon died, leaving an estate appraised at $2,700, and appointed a friend in San Francisco executor. This friend in speaking of it said to me, "I lost three weeks time from my business, in going and coming, and in court. I made no charges whatever; and all my poor friend's widow, who is in delicate health, got out of it, was $500, — not quite one-fifth. The court, lawyers, ragtag and bobtail, got the other four-fifths and over. The loss I personally sustained, from being absent from my business, was worth to me more than the estate was valued at."

A widow is not allowed to testify in her own behalf, although she may be the sole witness of value in the case. It seems that no one is permitted to testify for her benefit. In my own case, my sister, at whose house my husband died, was put upon the witness-stand; and, the moment she opened her lips to speak, the right hands of the three opposing lawyers flew aloft, accompanied by three stentorian voices, "Stop, stop, stop! that is a question of law, and therefore not admissible." And in that manner the entire evidence was stifled, as mine had been the day before. The following article was read from the abridged Civil Code, to substantiate the position taken:—

"A husband cannot be examined for or against his wife without her consent, nor a wife for or against her husband without his consent; nor can either, during the marriage or afterwards, be, without the consent of the other, examined as to any communication made by one to the other during the marriage: but this exception does not apply to a civil action or proceeding by one against the other, nor to a criminal action or proceeding for a crime committed by one against the other."

Does this act extend to dead men and women? If it does, then it should be stricken from the statute-books forever, for it is an insult and an outrage to common sense, let alone common justice.

Women should have the same protection in marriage as men. But what would become of the vultures that draw their sustenance from the Probate Court in that case? The pompous officials, professional and loathsome parasites, would have to seek fresh fields and pastures new,—the judge, with his $5000 a year, at four hours *per diem;* the army of clerks (but never a woman) with their fat salaries, wrung out of the hearts of oppressed mourners; the lawyers, whose name is Legion; the despicable leeches, hanging by their eyelids to the outer walls of this hideous Golgotha, starting up like an unseen pestilence wherever there is a forgotten heir, with, "If you please, y'r Honor, there's a *minor* in the case, which I'll represent;" then the judge with a knowing smile answers, "Yes, there is a minor heir," and allows this sneak-thief to write down his name as the legal representative of the minor heir; for which laudable act he is paid, out of the rapidly evaporating property of said minor heir, fifty dollars to start with. Verily, the ways of the Probate Court are mysterious and past finding out!

There is a widow in San Francisco, who has been in probate for five years, at a cost of $10,000, whose husband tried by every device known to law to protect his wife and children, in case of his death, from being subjected to the depleting process of the Probate Court. All appeared to be safe at his death; but, lo and behold! at the expiration of seven or eight months a child was born, which at once took the position of the "minor heir." And then began the probating in terrible earnest, and the poor tortured mother is still upon the rack. The lance struck deep, for "there was money in it."

I met a woman in the outer court of the probate prize-tribunal, a widow of a prominent judge. She said to me, "Seven years have I been fighting this godless abomination, misnamed a court of justice. I have spent thousands and thousands of dollars, besides the loss of time. My soul is filled with the gall and wormwood of all bitterness; but I will fight it till I die, and, like Macbeth, die with harness on my back."

This woman looks twenty years older than she did seven years ago. She has grown gray in the warfare. Heartless men jeer and taunt her heroic efforts. It calls for heroic courage to combat with long-established errors. Men, scoffing, say that she has had every lawyer in San Francisco. What of it? That of itself should move the stoniest heart to pity.

A Mr. Beal recently died in Oakland. He was a wealthy man, and left the palatial family residence to the widow, with an income of $600 a month for her support, until such time as she should desire to marry again. But, when she ceases to be Widow Beal, she is to be turned out of doors, with the stupendous sum of one dollar. And further, "this curious instrument" — that's what the dailies call it — dictates that if the children, who are also well provided for, should dare to change their religion, and forsake the gods of their father, they are to be sent adrift with a like sum, — one dollar. What kind of absolutism is this to wield in a land full of spread-eagle freedom, equality, and justice?

There are various kinds of widows in this Golden State, — peaceful and refractory, mild and belligerent. The former are full of self-abnegation and self-abasement. They would not break a will to establish their rights, and secure what belonged to them by law, because the husband had stolen from them for memorial aggrandizement. Oh, no! They wouldn't do such a naughty thing!

This is the style of wives and widows that men dote on. As wives, they always meet a dissolute and depraved husband with faces wreathed in winning smiles; and words of honeyed sweetness fall from their lips, while the heart is full of irrecoverable stabs, and bleeding at every pore, and the head is a fountain of tears. I am familiar with the history of one such. She and her lord came to California when it was a howling wilderness of sand, lions, and wild-cats, and settled on a ranche. There she bore him six children, doing all her own work indoors, and at harvest-time assisting in the fields. Thus they lived away their youth and early maturity. One day the messenger called for the husband to cross to the other side. When they thought him safely over, the will was opened, and divulged the fact that he was a far-seeing humanitarian; for he had willed nearly all the joint property to benevolent institutions, and left his wife only five thousand dollars.

She could break the will; but, as I have said, she preferred to *abnegate* rather than go contrary to the wishes of her august and ancient Adonis. The estate was valued at several hundred thousand dollars; but the peaceful widow ekes out a meagre existence on the income of $5000, because she would scorn, at her time of life, to be anathematized by all old-time husbands and old-time husband-abiding wives, as a woman's-righter, crusader, or any kind of a rebel.

I have personally lost over $10,000 in my two years' probating; that is, if I count my time of any value, which I certainly do, let alone the wear and tear of clothing, and that which is priceless above all wealth, health and good feelings; while the community estate is turned out of the probate disintegration-mill, in the usual form,—insolvent.

Mr. Pringle said to me, in that pleasing hesitancy of voice peculiar to him, one day when we were gathered in the court-room,—

"Mrs. Stow, you must be a very unhappy woman: you seem to have no faith in men or law." I replied, "I have such strong reasons to have faith in both, that it is rather surprising that I complain. Just men, and just laws made by just men, have taken every thing of worldly goods which were the joint property of me and mine; they hold me here in durance vile when I wish to be elsewhere. My precious time, my precious substance, and my precious good feelings, are trailed through this Barbary coast court day after day. Each day my substance becomes smaller by degrees and beautifully less; each day my wrath and indignation augments and blazes with a fiercer, hotter glow; and you wonder why I am not amiable and altogether lovely (which would be a physical impossibility) under such circumstances. You will have to be a widow, flayed alive, ere you can appreciate the situation, ere you can taste the gall and sip the wormwood."

Edward opened his mouth to speak; but just at

that moment the judge came softly out of his den, like a tiger-cat, and with a wary look and supple step mounted the official platform, and took his official cushioned seat, — called a bench, — which official cushion is stuffed with male votes. If one feminine vote helped to soften that padded chair, upholstered with crimson velvet, the judge would not be so fearfully exact with widows.

Women are realizing daily how powerless is the hand that holds no ballot. The sixteen thousand women of Chicago, who petitioned the mayor and common council to close the rum-holes on Sunday, are a standing army of evidence to this fact. They were assailed upon the street by a mob of *voters*, with their mouths filled with obscenity and profanity that was enough to make Billingsgate shudder. Mayor Colvin is an honest man, for he spoke the truth to those sixteen thousand disfranchised petitioners. Said he, "Ladies, you have no power to help to lift me into office again. I was elected with this one thing expressly in view; and I shall obey the behests of my constituency, and sign that ordinance to-morrow morning, though a million women were appealing to me." Probate judges are as outspoken in deed, if not in word.

Again: "A guardian of a child born, or likely to be born, may be appointed by will or by deed, to take effect upon the death of the parent appointing." This monstrous law has its iron grip within the body of the mother, upon the babe beneath her heart.

Could there be a more frightful barbarity than this? It is not surprising, with such savage laws, that so many men are lower than the brutes, or that there are so many wives murdered by husbands.

And these are the boasted laws of California, *so just!*

> "Go, ring the bells, and fire the guns,
> And fling the starry banner out;
> Shout 'Freedom!' till your lisping ones
> Give back their cradle shout."

Yet again: "The husband, with his last audible breath, may place an executor over the community property," who may be the wife's bitterest enemy, and who may have obtained — during the last sickness — a perfect psychological power and control over the dying man. The wife is thus robbed of the money paid for the administration (which money is most wisely and humanely paid before the family allowance), and it flows into the pockets of her foe; and the just laws protect this creature in his ill-gotten power. He may act without bonds; and there is no possible way to know whether he is dealing honestly with his enemy the widow, or not. The court supposes that a man in the throes of death knows what he is doing, and that he would not appoint a dishonest person to sit in state over the financial affairs of the widow. Men are so very honest nowadays that no one ought to question such childlike faith in an executor. Still the widow may feel that her own judgment might satisfy her better than the questionable judgment of an implacable foe.

Is it just or right that a husband should be armed with such an unbalanced panoply of power over the joint estate which has been earned together? By the wife's efforts and economy she has, most likely, contributed her half toward the family estate. Which leads the hardest and most dangerous life, the woman who runs the intricate machinery of the household, bears the children, and does battle with crude, uninstructed servants, or the man down town with his educated clerks or posse of trained workmen? Men need but to exchange places with women, for ever so short a time, to fully realize that the larger number of them bear half life's burdens, without the additional weight of cruel and oppressive laws. It is a criminal law that creates a power which is capable of placing either the husband or the wife at the mercy of a foe, after the death of the other. I hold that an enemy is bound, in all reason, to be false to his trust. He looks out for his own profit, not the foe's.

"Mankind is ever weak, and little to be trusted:
If self the wavering balance strike, it's rarely right adjusted."

If it is right for a man to put an executor over an estate at his death, then it is just as right that a woman should have and exercise the same prerogative. She would be just as wise as he, at the last moment. She should be permitted to choose a guardian for her children, as well.

Sarah Siddons — the queen of tragedy — said to

her inferior husband, whom her talents supported, and who prodigally squandered her money in foolish speculations, "Be the *master* of all while God permits; in case of your death only let me be put out of the power of any person living."

I think the same prayer may be safely reiterated by every wife to-day. Here was a poor stick of a man, an invalid, and a great expense upon his wife's time and purse, besides his passion for speculation, wherein he lost large sums of her hard-earned money; and yet he was the lord and master, — the supreme dictator of the noble woman he called wife.

The old Romans used to put their wives to death if they drank wine. The same tyrannical spirit is extant in this age. It is true that women are permitted to drink wine, but they are denied all voice in the government. I would rather help to make the laws by voting honesty into office, and putting corruption out, than to drink wine, if I am to be denied either privilege. A husband can ill-treat the wife in such a manner that to remain under the same roof is daily suicide; and, to escape this lingering death of torture and persecution, she flees for shelter and protection elsewhere. The just law, in this case, not only gives the legal brute, the husband, the entire property, but the custody of the children also, unless she can bring indisputable proof of his cruelty; and that she is not always able to do, for a wife often suffers from nameless wrongs inflicted upon her by a husband who, to all appearance, is among the best of men and a worthy citizen.

Without proof she can get no pay for her many years of hard labor ; and, as though this were not inhuman enough, the fiend of a husband publishes to the world that he will not pay for her support. He pay for her support ! He is a law-protected thief, as well as an inhuman tyrant, fit for nothing but a chain-gang, who has stolen her youth, her children, her earnings, and branded her good name by posting her through the press of the country.

Oh, shame ! shame ! ! shame ! ! !

CHAPTER IX.

THE LAW LIBRARY.

Quo jure.

THE California Civil Code and Belknap's Probate Digest had been my inseparable companions for weeks, when one day, after the perfume and flame of the condensed extract of masculine wisdom had somewhat palled upon the taste, a bold thought possessed me. I would steal into the camp of the enemy, — the Law Library, — and discover that "swan's nest by the river," Schouler's "Domestic Relations."

With a firm step I ascended the stairs, resolutely paced the hall, boldly pushed open the door. No lawyer fainted; and the polite librarian instantly came forward, and seated me at the judge's table, and placed the open "Domestic Relations" before me, with a hard-nibbed pen, and a cruse of ink the color of Sheridan's trusty steed.

How courageous I felt as I sat there taking notes, — galvanized corpses of past ages, — and heard the suppressed and terrified whisperings and mutterings (I was near the door) as some timid foe peered through the half-open portal, but dared not enter! Hearing the deep orotund of one of San Francisco's shining bar-lights, I coolly faced about in the judge's armed chair, and begged him — the rosy lawyer — to advise me in regard to some perplexing legal difficulty. He expressed no surprise at seeing me there, and gave the desired information gratuitously, which showed a heart commensurate with his voice and fame.

He further informed me that Schouler's "Domestic Relations" were *old relations*, and therefore not wholly to be trusted. In other words, they were as variable in their application nowadays as the changing whims of grand-jurymen; that the Supreme Court might give one version as law and gospel to-day, and another to-morrow, &c. Then I lost confidence in those "Domestic Relations," and closed my book, and gathered up my notes and wraps; and that seat at the judge's table and that Law Library have known me no more since that daring and memorable day — greatly to the peace and joy of the cautious and uncertain enemies. Before I had seen the probate judge, I was warned by an anxious lawyer, that I must be very careful not to offend *his Honor* by look or word; for, if I did, it would go hard with me. In other words, he was to be handled with gloves on, or with the tongs. However, like the woman who dared, if I might not aspire to speak to him, there would certainly be no harm in writing him a note, setting forth my grievances and necessi ties; and I did. But woe was me! the judge handed that private missive to my lawyer; and my lawyer immediately passed it to the warning lawyer, who came to me (I was in court) with a face — I won't say as long as a broom-handle, for I don't mean to exaggerate: the truth is bad enough — but it must have elongated an inch; and said he to me, in a sepulchral whisper, "Didn't you know better than to write to the judge? If you were a man, you would be sent up for sixty days for contempt." How I hugged myself, and rejoiced that I was not a man to be sent up! But then, if I had been sent up for two months, my board would have been thrown in, and that was an important item just then. Perhaps, after all, it was better to have been a man, even under the questionable conditions of being sent up.

Why is it contemptible to write to a probate judge? I have, nothing daunted, written him since, or the court rather, and thereby caused much merriment. When I was sick unto death, I wrote a note addressed to the Probate Court, and asked it to "show cause" why my allowance was withheld from me, stating that I was very ill, and in great need of money; and begged that honorable body the court to issue an order for the payment of the monthly allowance that the judge had awarded me.

Now, over this "show-cause business," I learned by the warning lawyer that he and some brother lawyers, joined by the judge, laughed themselves nearly sick in the court-room. A grand cause for merriment, surely! Most worthy the time, place and circumstance! Very funny!—a widow of a prominent citizen, in sickness, begging for enough of her own substance to buy medicine and bread, and pay for a nurse; and this, too, money previously granted for her support. A most laughable thing! But the cream of the joke, however, was that there was no further notice taken of my plea. What mattered it to them, after their laugh, whether I died of hunger or the want of sick-room care, or got well to pester them further with my unprovided needs?

The executor's lawyer said to me, in the office of the non-executive executor, "Mrs. Stow, you seem to blame me and the creditors because we cannot depart from the strict letter of the law. If you were actually starving, we couldn't help it. I *must* take away your allowance to cancel this letter of credit if I can. *This is law.* It may seem hard to you, but I am compelled to do my whole duty in my profession: it matters not whom it hurts. You must blame the law, and not me. Besides, we don't like your calling us Mr. Stow's Cæsar friends. That, you know, casts opprobrium upon our regard for him."

"True friendship extends beyond the grave," I made reply, "and it rarely bears upon its branches the bitter fruit of persecution. For over three months you withheld from me my hundred shares of tobacco stock, my Christmas present from my husband. Was that honoring the memory of a dead friend?

"You say that he had no right to make his wife a Christmas gift when he was in debt; that he was not a free agent. Yet he owed me the value of that stock, many times repeated, for household services. I claim that a wife, housekeeper, and sick-nurse, earns some money that a husband is bound in all honor, if not by law, to respect, and that he should pay her for such services. The law protects the servant's wages, but not the wife's. Besides, this stock never cost Mr. Stow a farthing. It was given to him for the use of his name, as you well know, when the company was organized."

What kind of a monopoly is this one per cent, which dictates to a husband whether his wife shall have any payment for services or not, or a present at Christmas? A monopoly of manhood is worse than serfdom. This frightful curse of manhood-monopoly is sapping the foundations of our nation to-day. Men are bought and sold like human chattels in the market-place, like beasts in the shambles. Here and there sit human vampires, with their subtle meshes woven so closely around their victims, that to stir without their permission is certain financial death. *O Freedom! where art thou fled? O Liberty! where is thy abiding-place?*

The traffic and monopoly of manhood extends from the highest to the lowest offices of the States and nation. Men to whom the people have committed the national interest, and who conduct the national affairs, are not freemen. This plague-spot of corruption permeates even to the public-school department, until what looks fair may be but seeming. The whole system is rotten at the core, and festering upon the surface. Right is down, with dust and blood upon its brow, while Wrong runs rampant up and down the land.

"Woe, a thousand times woe, to mankind, should there be no force on earth to maintain the laws of justice and humanity! Woe to freedom, if every despot of the world may dare to trample down the laws of humanity," desecrating and pillaging the hearthstone under the guise of legality, unhousing and prostituting widows and orphans!

Just here I would say to every woman who is earning money, and about to be married, that she had better come to some business understanding with her dear Charles Augustus, or she will find, too late, that she is working — after marriage — like an apprentice, for board and clothes, and that the money for clothes comes like pulling molar teeth.

That old fossilized idea holds its place in men's minds with a tenacity worthy a better cause, that wives earn no money. A housekeeper is paid good wages, while a woman in that capacity, fulfilling the duties of wife and mother, earns nothing, — is supported by the husband. What an absurdity! If a woman earns nothing fulfilling the duties of wife, then all women had best look to it in the future, so they may not take a hasty leap in the darkness, to have time to repent at leisure in the sad light of dawning truth.

If husbands wère more generous with their wives in money-matters, there would not be so many destitute widows and orphans in the world, whose only avenue of escape from starvation lay through the ever-open door of prostitution. Women, as a general thing, are far more conservative in money-matters than men. Whenever money comes hard it is spent with thoughtful care. The money of most wives comes very hard.

The Probate Court is a high-school of prostitution. It furnishes the widow and orphans support for one year only, if by any possibility it can proclaim an anticipated insolvent estate (with it all estates are insolvent until they are proven otherwise), meanwhile holding it for years undistributed, thereby letting the interest on debts and its own pay absorb every thing, while the widow and orphans work, if they can get employment, beg, starve, or prostitute themselves, for a livelihood. And this is justice!

When the estate is intestate, should there be an all-powerful creditor who objected to the widow serving as executrix, the court respects his wishes; and she is thus robbed of the price paid for the administration of her own substance. And *this* is justice!

Women have endured this state of things unrepiningly, because they have dwelt in a perpetual childhood. Children cling to leading-strings as a necessity, and feel it a benefit to be led. Out of the childlike attachment for the fancied protection of man, the duty of blind obedience was framed by the cruel hand of oppressors. The scene is slowly changing. Women are becoming, day by day, conscious of their disabilities, and the heavy burdens laid upon them by their long-time protectors. They would be free. The spirit of freedom moves through the air, and ought to rouse every manacled soul to action.

In the great struggle between liberty, human rights, and male absolutism, they will be compelled to act an heroic part. When the struggle is about principle, indifference and inactivity is suicide. He who is not for freedom is against freedom. There is no third choice. Every one who pleads for liberty for women pleads for humanity; and every blow struck for liberty is struck for humanity. Without justice and freedom, life is only a mockery; and peace purchased by servile submission to tyranny, a delusion and a burden.

There is a just God in heaven, and there will yet be justice on earth. The day of retribution begins to dawn; its shafts of light pierce the darkness which has so long hung like a pall over the path of woman. She is beginning to walk by her own light; or, rather, the divine light, which radiates above every human pathway if we will but see it, instead of ever groping our way by a borrowed or reflected light. There is nothing more intimately associated with the idea of freedom than the right of every mind to search for truth in its own way, and by its own individual light, — the right of private judgment.

CHAPTER X.

PROTECTION AND SUBORDINATION.

Ex ungue leonem.

It is claimed that most women have no intellect, or ability for self-support or self-government. If this be true, then why are men so alarmed at their using what little they have? The soul grows by what it feeds upon, which either broadens or narrows the mental calibre. Women should have every opportunity to expand their views by direct contact with the discipline of life. I would say to men, "Open wide the doors that have so long debarred women from a seat by your side. Take nothing for granted without a fair trial. The fountain will not rise higher than its source." Macaulay said in the English Parliament, "Throw open the doors of the House of Commons, throw open the ranks of the imperial army, before you deny eloquence to the countrymen of Isaiah, or valor to the descendants of the Maccabees."

If we are weak, why add to our misfortune by protective and oppressive laws? Take away your protection, — we have had enough and too much of it,—and give us the other extreme for variety.

Nations have been protected, and have suffered just as women are suffering to-day, in consequence thereof.

Protection and subordination are synonymous terms.

Literature in England, in former times, enjoyed the protection and encouragement of the patrician classes; and authors became the servile slaves of the crown and aristocracy. They begged for the patronage of the great as a tramp begs for a crust of bread, or as woman has plead for justice at the hands of man since time began. A protective policy is based upon ignoble dependence and subordination, and not upon the principles of freedom and equality.

During the fifty years that Louis XIV. wielded the sceptre in France, every man of letters became a vassal of the crown. Every book was written with a view to the royal favor; and to obtain the patronage of the king was considered the most decisive proof of intellectual eminence. Le Vassor bitterly said of that time, "The French are so accustomed to slavery that they do not feel the pressure of their chains." Most women have been accustomed to political slavery so long that they do not feel the pressure of their chains.

Religious protection in the reign of Louis XIV. cost France half a million of her most industrious inhabitants, who fled to different countries to escape death. Every vestige of liberty was destroyed, and a despotic system of protection and persecution deluged the fair land in blood. Religious protection was forced upon them just as special legal protection is forced upon women in the nineteenth century after they have outgrown it. The Church protected, and prohibited, men from taking the trouble to think for themselves. They were burnt at the stake, and drawn and quartered, if they dared to have a mind of their own.

The church policy and the feudal system were alike degrading. Men looked up to the Church or to the nobles. Thus aristocracy had its birth in feudalism, which gradually supplanted the Church in power, in the older nations; but in this more youthful nation we have a metallic or moneyed aristocracy, and an aristocracy of sex, which is world-wide with but one exception, and that of blood. Nothing but high birth can remove the stigma of sex. Royalty and patrician blood pull down the bars that exclude sex; but to plebeian blood and simple worth they yield not.

Marks of favor during the reign of Louis XIV., both in England and in France, were but the badges of servitude. The recipients were no longer free agents: they were only the pliant tools of the Protectors — just as women have always been the pliant tools and creeping-vines to their male protectors. The most noble and satisfactory protection that any one can have is self-protection. That is God-given to all the animal creation, if they are permitted and taught how to exercise it. "Whoever begins the world for himself by losing his independence, will end by losing his energy," is a most truthful maxim.

King George exercised his protective policy on his New World colonies, a hundred years ago; but the colonists had no more taste for protection then than some of their grand-daughters and great-grand-daughters have to-day. They — the colonists — didn't like it, and made a somewhat palpable demonstration of their dislike; just as women are now doing, but with different weapons. The sword, hand, and brain bring quicker results than the pen, hand, and brain; but no more certain, as the near future will prove, I trust, in the emancipation of all women from political bondage. Taxation without representation did not succeed in those days, any more than it will succeed in the good time coming.

One of England's greatest historians speaks of King George's trying to tax the colonists who had no voice in the House of Parliament, as "a scheme of public robbery, which the independent spirit of the colonists manfully resisted. And, in order to enforce the monstrous claim of taxing a people without their consent, open war was declared." Women are taxed just as wrongfully to-day. The male descendants of those stubborn old rebels have wielded King George's sceptre over women ever since the glorious victory. Like the man in Biblical history, as soon as his own debt was forgiven, he went straight and laid violent hands upon one, for like offence, inferior to himself in power.

The English historian further remarks, "This brave people, provoked by the injustice of the English government, rose in arms, turned on their oppressors, and, after a desperate struggle, gloriously obtained their independence. In 1776 the Americans laid before Europe that noble Declaration, which ought to be hung up in the nursery of every king, and blazoned on the porch of every royal palace In words, the memory of which can never die, they declared that the object of the institution of government is to secure the rights of the people; that from the people alone it derives its power."

A century ago men felt the need of being free, and rebelled against intolerant arrogance and usurpation. The same feelings are slowly but surely rousing in the breasts of the wives and mothers who have waited a hundred years for their wrongs to be redressed. Supplications and prayers have proved abortive. Now they demand their rights with a dauntless eye and firm lip. They have armed themselves with the panoply of true faith, and have stepped forth with a challenge to men, to "show cause" why their demands are not fully and speedily granted.

Call it rebellion if you will. They who sow injustice must reap rebellion. There have been various kinds of rebellion among men of all nations, classes, and creeds, and all fought out at the bayonet's point and the cannon's mouth; but this feminine hearthstone rebellion shall be the greatest of them all, — a sex rebellion which embraces all Christendom, and upon whose banner shall be embossed the emblems of all nations.

Webster said, in one of his great speeches, "Government owes high and solemn duties to every citizen of the country. It is bound to protect him," not her, "in his most important rights and interests." Women are not citizens: therefore they are not protected. "But human reason — that divine spark which even the most corrupt society is unable to extinguish — is beginning to display its power, and disperse the mists in which it has been so long enshrouded," as regards one-half of mankind. Women are beginning to take in the entire situation with wide-open eyes. They have commenced to think and act for themselves. They are weary of proxy and verbiage, and are groping their way in untried paths, in search of the temple of honor and justice, which ought to be seated on an eminence. "If justice itself were the great standing policy of the civilized world, as it is claimed to be, there would be no marked departure from it, under any circumstances; for that lies under the supposition of being no policy at all."

Lucy Stone, in speaking of the centennial celebration at Concord and Lexington, says, "The occasion which comes only once in a century, and which, by every sacred memory, should have summoned men far and near to carry out and settle on peaceful fields the strife begun in blood and war, has passed. All that was worthy and beautiful and true — and there was much that was so — is history now. But so, too, is the fact that *half* the people are still taxed without representation, and governed without their consent, and no one remembered to mention it.

> 'Earth, render back from out thy breast
> A remnant of our Spartan dead!
> Of the three hundred, grant but three,
> To make a new Thermopylæ!'"

"There is a courageous wisdom, says an old proverb: there is also a false *reptile prudence*, the result not of caution, but of fear." This false reptile prudence gives expression to just such sayings as these: "We have all the rights we want: we enjoy this protection; we are satisfied." But courageous wisdom says, "What is good and wholesome for my brother ought to be good and wholesome for me: therefore I ask that the same rights and immunities may be extended to me. What right has he to obstruct my way?" This will not debar any of the weak, characterless clinging vines from having the protection of man. Ah, no! far from it; and men will have to be regenerated before they will deny the dear, confiding creatures the pleasure of their protection.

Never fear, timid sisters! the dominant power loves authority too well to deny you the sweet boon you crave. They will shield you from the wanton breath of heaven, and its sunshine too if you are not careful. Did you ever notice an apple that was streaked with gold and red on one side, and was gnarled and green on the other side? I have; and knew that the puckered-up side had been nurtured under the protective policy. One-half was full of gathered sunlight; it had been drenched by the rains, and tossed and buffeted by the gale, and yet it was beautiful to the eye, and luscious to the taste; while its other half had been securely shielded by the sheltering leaves, which gave it a shrivelled, dyspeptic look and a bad taste.

When I see a man who is broad and catholic in his opinions in every good work — excepting the legal emancipation of woman — and his wife narrow and pinched in her views of life, I mentally exclaim, "She cannot help it: is she not protected, sheltered, hedged about, by the accumulating fossils of centuries — the antiquated must of ages? What wonder that her mind is gnarled, puckered, and twisted out of all reasonable growth? There is no growth: it is standing still, stagnation, a living death. He — the husband — is full of sunshine and strength, gathered from daily battles fought and won. He has braved the elements, and rollicked in the sunshine, ever since he emerged from his swaddling-clothes. No wonder he is bubbling over with the milk of human kindness. It has not been kept, in his case, in a cast-iron bottle hermetically sealed and stamped, with time-honored custom. The wife of such a man is not a partner, in any true sense. The higher and nobler attributes of life are all shut away from her. She is simply a physical companion, a ministrant to material needs. The husband seeks mental food elsewhere, in books, at the club, and in his daily intercourse with men; while she is left at home to feed her mentality on husks. A home is a place for him to rest in at night, to recuperate for the morrow's fray."

It is most astonishing, what deep-rooted prejudice pervades the minds of most intelligent women,—in other respects,—as regards this babyish helplessness. When I was returning from Europe, I made the acquaintance, on the steamer, of an exceedingly intelligent lady, who was born and reared in the State of Louisiana. She spoke several languages fluently, and had greatly amused me by her graphic description of her daring travels—she was alone—through France, Germany, and Switzerland; and her persistent warfare against being overcharged by custom-house officials, hackmen, shopmen, and in the settlement of hotel bills, &c.

The day we arrived in New York, she came on deck, looking like a butterfly escaped from its chrysalis (we experienced a rough passage, and had not been over-particular about the appearance of the external woman), and exclaimed, "How glad I am we are nearing port! When I'm in New York I'm not obliged to know one thing after I have pointed out my baggage to husband or brother; and that is such a relief!" — "You surprise me," I exclaimed. "Oh!" she continued with a coquettish toss of the head, "you are a *Northerner*, and think differently; but when I'm at home I'm just the same as one of the children in my own house. *Husband* is consulted about every thing. I know nothing, absolutely nothing, of myself. It is such a relief not to be obliged to think about any thing, to be so tenderly cared for! I enjoy this thoughtful attention so much! I have one of the best of husbands."

This woman was no longer young, never had been handsome or even pretty; but she liked to play baby in her own home, nevertheless, with the younger babies which she dandled upon her knee. "Well," I mentally ejaculated, with a returning qualm of sea-sickness, "a most eminent man has said that 'all's well that ends well,' and it may be so in this case."

Later, as I was frantically searching among the baggage on the wharf, for a missing valise, — *I* had no husband or brother there to do it for me, — I saw her calmly seated on a dry-goods box, "with a far-away look in her eyes," as the custom-house official held up gowns and other female paraphernalia — *à la mode* — before the wondering gaze of the astonished husband. The veritable husband — she had told me so — was on hand to take charge of his baby wife.

When the officer demanded my keys, I said, "I

nave nothing, sir, in these trunks subject to duty. I have a sick sister in San Francisco, and am most anxious to leave for there on the first train westward bound. Won't you take my word?" He called another officer, and after a brief consultation they said "Go in peace;" and I went, leaving my Southern acquaintance still seated upon that dry-goods box, with the officers still unearthing boxes, bundles, and switches (she had informed me that she had six of the latter), and her liege lord still looking on with amazement intensified in every line of his handsome face: he was a handsome man.

I did not have my baggage opened but once in Europe, and that once was at Cherbourg, on my first landing; and I travelled quite extensively upon the Continent and through the United Kingdom; and I gave no bribes. The officers at Cherbourg unlocked both my trunks, and then asked me if I had any cigars or tobacco in them. I answered, "No; but my husband is president of a tobacco company in San Francisco, United States of America." That seemed to satisfy them; for they immediately locked the trunks, and ordered the subordinates to restrap and cord them.

CHAPTER XI.

DOUBLE LAWS AND VALUABLE DOCUMENTS

Dulce est desipere in loco.

MEN make laws, — two kinds of laws; a double deal all round, as far as women are concerned, — a male code and a female code. Women are ruled by the rod of law, cut from the great tree of male arrogance; and yet men say that we are all free. They forget that freedom without equality is a fraud; and both therefore, without justice, a snare. What is the meaning of freedom? Is it to have absolute control of our persons and property? "Does history teach us that we may reasonably hope to see a large disfranchised class receive justice at the hands of its rulers?" The key-note of our Declaration of Independence is, that governments derive their just powers from the consent of the governed.

This great idea, "the consent of the governed," is the one upon which the whole structure of our government is *theoretically* built. But in practice it falls far short of it. Congress takes from the women of the nation millions of dollars every year. According to the Declaration of Independence, this is absolute tyranny, because the women have not consented to this taxation. These law-making despots have not the chivalric courtesy to say, "By your leave." By the theory of our government, taxation and representation are inseparable correlatives.

Why not remove at once, may I ask, every restriction that weighs upon women? All adults should be governed by the same laws. No part of maturity which years bring should be hedged around by other laws than are made by the united voice of the whole people; not the half, for, if but half is used, it — the law — will go halting. It will lack that just equipoise which is found throughout the great physical balance of Nature. She never deals in fractions; therefore the harmony — the beautiful equilibrium — of her laws.

Men have continuously made laws for women, and therein lies the secret of their failure. They have constantly sought to separate and divide what God ordained from the beginning should go together. What just cause is there for the requirement of separate laws to govern the lives of adults? Does not the same sun light us by day, and the same moon and stars by night? Are we not nipped by the same frost, and warmed by the same fire? Wherefore, then, this waste of time in making laws to cover two distinct classes of human beings that should be one, inseparable and undivided? Are not the laws complicated enough without this? How much wiser it would be to make one code of good laws, that would reach adult humanity regardless of sex, color, or previous condition! Then, when the husband dies, the wife can attend to the joint estate of husband and wife, the same as a man does when a woman dies. The family in this case would not be broken up, and in no way disintegrated, as it is in most of the cases, at the death of the father and husband, thus outraging and profaning the great law of humanity.

A most annoying, ridiculous, and amusing (using an anomalous trinity) thing occurred, in my own case, in relation to the abominable and absurd laws made for the control of widows. I received a postal card from Crabb & Co., a prominent business firm in San Francisco, advising me that they were in possession of valuable letters addressed to my late husband. I at once waited upon the said firm, and asked for the letters. I was met by the pertinent inquiry, "Are you the widow of the late J. W. Stow?"—"I am," I made answer. "Oh, ah!" continued the questioner. "I hadn't the pleasure of your acquaintance, Mrs. Stow. Are you the executrix of the estate?"—"No; but I am the widow, and the one most interested in the finances of the estate. I am the *one*, in fact," I continued, somewhat earnestly, "now that Mr. Stow is dead. During his life, the law says that we *two were one*, and that he was the *one*; but, now that he is dead, I take his place, and represent the one. If I was not to be trusted with the letters, why was I put to the expense and loss of time to come over the bay" — I was living in Oakland at the time — "to meet with a refusal? I am going to the office of the non-executive executor, and I will place these important missives in his hands with the seals unbroken." — "Oh, ah!" broke in my polite interlocutor: "allow me to accompany you, Mrs. Stow. I shall do so with the greatest pleasure."

"You are exceedingly kind," I replied, reaching out my hand for the coveted prize.

"Excuse me, Mrs. Stow: I will not trouble you to carry them. I will retain possession of them, if you please, for they are evidently most valuable documents, &c. It is very necessary, you know, on account of the reputation of our house, you know, that we should do every thing in a strictly business way, you know."

When we arrived at the non-executor's office, we found that blooming gentleman out.

"Ah! this is a most unfortunate circumstance," exclaimed the dyspeptic representative of the Crabb house. "My time is most precious this morning."

"*Indeed!*" I replied, with a prolonged look of exquisite delight. How I nursed my well-earned happiness, and rejoiced that I had that pertinacious individual in a tight place! and at once commenced an impromptu disquisition on the charming laws made by men for the suppression of women generally throughout the world, and in California in particular, with a sweeping review of lawgivers since the time of Grotius.

Oh, my! how this wary fish did struggle and suffer during the uninterrupted harangue! From the way he squirmed around in that arm-chair, one would have supposed he was sitting on a hornet's nest instead of innocent cane. When he could endure the continuous fire no longer, he rose up with a desperate determination to hear no more. He paced madly up and down that office (it is a large one), grasping the letters in one hand, while with the other he mopped his hot forehead with his snowy cambric, as he hurled question after question at the luckless wight of a clerk:—

"When did you say you thought Mr. Blank would be in? How long did he say he should be out? Does he usually return promptly at the hour named? Do you know whether it was a funeral" (evidently he was anticipating his own demise if he had to remain there much longer) "or a wedding that took him out this morning? Does he ever go fishing so early in the day?" (consulting his watch, and casting a furtive glance at the solemn-faced clock, which ticked on unmoved). The thermometer of his misery rose with my delight at his ludicrous position. The clerk bit his lips, as he answered straight, and tore his pen over the paper at an awful rate.

Just at the moment when he, the gallant representative of the Crabb house, was about to pass into a comatose state, the door opened and discovered the head of the office, to the unspeakable relief of the eager and thoroughly demoralized representative.

He made a lively dash at the new-comer, and said, "Ah! Mr. Blank, I presume? Mrs. Stow had the *ke*-indness to call for letters intrusted to our care, addressed to the late J. W. Stow; but, as we didn't *know* Mrs. Stow, we didn't deem it prudent to deliver such valuable documents to a *woman*, upon her individual statement."

"Oh!" cried I, "why didn't you explain this to me? There are plenty of people in your block who do know that I am Mrs. Stow, and in this building also. I could have saved you all this delay if you had spoken thus to me." He condescended no reply, but, with a theatrical bow, said,—

"I wish you a very good morning, madam. I believe my whole *juty* in this important matter is honorably discharged."

Mr. Blank sat down at his desk opposite me, holding fast the important documents. He poised them upon his finger-tips, to feel their exact weight; then he looked sharp at the superscription; then turned the envelope over, and gazed long and earnestly at the convex streak of mucilage which held the edges together. At this point I began to grow uneasy, and said, "Mr. Blank, the two letters from some unknown land, addressed to Mr. Stow, are within the large envelope. That, you see, bears the coat-of-arms of the Crabb house. They, the members of that house, have most generously furnished it. Will you please to open it, or allow me to? I authorize you to do it."

"I don't think the law will protect me in so doing," said he, "when the active executor is out of the State."—"But it does," I replied: "Hittell"—"You needn't quote Hittell," said he, rising in apparent haste: "I'm not a lawyer, but I'll send for one."

The executor's lawyer was soon upon the ground,—or floor, rather,—and the mystery of the sealed letters duly explained to him. He reached forth his hand, and took the Crabb envelope, which contained the two important letters, and "with a smile child-like and bland," gallantly handed it to me, saying,—

"We certainly can let Mrs. Stow gratify her *woman's curiosity* by examining the contents of these letters in *our presence*."

The open letters proved of no consequence to any one, excepting to the parties who wrote them. Then I said, "I am very glad to meet you, gentlemen, together. I am in very great need of my allowance money, which is now several months overdue. Will you explain to me why it is not paid?" The lawyer made answer, "This matter is to be discussed with your attorney: you know nothing about it."—"More's the pity," I replied; "but this much I do know,—that I am in very great need of the money; not to buy handsome apparel, but to pay my honest debts. Hittell"—"Mrs. Stow," he broke in, "don't quote law to me: *that's my profession!*"—"But I cannot afford to hire a lawyer every month, to arbitrate for my meagre hundred," I urged. "It seems very hard, and like unjust persecution."

He rose majestically from his chair, and turning to the executor said, "I don't think there can be any thing done in this matter of allowance, until the return of Mr. Blank number two from New York."

"When will that be?" I inquired. "I cannot exactly say: he may be absent several weeks longer," answered the smiling friend of my dead husband.

The withholding the allowance money which the probate judge had awarded for my support was in open defiance of the written and published laws of California. The probate law says, "Any allowance made by the court or judge must be paid in preference to all other charges, except funeral charges and expenses of administration." The judge awarded me one hundred dollars a month, but declined to give an order for the payment of the same, because it was contested. If there is any truth in probate law, he had no right to do that. The first money I got was after a sharp skirmish, a sort of legal tilt, between the judge and three lawyers, while I acted as dummy (women are usually dummies in court), but came off with four hundred; then, after another hotly contested siege, I got two hundred. After that I could get no more. Seven months, eight months, nine months, went by; and then I said to myself, — for I had no lawyer, — "This won't do: we must have a great battle of words, and compel a surrender." Then I prepared a speech, and sounded the bugle-call, and, lo! the enemy appeared upon the outer walls, and capitulated ere a word of my speech was spoken. The judge gave me, then and there, an order for the three hundred; and the last three came in due order, monthly. It was the speech that did the business. Let all widows prepare speeches, whose allowances are contested.

CHAPTER XII.

BROTHERLY LOVE.

Nefasti dies.

THE legal fraternity of San Francisco are very sensitive about any question being raised as to the justness of the laws made to govern peaceful or refractory widows — more particularly the latter. I went into an office one day, — not a law-office, — and was freeing my mind somewhat *earnestly* about the outrages perpetrated on all widows by the heinous laws made by men for the suppression of women; and, among other facts, I mentioned that the Probate Court was created for the special purpose to rob widows and orphans.

In an instant I was confronted by a hay-colored specimen of humanity on two sticks, whom I had noticed sitting at a desk, reading in a half-audible tone, to let me know, I suppose, that there was one individual present who didn't listen to such heresy. However, his splenetic wrath betrayed him. Assuming a terrible attitude, and removing his specs, — he wore glasses, — he said, "Madam, do you wish to insult ME?" — "Why are you insulted?" I inquired. "Who are you? What are you?"—"I have the honor to be a member of the San Francisco bar, madam; and I will not sit silent when I hear it thus assailed by a *woman*."—"Ah, indeed!" I exclaimed, with a genuine stare of amazement: "that's bad for the bar. But you must bear in mind, my friend, that, in polite society, present company is always excepted; and then, again, I cry pardon! for I didn't recognize the *lion in the ass's skin.*"

San Francisco lawyers not only protect themselves, as a legal brotherhood, but they also endeavor to protect the profession from any encroachment on their classic borders by laymen; and, above all, do they shut fast the doors of their stronghold to keep women—the feminine wolves—out of their sheepfold.

I wrote my lawyer, when I was very sick, and begged him, as my allowance money was overdue, to make all the haste that was possible, which would not interfere with legal dignity, to get it. I quoted from the probate law, about the right of its being paid at once. But my law lore caused my ruin. This lawyer, whom I thought ere then a friend, took this private business note, with his wounded *amour-propre*, to my brother-in-law, so he said, and urged him to read the note, saying, "I don't permit any client of mine to quote law to me. Mrs. Stow will have to employ some one else: she is in too great a *hurry* about her allowance." That appears to be a specimen of the California "code of honor" among some members of the fraternity. I afterwards went to another lawyer, and engaged him to transact some legal business for me, and fixed upon the price at twelve o'clock noon. He told me to return in two hours, and the paper would be ready to indorse. I was there promptly at the hour named; but to my astonishment, he had made the discovery, during my absence, that it would cost half as much again as the sum agreed upon. Then I said, "I am not able to pay so much. If you had named this price, I should not have had it commenced. I cannot go forward with it now, it costs too much: keep the paper until I can, and, in case I do nothing further in the matter, I will pay you as soon as I can for this two hours' work." He went out of the office, and I said to the clerk who had done the writing, "How much do you think this will be?" He replied, "About twenty-five dollars." — "Well," I exclaimed, "I think that I will study law, and open an office, and employ a clerk to write, if he can command twenty-five dollars for two hours' work."

This lawyer went to my brother-in-law, so he said, and told him that he had done work for me equal to seven days' copying which my sister had done one time for her husband, and that then I had thrown it up. He forgot to state, however, the reason why I threw it up, — the cause of its turning on my stomach; how he had agreed upon one price, and then, when he thought he had me in his power, had charged another. Thus it is that every widow is plucked on every side. A widow acquaintance of mine said to her lawyer, "It is impossible for me to get along with so small an allowance. I must have it increased." His reply was, —

"Well, *Mrs. Tribulation*, how much can you get along with? I mean, of course, the very *smallest* amount."

"Mr. Skinbones," she indignantly made answer, "I employ a lawyer to get the very *largest* amount for me, not the *smallest*. Understand me! I wish you to get all you can, — yes, to the last farthing. That will be meagre enough, coming as it does through the all-absorbing maw of the Probate Court."

For a long time I had no lawyer (I found them too expensive a luxury for a widow on a hundred dollars a month), to the insufferable disgust of all concerned. Men do not like to transact business with women. The first question asked would be, "Who's your lawyer? Send him round to fix this thing up." When I divulged the dreadful fact that I had none, and that I was pleading my own case, there would be an awful pause, after which my questioner would usually say, —

"Excuse me, Mrs. Stow, but you must not forget the old proverb, that 'he who serves himself in law has a fool for a client.' Now, I would advise you, as a friend, to get a lawyer by all means; and, while you are about it, get a good one" — as though any of them were bad. I listened to their advice, but kept my own *counsel*.

The judge said to me one day, that I did not need a lawyer; but at another time, when he was not quite so amiable, he said I must have one, for he could not act in the capacity of judge and lawyer both for me. I wrote several notes, at different times, to the judge, executor's lawyer, and the executors. Each and every one of these private notes were reported at once to my brother-in-law. When he came home at night on these grave occasions, — I was in my sister's house, — he wore a dark and ominous look, which heralded the coming storm. Then he would say, — usually after we had sat down to the table, and he had served me with my dinner, to improve my appetite, I presume, — "You" (meaning *me*) "have been writing again to Mr. Smudge, Fudge, Mudge," as the case might be. "Yes," I would make answer, before the comments could escape: "what of it? That's my business." And then the dinner would go forward in black silence, which was very bad for digestion.

I at last added to my letters, by way of postscript, which it is said a lady always has, "Don't trouble my brother-in-law about this matter: he is very sensitive; and, besides, he is not my legal adviser or guardian, never has been, and never will be; we are too well acquainted for any such relationship."

The moment a woman rebels against subordination to the rule of some man, it matters not how much her inferior he may be, there is an uproar amid the powers that be. When the husband dies, a father, brother, uncle, brother-in-law, nephew, or son even, — any *masculine* creature in human form, — assumes the sceptre of control over the widow; and if she kicks over the traces, and holds the bit between her teeth, and won't obey the lash, then she is dubbed "a monstrosity, a disgrace to her sex; ought to be put in a mad-house," &c.

When my lawyer abandoned my case because I dabbled in his profession, there were among the papers returned to me some that he knew nothing whatever about, — papers that the veriest ignoramus ought to have known were not for him, for they had nothing to do with the case in hand; and it is a marvel how the parties that executed them knew who my lawyer was.

That the machinery of justice works slowly, and produces unreliable, unsatisfactory, and uncertain results, is apparent to every one who has had the misfortune to come under its power. Through a confidence operation I lost several hundred dollars. I commenced suit to recover the money; but, during the many months' delay ere the trial, I learned so much about law and lawyers, that I went and dismissed the case, and paid the costs of court, rather than continue the contest. I should have won the suit in the first trial, without doubt; but it would have been taken to the higher courts probably, and I had no time to waste in litigation.

It seems that it is not worth while to sue for less than five hundred dollars: therefore one must have a sharp eye to small debts, leases, &c., unless amply secured against loss. Knowledge is power, money, health, and happiness.

The various professions have held the masses in ignorance long enough. It is high time people began to investigate for themselves. Physicians have often declined to attend my husband in sickness, because they said that he was too intelligent in regard to medicine and its effect upon the system, and the condition of his own case.

People swallow all kinds of poisonous concoctions, and then wonder why they are always ailing. They are caught in the relentless grip of the law, and wonder why they are always poor. The exercise of a modicum of common sense might save them from the horrors of the former, and the terrors of the latter. Practical knowledge appears to be purposely withheld from the people. I went to the Mercantile Library in this city, in search of works on law; the Civil Code and Probate Law I certainly expected to find there. But no! The librarian said that these were books that were seldom or never called for: consequently they were not furnished by the society. That is no good excuse. Works on medicine and law, as well as theology, should be found in abundance on the shelves of every library. Sound Christianity depends upon sound health, and sound health depends upon potential knowledge, kept bright with daily, hourly use.

Will not some humane lawyer, who has outwitted

want with "*fat*" cases, write a book on how to avoid litigation; give the *modus operandi* of all the courts, how many times suits can be appealed, and how, when they have gone to the length of the elastic tether in one form, they can begin all over again *ad infinitum?* If some one will write such a book I will sell it. I would endeavor to prove that no library was complete without it, — and "Probate Confiscation," — that every married man and woman should have copies; that every bachelor and spinster, young and old, should have copies; and that every male and female child should memorize them in conjunction with their catechism. Legal ignorance cowers in garrets and tenements, while legal wisdom rolls in carriages and is housed in splendor. An intelligent man makes himself familiar with general law; but when he sees his wife conning over its pages he turns her desire of gaining a little knowledge of its devious ways into ridicule, and says, "Well, little puss, what can you understand about law? What folly to waste your precious time on such a dry pursuit, that will amount to nothing!" Why do husbands do this? I will tell you why. Because they want to keep their precious simpletons, in this respect, in ignorance of the legal power they hold over them. Mine said the same to me, yet I argued in this wise: "If Hittell is good for you, Hittell ought to be good for me," and continued my explorations among the dry bones. A man whom I asked to buy my book replied, "No, no, Mrs. Stow! I have a happy home now, because my wife knows nothing about law. I would not permit her to read such a book as that, no, not if you paid me fifty dollars." Legal ignorance in wives is bliss to the most of husbands. "But," you may ask, "would you have all women study law?" Yes, to a certain extent. It would be far more practical than parallelograms and cube roots. I would have them familiar with the octangular rights of a husband during his life, and the hypotenuse of those rights after his death. If women would read only so much law as pertained to themselves, instead of trashy novels, they would soon wake up to its injustice towards them. Many of the laws which govern women to-day were codified by semi-barbarians, who slew their wives for committing adultery, or drinking wine, or other offences practised daily by the husbands. Those were not masculine crimes.

Law should keep pace, in its development, with progressive intelligence. This it has not done; therefore it is unjust. Justice is immortal, eternal, unchangeable, like God himself. The great field of jurisprudence is overrun with weeds and brambles; the tares have outgrown the wheat, because there was no one to use the pruning-hook, no one to strike a brave blow at corrupt practices and abuses, no one who dared defend the weak against the strong. This demands a radical change, that justice may be protected, rather than violated; for without justice there is no wisdom on earth, no everlasting principle, no escape from oppression, no individual freedom. In law, as in every thing else, long-established custom becomes as fixed and immovable as the laws of the Medes and Persians. Men say it is so much easier to jog along in the old ruts; but woe to the outsiders!

The cry goes up daily, throughout the length and breadth of the civilized world, for the freedom of one-half the race, the emancipation from political bondage, the pulling down of all bars and barriers, and the opening of all gates that obstruct the onward march of the whole people. Give to the sword and flame of reason and truth and progress, these corrupt laws, these time-honored prejudices, this rank undergrowth of usurpation, which have crippled the energies of woman since time began. Luther had his reformation, Cromwell his victories, and Bunyan his triumphs; but this overthrow of man-power shall be the greatest of them all. It is the war of right against might; the sharp, logical weapons of the mind, scintillating in every direction against the fossilization of the past, — hoary with the hallowed dust of ages, — this venerated idol, *custom*, which the irreverent finger of the iconoclast dares to touch in the last quarter of the nineteenth century.

The tools are being forged in the white heat of indignation, that will break these cruel bonds, and let the oppressed go free. Freedom shall be our banner-word and rallying-cry. We will leave no stone unloosed in the crumbling edifice of masculine power, so that when the earthquake of reason, justice, and humanity shall shake the foundation-stones, it shall topple over in perpetual and everlasting ruin. But, when the smoke and dust caused by the fall shall have blown away, the new builders shall join with the old forces, and reconstruct from the *débris*, and upon the old site, a new and more lasting edifice, a grand structure, beautiful and symmetrical in all its proportions, within whose walls no arm of might shall smite the brow of right.

CHAPTER XIII.

INSOLVENT ESTATE.

Aura sacra fames.

EARLY in my acquaintance with Mr. Stow, he told me that William C. Ralston, Edward P. Pringle, and himself were associated together in an enterprise for the treatment of refractory ores, known as the "Hagan Process for the Disintegration of Ores." He said, "Ralston furnishes the money, Pringle the legal advice, and I the brain or working power." The whole thing was an entire failure, at a loss to the trio of eighty-four thousand dollars. For several years Mr. Stow owed the Bank of California for a portion of his *pro rata* of the expenses; but he said, when the Metropolitan Gas Works were sold out to the old gas company, that he paid off his entire indebtedness to the bank.

Mr. Ralston had provided the money — some $400,000 — to build up the Metropolitan experiment of making gas from crude petroleum, which proved another *fiasco*. J. W. Stow furnished the mental part, officiated as president of the company, and superintended the whole vexatious enterprise, working day and night for many months to perfect it. The foundations of the building were not "laid upon a rock," but in a pool of odoriferous mush on Mission Creek. I saw men — fine handsome fellows too, some of them — standing in this filth (it was upon the site of an old hog corral and slaughter-house, and is known by the euphonious and elegant name of "Hog Town") up to their girdles, laying bricks and driving piles. It for a long time appeared to be "love's labor lost;" for each morning found both bricks and piles *non est* to all human ken. I heard Mr. Stow say to Gen. Alexander, "The very deuce is in the thing. We drove piles ninety feet long yesterday; and this morning we probed the spot with a ten-foot pole, but could not find a vestige of their whereabouts. I think the old gent vulgarly known as Satan is building another Sodom down there, and has use for many piles and much brick, by the way they disappear. It is the bottomless pit." After the walls were up, and the roof on, the entire building had a way of sailing round from one point to another, which gave the local engineer no end of quakes. The gas-holder looked as though it had been through the wars and was under hospital treatment, with a liberal supply of "d'Artagnan's baume," for it was swaddled like a newborn babe.

Although the old company paid over half a million dollars for the works, which took it into their head to blow up and explode the day after the consummation of the much-desired sale, it would seem that my husband was paid nothing — that is, nothing commensurate with his expectations, and for the labor performed; for the old claim of the bank is brought against the estate, with the accrued interest, which amounts to forty thousand dollars.

Before I left for Europe, in 1874, I had a thorough business understanding with Mr. Stow. He said, "We are worth at least two hundred thousand dollars, besides your separate property; and I owe no man a dollar. I squared up with the Bank of California when the gas-works were sold out in San Francisco, the franchise in Oakland, and the closing out of the Treadwell estate." Now, in the face of this statement, the old claim rises, clad in full armor, like the Danish ghost, and is awarded by the executors.

Mr. Pringle said in open court, that, if Mr. Stow had lived, the Bank of California would never have brought a claim against him, as he was a most valuable man to that organization. In other words, a live man would not have to pay his debts twice; but, dead, the estate is mulcted of forty thousand dollars.

Mr. Stow would have been alive to-day, and a rich man, instead of lying in Lone Mountain, with an estate which the executors and Probate Court have brought down to pay only sixty cents on a dollar, if he had attended to his legitimate business as manager of the Russell & Erwin Manufacturing Company, and not been led off by men who coined the products of his brain into money for their own aggrandizement.

I said to him, often and often, "You are committing daily suicide, personal and financial, in the course you are pursuing. You are not physically strong. You should not do one other thing besides the management of your legitimate business. You will be far richer in the end if you listen to me, and conserve your health and strength for years of usefulness. These men who lure you from the duty you owe this company, in whose employ you are, are not your friends in any worthy sense. They will kill you with overwork, while they pat you on the back, and say, 'You must not work so hard, my boy,' and beggar me by taking every thing I have when you are dead."

"No, no!" he would reply. "You mistake and misjudge my *friends:* they will treat you like a sister were I to die before you."

The sequel will prove whose prophecy was correct, his or mine. At this writing he has been dead over a year and a half, and there never has been an account rendered by the executors ready for publishing. The probate law says that there shall be various accounts published, quarterly, semi-annually, and yearly. I have risen for an explanation many times, but in vain — aside from some informal hearings in the judge's chambers. I have sought often to have Mr. Pringle and the executors meet me in open court, at a time when I was destitute of that necessary evil — in probating — a lawyer, that I might have the opportunity to express myself publicly in reference to my grievances. But no: in each and every case I was most graciously awarded a private interview. The judge could not tarnish the purity of his ermine by granting so undignified a request; and Mr. Pringle was not going to dull his polished steel by tilting with a widow in the presence of the vulgar herd of the court-room, thereby robbing some brother lawyer of a fee. No, no! A lawyer is the one thing needful for a widow. Without a piloting lawyer she is tossed upon the tempestuous sea of doubt and uncertainty. The very first question that is asked by every one is, "Who's your lawyer?" And when you — if you are a widow — reply, "I have none," the interrogator gasps for breath, turns black in the face, his eyes become fixed and immovable, and you imagine he has got a fit of apoplexy until he opens his mouth, when you are likely to be undeceived. A widow in Oakland, whose husband's estate was valued at a hundred thousand dollars, was probated; and, as usual, there was nothing left for her but a large vexation of spirit, and the insurance on the late husband's life of twenty thousand dollars. Strange to relate, there was some legal technicality about the policy; and the magnanimous company, seeing it was a woman, offered to compromise for half its value. She was so tired of law and lawyers — poor little simpleton —

that she preferred to take the half-loaf fresh when she could get it, than the whole loaf stale at the end of lightning litigation. However, friends — widows always have friends under such circumstances — advised her to employ some tiptop lawyer; none of your penny-a-liners, for good pay means good work. She accepted the advice, and procured the service of two experts, — thinking, no doubt, if one is good, two must be better. They only got the sum offered her by the insurance company, and the fee charged by them covered all of it; and she went forth into the great highway of life to earn her own living, a sadder but a wiser woman. She has no need of lawyers now, nor they of her. The admiration is mutual.

I have sat in the court-room (Probate), and heard the lawyers discussing cases (ere the judge was upon the bench — which, by the by, is no bench at all, but a soft cushioned arm-chair with a canopy behind it), and chuckle over the plump ones, as they said confidentially, "It's a good one: there's money in it." Then I thought of the widow sitting powerless, while the legal ligature tightened, day by day, round her neck and the necks of her darlings; and wished that she was as fortunate as the man I heard tell of when I was a child, who had been a cripple for twenty years, and who was not afraid of ghosts and haunted houses. Near him was a vacant house that all the neighbors said was haunted. But he declared to a robust friend one evening, as the shadows began to deepen, that he was not afraid; and that robust friend instantly seized him, and, lifting him upon his broad shoulders, carried him to the open door of the haunted house. A man came out of the open door, and said in an unearthly voice, "Is he fat, or lean?"—"Fat or lean, take 'im," said the robust friend, dumping his burden upon the ground, and taking leg-bail to safer quarters. The cripple lost sight of his infirmities from sheer fright, and, rising from the ground with one spring, bounded away after his companion in flight. The house was the rendezvous of sheep-thieves, but the courageous man was healed of his affliction ever afterwards.

Would that all widows, whether "fat or lean," could make as fortunate an escape from the open door of the thieving Probate Court, with its spongy excrescences and cruel extortions! It openly sets at defiance its own august laws, or, rather, the amendment to the Constitution of the United States, which says, "The right of the people to be secured in their persons, houses, business, and effects, against unreasonable search and seizure, shall not be violated; and no warrant shall issue but upon reputed cause, supported by oath or affirmation particularly describing the place to be searched, and the person or thing to be seized." In the face of this law, a widow's house is turned into a pandemonium the moment the husband is under the sod. It is overrun by the minions of the law, searched, and every thing of value sequestered, should the estate, under *covert* manipulation, be proved insolvent. And insolvency being the rule, and not the exception, this law is violated a hundred times each day, if the entire nation is included in the estimate. A widow has no protection in her own home against the marauding parasites of the Probate Court. Her house is ransacked, her children stolen from her guardianship, and her private grief dragged through the gutter of publicity. In her best estate of insolvency, if she is so fortunate as to have landed property, she is turned out of doors with the munificent dower of five thousand dollars at the end of one little year.

In Christian England, when the husband forges and swindles, the wife of the felon is robbed of all her private property to eke out the loss. She is left to beg or starve, as in the recent case of Winslow. How noble and humane! That English law ought to cross the sea, and court and wed our probate law. Then all our probate judges, special-probate lawyers, guardians, referees, executors, appraisers, clerks, publishers, posters, reporters, and probate scavengers, could dance at the wedding-feast.

CHAPTER XIV.

MOTHER AND CHILD.

Aude sapere.

THERE is one place in the laws of California where "children, women, and persons of unsound mind" have the advantage over male adults: they can contest the validity of a will after the year has expired. *Mark you how it reads!* Women are sandwiched between children and fools. Children include boys, therefore they are placed before mothers; for after the husband comes the son, to take precedence of the mother at the father's death. The son at fourteen years of age can choose and appoint his own guardian. A lad, by law, becomes at fourteen wiser than his mother at forty.

What a sagacious law, and how fragrant with masculine wisdom! Here is a mother who probably has all her governmental ingenuity taxed to control the exuberance of youthful America, without his having it within his power to turn upon her with a law-weapon, and say, "Oh! I don't care what you say nor what you think: *you* are not my guardian."

Again: as soon as she marries, she becomes disqualified to have the control of her own children. A premium is thus offered for widow-celibacy; for what mother wants to be deprived of the legal guardianship of her young children?

This is rather a paradoxical dilemma; for one would suppose from the hue and cry raised about the race dying out, or progressing in an inverted ratio of degeneracy towards its prehistoric ancestors, that every man would prefer to see every widow married again, and working out her true salvation — with a babe at her breast and another at her knee. Why is not a widower deprived of the legal control of his children as soon as he solaces himself with better half number two, three, or four, as the case may be? Surely motherless orphans stand in greater danger of abuse from stepmothers — if half the tirade of abuse waged against them can be believed — than when such children are subjected to the shortcomings of stepfathers. Nature ordained motherhood from the beginning the real guardian of its offspring; but more potent man perverts the natural order of things, and shows to the world that he is superior in judgment to the venerable dame. Nature admits of a feminine declension: therefore the departure, I suppose.

When a widow marries, a grandfather on the paternal side has the first right to the guardianship of her children. He is armed, cap-a-pie, with the full panoply of the law to step in and rule. No matter how old and decrepit he may be, or how much of a grinding misèr, or how non-progressive — as to the requirements of the age — in his ideas of education and choice of pursuits, for those whom the law has placed under him. The mother and the man that she has married have no voice in the matter. They are silent witnesses of the unbending arrogance of the legal ruler. His will is absolute.

A son may have all the requisite ability for a leading profession, or a fine mechanical genius; and the mother anxious and eager as himself, that he may be allowed to follow the inherent bent of his God-given faculties. But no! the inflexible, old-fashioned, treadmill grandfather puts his foot down with an emphasis, and says, "No! he's got'er foller in the footsteps uv his father and gran'father. It shall never be said I let the illustr'us house uv 'Grubb & Son' die out fur the want uv a lineal representative." And so the mother and son bow to the inevitable, rather than meddle with the gracious and time-honored law that has turned the current of their hopes up stream.

This heinous law of guardianship has its legal grip upon the unborn child. What marvel is it, in the name of highest heaven, that women resort to any means, and at any price, to rid themselves of such savage thraldom by abortions and the deadly preventive drugs and nostrums which are ruinous to health, causing barrenness, premature decay, and death?

There is no use in beating about the bush to discover the true cause of barrenness in American women to-day. That with the untoward, legalized licentiousness of men, who are often diseased from the crowns of their heads to the soles of their feet, because long-established custom permits and winks at debauchery in high places. Look at the fearful death-rate among infants up to five years of age! What causes the slaughter of the innocents? Corruption of blood, which, could it be traced, in very many cases would be found to originate in the licentiousness of men — male prostitutes, with the seeds of their crimes planted in the vitals of their children. And such men as Drs. Clark and Van de Walker charge home this guilt upon the innocent. They had better change the base of their investigations bearing upon female weakness, and carry their research into home-quarters, the unexplored regions of male weakness, with cause and effect.

Men sow their "wild oats" broadcast; and, when they come to harvest them, the crop turns out to be human tares in the shape of abortive children. Such children tear the hearts out of their mothers (those "physical beauties" which Herbert Spencer goes into raptures over) in the endeavor to control the corrupt blood inherited from diseased fathers, which breaks out in all kinds of ailments during infancy and childhood.

Said a beautiful mother who has three young children, and all sickly, to me, "I'm at a loss how to account for the continuous ailment of my babies: not one of them but has sore ears, eyes, or some kind of scrofulous disease, and I never had a sick hour in my life, excepting at their birth. There is no blood-taint in my family." What is the matter with these children? No one would dare claim that there was corrupt blood in that fair young mother's veins; yet she and her innocent babes pay the penalty of vice. She is not only debarred from society by the care of these three ailing, suffering children, but her loving heart is wrung every hour in the day by their sufferings, which she is impotent to relieve. This is paying a large price to perpetuate the race, and a very poor quality is obtained at an immense cost to the innocent, while the transgressor goes comparatively unscourged. The great want of the age is virtuous fathers; for if a clear stream is an outlet for a muddy one, are they not both contaminated as soon as the waters mingle? No pure breeding can come from any source unless the male is sound; and that can never be for humanity, until there is a moral code for man as well as woman. Give us pure fathers for a few generations, and the improvement in humanity will record itself in the constitutional vigor of our children.

I urge every woman who is in search of a husband to look out for physical health and manly beauty, "for the sake of the race." Do not bestow a glance on the lean, dyspeptic, cadaverous biped. Shun him as you would a pestilence. Remember that not the midnight student's lamp has caused this wreck, but the midnight debauch. Remember his "wild oats" and the inevitable harvest. Remember that many a wife is stigmatized as "barren," whose husband could not reproduce his species, were he to suffer the penalty of death for the failure. He has squandered his virility in riotous prodigality; the life of the fountain has run dry. And who is to blame? The woman, of course, — the oft-repeated story of the "apple," over and over again, *ad infinitum, ad nauseam.*

There are two kinds of law codes and two kinds of moral codes, — masculine and feminine, distinct and separate. Men have made and administered both kinds; with what success, the present disjointed times, as regards all manner of corruption, bear abundant evidence. But what else could be expected, where licentiousness has its most luxuriant growth and grandest efflorescence at the fountain's head?

My husband went up to Sacramento, once upon a time, to use his influence in some legislative matter; and on his return he said to me, "It is very dangerous for you to let me go to the capital *alone.* Mr. So-and-So, a State Senator, asked me if I would not like to have a lady share my apartments with me. I replied, 'No! I don't indulge in the luxury.' Then this modern Solon exclaimed, 'The dickens, you say! You're a veritable Joseph by nature, as well as by name. Why, bless you, there isn't a member in either house, if he hasn't his wife with him, but has his *woman.*'"

It is to be hoped that that member was a stranger to the manner of life of the most of those lawgivers. Still, from the sequence, I should judge that he was a "*bosom friend*" of them all. In Washington the lobbyists understand the nature and practice of men in high places, and know that the surest way to secure the passage of their pet schemes is to distribute large sums of money — thousands of dollars — among the sumptuous palaces of the courtesans, that these women may influence and cajole senators and representatives into favoring their public and private projects.

When women sit in the halls of legislation, a death-blow will be given to prostitution, and the loose governmental garment which men make to cover themselves and their dark deeds while they draw such a tight rein on woman. Women will not resort to prostitution for a livelihood when they are freed from legal serfdom. Four years (the average life of an abandoned woman) of gilded misery — with the dissecting-knife and the potter's field staring her in the face when the breath is out of her polluted body — will not prove a sufficient inducement then for a life of shame. This should not be an alluring picture even now; and yet I see daily upon the streets of San Francisco fair young girls, perfect Hebes in the matchless symmetry of form and feature, with the brand of infamy upon their brow, and I think an agonizing cry, — "O God! where are the desolated homes, and the Rachel mothers mourning because they are not; dead, yet living — dead to every thing but shame; mothers whose tears of love have fallen like rain in baptismal blessing upon their innocent baby faces, blessed by thousands of kisses, and sanctified by thousands of prayers!" For such as these estrays, out of the fold, men — fathers and brothers, husbands and sons — sit in the capitals of the States, and make it legal, this sale and barter in mortal flesh and immortal soul.

Talk of black, ignorant slavery! Unhand, unshackle, and unslave white, intelligent womanhood; take the foot of the law — shod with an iron heel — from off the necks of the free-born daughters of America, who are down, and struggling to get free; down in brothels, to be kicked and scoffed at; down in gilded mistress-palaces, to be ostracized by society; down as efficient educators, on half-pay; down, and half starving, as a great army of producers; down as non-producers — the real *paupers* of society; down as wives, unpaid and oftentimes unappreciated, whom the "*just*" law prohibits from selling even the smallest article of personal apparel, or from transacting any legal business, without the co-operation of the husband (unless it be her separate estate), even though he be entirely supported by her mental or manual labor; down as widows and mothers, whose sons at one and twenty push them from their stools.

Out upon such a state of things! I cry aloud to every woman in our blood-bought land of freedom — God forgive the standing lie! — to rise up and clothe herself in the stanch armor of determination, and give battle to this legalized usurpation. Forge the will-power into a Damascus blade, keen and sharp at the edge, and strike out from the shoulder, not caring whom it hits, until *double* laws and *single* vices are unknown; until what is unclean in a woman will be equally *vile* in a man. Let us go back to first principles, and have "one law, one faith, and one baptism;" the simple law of right, the white faith of the just, and a pure principle baptism. Special laws and special protection for one-half the race have proved a failure. There is too much law, too much legislation: cut away the useless part, and lop off the gnarled branches which protect women from the free sunlight of heaven. Oh for a modern Justinian, to simmer down two thousand law-tomes into the condensed extract of fifty modest folios! Oh for honest men who legislate for right, instead of power!

"God give us men! A time like this demands
Strong minds, great hearts, true faith, and ready hands;
Men whom the lust of office does not kill,
Men whom the spoils of office cannot buy;
Men who possess opinions and a will;
Men who love honor, men who will not lie."

CHAPTER XV.

A FATHER'S RIGHTS.

Empta dolore docet experientia.

SOME seventeen years ago, I was spending the day with a friend who resided in a small village in Northern Ohio. She had living with her, at the time, a little grandson between three and four years of age. He was a lovely child, with large blue eyes, shaded by long dark eyelashes; a mouth of rare sweetness, whose lurking dimples were a perpetual invitation for kisses; rings of flossy gold lay in thick clusters above his shapely brow; his ringing laugh was clear as a bugle-note: all the village knew and loved the happy child that brightened the home of the aged couple, bringing the gladness of spring to the threshold of winter.

"He is the sunbeam in my heart, and the joy of my home," said the proud and happy grandmother, as she caught him in her arms, and covered his laughing face and shining curls with kisses. "Next to his mother, he loves me better than anybody in the world: don't you, Birdie?" she continued.

"Me do, me *do* 'ove 'ou dearly, g'an'ma," replied the child.

About four o'clock in the afternoon, as we were sitting upon the piazza, and the child was at play with his little dog upon the grass-plat in front of the house, a carriage came dashing down the street at a furious rate, drawn by horses smoking with heat from fast driving, and drew up before the place. It had hardly stopped ere the door was pushed violently open, and a young handsome man sprang to the ground, and came hurriedly through the gate and up the walk. At sight of him, the child clapped his hands in an ecstasy of delight as he shouted, "Papa's come, papa's come!" The young man bowed politely to my friend Mrs. Brown; then he lifted the child in his arms, saying, "I have come to take you riding in the pretty carriage: will you go with me?"

"And g'an'ma too, g'an'ma too?" broke in the pleased child.

"We will see," replied the young man; and, turning to Mrs. Brown, he gave a command that curdled my blood.

"Get Willie's things ready as soon as possible,' he said. "I am going to take him where you and his mother will never see him again, until she keeps faith with me as a wife."

"For the love of God, you don't mean to carry out that dreadful threat, Mr. Vincent?" cried Mrs. Brown, in an agony of grief.

"Yes, I do; and if you cannot get his clothes together in ten minutes, without making a fuss about it, I'll take him just as he is."

For an instant Mrs. Brown stood with her hands pressed tightly upon her wildly beating heart, and her swimming eyes raised to heaven: then she said, in a tremulous voice, "Dear Lord Jesus, thy will be done!" With close-pressed lips, and a firm step, she moved about from room to room, and gathered together from drawers and closets the little wardrobe, the making of which mostly consisted of her own loving handiwork — the pretty dresses and warm jackets which she had cunningly fashioned for her darling. Every garment was made double. It was not alone the thread which held seam and gusset and band in place: they were woven through and through with the stitches of her love and motherly blessing; warm mittens and gay stockings, knitted before the ruddy firelight at eventide, after the busy day was done. How happy she was, planning for his future as she turned the tiny heel, turning over in her mind, meanwhile, the possibility that he might some time be a preacher of the gospel! That was the height of her ambition, and to her the height of all earthly attainment; for she was a devout Christian. And when she pressed the last good-night kiss upon his unconscious brow, as he lay rosy and beautiful in that blessed sleep of childhood, with what a consecration did she carry him up to the Throne of Grace, and lay him, with the burden of her love, upon the bosom of the Master!

When all was ready she said, "Come to grandma, Willie, and have on your cloak and hat: papa is going to take you to ride." "And 'ou too, g'an'ma," said the eager child, who had been diverted by the tick of his father's watch, as he listened to hear it strike, and had not noticed the grief of his grandmother. But when he saw the tears coursing over her quivering face he said, "Me won't go to 'ide, g'an'ma: me 'oves 'ou dearly, me does. Go way, papa! go way! me don't want to 'ide wid 'ou; go way! 'ou makes g'an'ma cry, go!" As he said this he kissed Mrs. Brown again and again, ever repeating, "Me 'oves 'ou, me 'oves 'ou," as he wiped away the fast-falling tears from her withered cheeks. "Go! me tells 'ou, papa!" said he, doubling his little fist, and shaking it angrily at his father, who stepped quickly forward, and with an impatient "Come to me!" took him from the arms of Mrs. Brown, who burst into an uncontrollable wail of sorrow as she tottered down the steps of the piazza after the father, who was midway the walk to the carriage.

At that moment another actor in the intensely thrilling drama burst upon the scene, in the person of the young wife and mother. She sprang to the rescue, through the open gate and up the walk, with the supple swiftness of a tigress bereft of its young, and, snatching the child from the father, with flashing eyes and white lips exclaimed, "How *dare* you come here to steal my child, break my mother's heart, and trail her gray hairs in the dust!"

"I came for my child, which the *law* gives me; and that is stronger than your *love*. I have an order from the court. I should like to see you fly in the face of that." "We shall see, Arthur Vincent, which is the strongest — the wicked laws made by men such as you are, to rob mothers of their babes, and the love which lives on through an eternity of bliss, after the criminal laws made and enacted here cease their diabolical power. We shall see!" "I shall take him away to-day, Mary: I have the first right to him as his father; and, besides, I have the order from court. You cannot circumvent that." "Have you *truly* an order from a court of *justice?*" "Yes, I have: would you like to see it?" "No, I spit upon and defy this *court of justice* and its vile orders. And *beware!* I give you warning, the moment you and your just law, and just court which enacts this just law, steals my child, prepare to die; for at that moment you are a doomed man. I swear it by highest heaven and lowest hell, you are a doomed man!"

"Amen and amen!" I responded audibly. The baffled man turned upon me a look of insufferable disgust, as he hissed between his clenched teeth, "We *shall* see! If that cursed bolt had not been lost, I should have been gone an hour before you could have arrived. The next time I come for him you will not have a fool's warning, as you had this time. I shall keep my own counsel hereafter." "Why do you take him from his grandmother," she continued, "and put him with a strange nurse, where he will be exposed to every evil that childhood is subject to in cities, and where he cannot be as happy as he is here with those that love him?" "I will leave him now, rather than prolong this controversy. But," said he, turning to the grandmother, "Mrs. Brown, I charge you, before this witness," pointing to the burly coachman, "do not let Mary, until she returns to me like a true wife, take him out of your sight. If you do you shall suffer the full penalty of the law."

"Arthur," said the young wife, stepping close to his side, with the child still in her arms, "when you love me better than *rum* and *harlots* I will live with you, but not before. You have your choice, but my child you shall not have." "How can you help my taking him? He is more than three years old, and at that age the law gives him to me."

"Yes, there again! the *law!* In the face of drunkenness and all kinds of licentious debauchery on the part of the husband, it nevertheless takes the child out of a virtuous mother's protection, — if she refuses to live with one whose touch is moral pollution, — and consigns him to a father whose only claim upon him is that of the pleasure of begetting. And this is *called* justice!"

"'Until you can rail the seal from off the law,' Mary, 'you but offend' — you know the rest," said Vincent with a scornful curl of the lip. "I shall surely take him."

"Take him at your peril! I dare you touch but the hem of his garment to rob me of him! and I repeat, you are a doomed man, though I suffer perdition for it; though my soul writhe in nethermost hell till the end of eternity — I will slay you at my first opportunity. Like an avenging Nemesis, a thirsty bloodhound upon your track, my vengeance shall be swift and certain."

The man had turned deadly pale while she spoke, for there was a dangerous glitter in the woman's eyes; and when she paused, he laid his hand upon her arm, which she shook off as though it had been a viper's and the touch deadly, and said he to her with a pleading look in his eyes, —

"Come, Mary, let us be friends. You know how I love you both, and how hard it is for me to live without you."

"Very hard," she replied with a mocking laugh. "You suffer the same now, probably, that you did in being separated from me when I carried this child beneath my heart, in loneliness and sorrow; while you were in a distant city, living as you and your God alone know how. Your life flowed on as best pleased you, far from your young wife, who was left to starve or find means of support other than a husband's, or become an object of charity among her proud kindred. This child of contention might have first seen the light of heaven in the gutter, for all the care you had about it or me, so long as you could squander your earnings on lewd women and wine.

And since that bitter time what have you contributed towards our maintenance?"

"Nothing," doggedly replied the man, impatiently tapping the toe of his boot with his cane, "because you refused to live with me."

"Here in my mother's house," she continued, "I found that love and hospitality which my husband failed to furnish me in the most tragic hour of a woman's life. Here my babe was born, and cradled in my mother's bosom, as I had been before it. Here it has the best of care, the best of food, — both physical and mental, — and the best love; and here it is going to remain, in spite of father-rights, law-rights, or Satan-rights. Divine rights are over and above them all; and they give the child, regardless of sex, to the mother, particularly if she has always supported it, is able to continue to do so, and is in every respect a true, pure woman."

"These are pretty theories, prettily spoken, Mary," said Vincent, with a look of tranquil superiority upon his face peculiar to men; "but they won't hold water; they don't belong to solids."

Without heeding the ironical interruption she continued, —

"To my mother I am indebted for life to-day. She gave me a refuge in my bitter need, and she has sheltered and provided for my child — with such assistance as I have been able to render — ever since. But now the just law has power to steal him out of her bosom and mine. And for what, forsooth?

Because he is a male child, and I refuse to live with his father for crimes that Christianity and virtuous society wink at in a man, but which in a woman they brand as *fallen* and *outcast;* which give a wide space in passing, lest their holy and sanctimonious garments be smirched by contact. O Christianity, justice, and consistency, what jewels thou art!"

"Mary, you can safely count me out as a henpecked husband, or a fit subject for petticoat-rule in any form of canting homilies. I've not been used to them. I shall never turn teetotaller to please any woman; and there are some other things necessary to the health and enjoyment of men, which I don't think incompatible with good husbands."

He waited an answer, as he gazed at her with a look of mingled admiration and defiance. It was a beautiful picture to *look* upon. She had unconsciously taken the exact pose of the *di San Sisto* Madonna. The child in its play had untied her bonnet-strings, and it had fallen upon the grass at her feet, leaving the head uncovered save by its own wealth of auburn hair, which was gathered in all its wavy luxuriance in a loose knot at the back, from which escaped here and there a curl that the wind moved gently with a loving touch. Her form retained all its girlish, symmetrical beauty, while the crown of motherhood sat upon her brow with a matchless grace.

She was looking far out beyond the line of the village, upon the billowy meadows and sloping hillsides, where the long shafts of the setting sun lay like glory-rays, throwing over the whole scene a golden halo.

What a picture! and what a grouping!—that gathered family of three generations, riven by vice; the father and mother so young and so beautiful, and should have been so happy—so capable were they of receiving and imparting happiness; the lovely child; the aged mother and grandmother, touched by the frosts of many winters, scorched by the rays of many summers, and withered by the breath of many sorrows; the little dog sitting upon the door-step, impatient and anxious, waiting to have a frolic with its young master; the surly coachman, whose looks plainly showed that he would like to see *his* "wimmin-folks" making such a fuss; the tired horses; the dusty road; the pretty cottage, with its vine-clad veranda. How peaceful and happy it looked, all save the *dramatis personæ.* It made an ineffaceable impression upon my memory, stamped in with imperishable dyes, never to be obliterated by time.

The father broke in upon the mother's revery, by saying to the child, "Come and ride in the pretty carriage with papa?"

"No!" answered the boy. "Me 'ill stay wid mamma an' g'an'ma. Me s'ant 'ide to-day. Go!"

"Yes, I will go; but the next time I come *you* will go too, I'm thinking, and you won't come back either." Without another word he entered the carriage, and drove rapidly away. His last prophetic sentence was spoken in anger, resentment, and brute-force power, strengthened by brute-force laws to subordinate the physically weak. Ah! how little he divined its import, its terrible significance! The next time he came, little Willie did go to ride in a "pretty carriage;" but it was long and narrow, with black plumes waving over it. The father followed, speechless, in the ashes of his supremacy, a sadder if not a better man. Man proposes, but God disposes.

CHAPTER XVI.

SPLIT-WOOD AND THIRDS.

Jure humano.

GRANNY GREEN sat spinning on her little wheel, one summer afternoon; and as the shining flax slipped through her fingers, and was twisted into a thread that would make the warp of the crash-towels that were wanted up at the big house on the hill, she crooned an old love-ditty, ever and anon glancing over her spectacles at Tab, sitting bolt upright by her side, with his tail comfortably wrapped round his toes to keep them warm. They both appeared to be buried in their own thoughts: Tab's probably ran on the habits of mice and the prehistoric gopher, while his mistress's were wandering among the living memories of the dead past, thinking of the pretty picture in the looking-glass and mirrored in the still pond sixty years ago, when she first knew Obadiah Green, — Obadiah, whose last resting-place is marked by the swelling mound under the willow on the other side of the brook which comes tumbling down the hillside, laughing and purling in a thousand sparkling eddies as it hurries toward the river, —

"For men may come, and men may go, but it laughs on forever," — thinking of the day when she stood in bridal white, with snowy blossoms in her hair, and promised to love and obey Obadiah Green "till death do us part."

She had kept her vows — not a hard thing for her to do at that period of the world's history, for Granny Green spun her last skein and sung her last ditty fifty years ago. In those non-"*evil* days" a wife and children knew no law but the law of blind obedience to the legal master, the father and husband. Against these laws of the "Medes and Persians," Granny Green never rebelled. She loved Obadiah: to her it was "a pleasure to do his bidding," and "pleasure physics pain." They had lived in peace with each other, and with all the world beside; blessing God when a little child was born unto them, and not repining when it was laid away, like a withered flower, under the daisies.

Granny Green was comely in person at fourscore. She had grown old gracefully for one in her humble sphere in life. Trials she had had, for those none can escape; but she had borne the most of them with meekness, and the expectant trust of the true believer in the joys of the life to come. But there was one trial in reserve for her, during all those years, that, when it came, was most distasteful to her; and she, with all her Christian philosophy, was unable to reconcile it with dutiful forbearance.

At the time of Obadiah Green's death, she was

living in the big house on the hill. That was her home, and there she expected to dwell the remnant of her days on earth; and from that house she expected the messenger to call for her; and from out that door, with baptismal blood of ownership upon its lintel, she expected to be carried in white robes, with folded hands and placid brow, and laid beside the husband of her youth, the tried companion of maturity, and the father of her children, there to rest till the sound of the trumpet should bid her "come up higher." But she was mistaken. She had trusted in God's divine laws of right and justice, not man's; but on earth it would seem, as regards marriage law, that God proposes and man disposes. Obadiah's testament ran thus: "I will and bequeath to my beloved wife, Sally Green, the third part of all my possessions, houses, lands, live stock, furniture, &c., to use and to hold for her benefit during her natural life; the which, at her death, must be equally divided between my two surviving children, Obadiah and Sally. To my son and daughter I bequeath an equal amount, one-third of all I die seized, to each — share and share alike. I further will that my son Obadiah, immediately after my burial, move into my house, and take my place in regard to my wife and his mother, paying, as soon as convenient, my daughter Sally — wife of John Wood — the value of one-third of the house and the furniture therein."

Obadiah, jr., was living at that time in the little

house where Granny Green was accustomed to spin, and philosophize on the ups and downs of life in her old age.

The mandates of the legal instrument were carried out to the letter. For one year Mrs. Green — *old* Mrs. Green: no one thought of calling her *Granny* when she lived in the big house on the hill — made her home with her son. Although the house had nine rooms besides the kitchen, old Mrs. Green soon found out that a third of nine rooms, plus the kitchen, meant one small bedroom off the general sitting-room, where the youthful Greens, sons and daughters of Obadiah, jr., were ready at all times to pounce in upon her quiet, upturning her work-basket, upsetting her wheel, and upheaving all peace and good order, besides engendering an uprising of hostile feelings in the breast of the grandmother against the encroachers and transient squatters upon her limited territory.

At last there came a day when patience had ceased to be a virtue; and old Mrs. Green had a "*serious*" talk with Obadiah, jr., the result of which was a removal of the disturbing element in that gentleman's household to safer quarters, the little cottage known as "Granny Green's cottage." She got the pleasing *sobriquet* of "Granny" from her grandchildren, who always spoke to and of her as "*Granny*" ever after the removal.

Her son rarely visited her, unless she was sick; his wife, never; and, when the children came, they were, as ever, an affliction and a perpetual torment as long as they staid. Tab took to the ridge-pole of the cottage as soon as he saw one of their noses poked through the gate; he having great respect and consideration for that member of his body-corporeal which the "guid mare Meg" lost on the "Brig o' Doon," by an unlucky contact with a near kin of theirs. Towz would suddenly remember that he had not paid his dead master a visit in "mony" a day, and go trotting off down the well-worn path and up the knoll, where he would stretch himself at full length among the myrtle which covered the mossy mounds. There was more than one to cover. Standing in the space between the longest and shortest of these graves was an old-fashioned splint-bottomed chair. In that chair, every day when the sun shone, sat Granny Green, with Tab in her lap, and Towz at her feet, thinking, always thinking. She was not obliged to do much but think nowadays, for Maggie, the maid-of-all-work at the big house on the hill, came every morning to "rid" things up; but she always came too late, and found every thing in spick-span order when she got there. Granny Green was the soul of order, and her physical wants were few and easily supplied; but she was human, and, like the most of us, she often got very tired of *thinking*. Then she would spin and knit for the thankless people in the big house on the hill; but she could not drive away thought by the hum of the wheel, or the click of her knitting-needles. Wearying of both, she would call to Tab and Towz, and bid them listen to what she had to say to them. They were intelligent companions, and knew the history of the last three generations of Greens, all by heart.

On this particular afternoon, when Granny Green sat crooning at her spinning-wheel, she heard a light footfall upon the brick walk, and looking up, she saw Hetty, her favorite granddaughter, a rosy lass of nineteen summers plus nineteen winters, but to the grandmother still a child who ought to be in short clothes and pinafores, instead of indulging in sweethearts and long dresses. The song and the wheel stopped at the same instant; and, putting out her hand, she said, "Where've you been, child? I've not seen you for a fortni't."

"I wanted to come and see you, Granny," replied Hetty, pressing her fresh red lips to the faded cheek of the old lady; "but we've been very busy up at the house,"—as it was usually called by members of the family,—"and I couldn't find a spare minnit till this afternoon." "Why, what's up now? No more weddin's, I hope," sighed Granny Green; for although the children of her only son were far from being all she could wish, yet when they dropped out of her uneventful life, by death or marriage, their places left a vacancy which could never be filled. They were of her blood; and blood is stronger than water, if it has not been perverted — adulterated — beyond all recognition.

In spite of her constant companions, the dog and

cat, Granny Green led a very lonely life among the memories of the past, and the graves of her dead; and, in spite of her trust in God, she oftentimes felt very rebellious over her unnecessarily hard and cheerless lot. She was in this mood when interrupted by the coming of Hetty.

The young girl dropped down upon the grass before the spinning-wheel, and, throwing off her gingham sun-bonnet, patted Tab on the head, as she answered the query of her grandmother in the shortest possible way.

"Yes, Granny," she made reply, while her face turned crimson, "there *is* to be a wedding up at the house."

"Who's trapped this time, — man, or boy; woman, or child?" almost groaned Granny Green.

"I don't know what you call *me*, Granny, but I'm the bird that's caught," said Hetty, laughing, and bending over Tab, who had curled himself up in her lap, to better hide her blushes. She and Tab had been on the most amicable terms ever since she had eschewed short frocks.

"*You*, child!" screamed Granny Green, throwing up her hands, and sitting back in her chair so suddenly that her spectacles flew over the top of the distaff, happily lodging in the ample tuft of flax which adorned it, and thus saving their owner the price of a new pair; for, had they fallen to the walk, they would have been dashed to fragments. Her cap-frill fairly bristled with excitement. As soon as she recovered her breath, she continued, "Why, it's only yesterday, as it were, that you were born; and now to be married! What is Obadiah thinking about?"

"How old were you, Granny, when you were married?" demurely questioned Hetty, as one who knows that he has the head of the nail in sight, and the hammer in hand ready to strike.

"I? lem'me see: I — why, bless me, I was eighteen!"

"And I am *nineteen*, a year older than you were," said Hetty triumphantly.

"That's nothing whatever to do with it, Hetty Green. That was sixty years ago, and people ought to learn something in sixty years. You are no more fit to git married than a baby: you never have spun a skein of yarn nor wove a yard of cloth in your life; you don't know how to cook a meal of vittles, nor wash dishes, nor make butter, nor turn the heel of a stockin'."

"I don't need to," said Hetty, with a satisfied look at her white, shapely hands, that were never to lose their beauty by hard labor and uncongenial pursuits, "for we are going to live in the city, and board."

"Heaven help you, then!" continued Granny Green, "for that's no life at all. Every one ought to hev a hum ov their own, an' stay in it till they die, an' they should be content to live single till they git it. I tell you what, Hetty Green, no woman's fit to git married in these degen'rate days, when it's all book-larnin' and no practicability, under twenty-five."

"What's amiss now, Granny?" chimed in a man's voice; and looking up she saw, leaning over the low fence at the side of the house, a man who had been hunting, judging from his appearance, for he had a gun upon his shoulder, and a brace of ducks in his hand. "Who's dead, sick, or married? What's the matter?"

"Matter enough, Caleb White," replied Granny Green, as she asked the new-comer to get over the fence, and take a "chair," saying in her thoughtful way, "You must be all fagged out after such a long tramp as it is to the Salt Marsh an' back agin." The man did not wait to be urged further, but scaled the fence at a bound, and, coming forward, took the proffered chair, and with a friendly nod to Hetty said, "I hope nothink's goin' wrong wid you an' the young lawyer, miss."

"Nothing," responded Hetty, with a sly laugh: "we're not married yet."

"Before you are, Hetty, if you take my advice," said the old lady, "you'll make this gay young square promise that you shall have the hum, unmolested, as long as you live, an' in case of his death the half of the property shall be your'n. If he won't do this, give him his walkin'-stick; for I tell you it's very hard, when you're old an' gray, to be turned out of doors on a third ov what you an' he hev arnt together, an' hev to be content for the rest ov your days on split-wood an' thirds, — *split-wood an' thirds!*"

What Granny Green meant by split-wood remains a mystery to this day. True, the ample fireplace in the little cottage took in a big backlog, which would last a week, and that was always round; no desecrating axe or wedge had cleaved off a fibre of its rotundity; but upon the polished fire-dogs in front of it was piled split-wood, which crackled and snapped on a cold night in midwinter, sending up myriads of sparks that whirled in an eddy above the roaring chimney-top, and fell in a fiery shower upon the snow-covered roof of the cottage. Perhaps her own symbolic life had suggested a simile; for at eighty she stood alone, a riven trunk, cleft and storm-beaten, without one green leaf or branch upon it, waiting, waiting!

CHAPTER XVII.

"THRITEN'D WID A CONTINUENZE" — IN PART ALLEGORICAL.

Le renard prêche aux poules.

GROPING my way one morning through the clouds of tobacco-smoke and bad air of the Probate Court-room, warily guarding against being upset and falling prone upon my face in consequence of various and sundry masculine appurtenances called spittoons — before the throne of *his Honor*, the high and mighty judge of the quick, and the *will* of the dead, I suddenly came in contact with a little woman, all up and down. I mean by this, that the space she occupied was mostly perpendicular space. She was thin as a knife-blade, double-edged, and her dress was as meagre as her person. It was composed of a linsey-woolsey gown, very narrow in the skirt (statuesque), with an old mangy-black shawl so tattered and worn that it was a marvel how she got to the court-room that breezy morning with a shred of it left upon her shoulders. A cap with a full frill, which looked as though it had been mislaid in the coal-scuttle for a month, adorned her head. The only ample thing about her, in the line of dress, was the shoes she had on; and they evidently belonged to some one else, — her "old man" probably, — for they were of the heroic gender of shoes, made of cowhide, and called brogans. A pair of small, twinkling gray eyes looked straight ahead along the bridge of her nose, and shot off the end of it in a parallel line, piercing the murky atmosphere like an arrow, until the course of vision was obstructed by the judge's chambers — which, by the by, ought not to be pluralized; for they (or it, rather) consist of one diminutive room. It is long and narrow, like a coffin, and has the stifling, unwholesome odor of a charnel-house; for every nook and cranny, from floor to ceiling, upon the chairs and under the carpet, clinging to the walls and festooned over the windows and doors, are the dead hopes of widows and orphans mouldering and rotting away. It is full of sighs, and damp with ever-falling tears. The pall of death broods above it. I *hate* that room, with all its tyrannical mortmain associations. In it I have been lectured upon widow-propriety, the quintessence of female modesty, the necessity of possessing my unruly soul in patience, the beauty of bending a stiff neck to the yoke of circumstances, the holiness of humble submission to probate rule, etc., etc. It is the only place where I have shed tears before the mighty; but, thank God! there was only a drop or two wrung out. That was enough to mollify "his Honor" somewhat; for there is nothing which an arbitrary man delights in so much as to see a woman cry, particularly a strong-minded one. I am ashamed to chronicle this momentary weakness; but I was sick and needy, had no money to buy bread, medicine, or *gloves*, and was threatened to be sued by another sex autocrat. What marvel that I wept? It is a marvel that I did not flood the place, and drown "his Honor" in a deluge of tears.

But to return to the little long woman with the fiery eye, the scant gown, and the big shoes, who is waiting outside of the judge's charnel-house of withered hopes; outside of it, but inside of the railing which separates the court from the lobby. The Probate Court has a lobby, where sit the uninitiated and the "great unwashed." In this lobby, on that particular morning, stood a small specimen of humanity, — a kind of an apology for a boy, but a poor one. He was a species of the "Lost Heir" genus, which suggests the "missing link;" hatless, shoeless, and friendless he looked, uncombed, dirty, and ragged. What did he want there? He was not a widow. He might have been an orphan; and yet that would have been a preposterous supposition, for where was his male guardian? Where was the lynx-eyed protector of his orphan rights against the marauding propensities of his mother, — the widow mother, eager to squander her child's substance? I was interrupted in my cogitations over the small boy by the perpendicular woman, who punched me in my side with her elbow, which was as sharp and incisive as an uncapped foil, and said, —

"Are yez a widdy, too, darlint? and hev they tied up all what yersel' and yer ould man arnt in his life? God rest his sowl!"

"Yes, all," I replied.

"Och! God help yez, thin," she continued, "for it's gon *intirely*, an' there's no help for't."

The uncovering of potential heads, and a slight stir like the ripple of a summer wind through a forest, warned us to be silent; for the judge was enthroned upon his seat, which is a soft cushioned chair — a *revolver*. The moment my neighbor, my sister-widow-in-affliction, caught sight of this mortal-immaculate functionary, she nimbly placed herself in front of the throne, and with a hand on either hip, and an old-fashioned courtesy, — which must have originated the idea of a baby-jumper, — she said in a piping falsetto, —

"Jidge *May*-rick" — "*My*-rick," chimed in the judge parenthetically, putting a strong accent on the "*My*," and getting very red in the face. ("What's in a name? A rose by any other name would smell as sweet.") "Yer Honor," she continued, taking no notice of the momentary interruption, "will yez hev the graciousness to giv an ixthra illowanze for sick ness?"

Judge. — "Who's sick now?"

Widow. — "Little Patsy, y'r Honor."

Judge. — "What's the matter with him?"

Widow. — "He's thritened wid a continuenze, y'r Honor."

Judge. — "A *continuance!* what's that?"

Widow. — "That's for the docthur to tell whin he lucks at 'is tung and fales 'is pullse, y'r Honor."

Judge. — "Give him a dose of pikery, or salts, or Hull's physic: his blood's bad."

Widow. — "No, 'taint, y'r Honor; we've not had the docthur yit: so plaze gim me the ixthra illowanze, an' long life t' y'r Honor!"

Judge. — "But, my good woman, the estate *may be* insolvent; and in that case I cannot grant a further allowance, unless it is an emergency of life or death."

Widow. — "Niver throuble y'rsel', a divil a bit, y'r Honor, aboot the '*May-bees;*' for, hiven save y'r Honor, they niver flies this time o' the year. So jist gi'm me the ixthra, so that I may be afther goin' t' me pure sick darlint, who is a-waitin' on one fut outside o' the ralint."

Judge. — "But, madam, I cannot do it: it might defraud the creditors."

Widow. — "The credithors, indade! What hev they to do wid the nades uv me sick Patsy?"

Judge. — "No, madam! I must protect the interest of the creditors; they sustain me in office; they are rich and powerful, while you are only a poor miserable woman, without money, without influence, without votes, — the three things most needful for judges to guard with jealous care."

Widow. — "Oh, plaze, Misther Jidge dear, do give me a wee bit uv ixthra illowanze, that I may be goin', for shure Pathrick would cum out uv his grave to plade wid yez if he only knew how disthressed I wuz. Faix, y'r Honor, he declared to ma wid 'is last breath a'most—God rest his sowl—that he owed no craythur on arth a pinny; an' now Michael O'Rooney, 'is best buzzom friend, taks the ruff frum over me hed an' the heds of the darlints that Pathrick would hev spilt 'is last dhrap of blud fur. An' y'r Honor calls this *justice* an' a fra counthry!"

Judge.—"Yes, madam: every creditor is *free* to demand his share of the estate, if he presents his claim, which I must in justness approve."

Widow.—"And the pure widdy an' orphins is to git nothin', bekase, forsooth, there is no rale estate, no house and lot, no pig in the pen an' cow in the lot that belonged to Pathrick an' ma. I've kept hous fur Pathrick McGee fur twinty yers, cuck'd 'is males, washed 'is close, an' nussed 'is babies; who will pay ma fur this woruk? Will yer Honor appruve *my* claim whin I brings it in?"

Judge.—"No, madam. You were supported, clothed, fed, and housed for your services. That ought to satisfy any *reasonable* woman."

Widow.—"That don't satisfy *ma*, an' it wouldn't ha' satisfied Pathrick McGee, y'r Honor."

Judge.—"You are difficult to please, madam."

Widow.—"But, y'r Honor, the credithors be rich; they wouldn't miss the wee mite to them, but a big mite to the childer an' ma if it be left to us in pace."

Judge.—"That is irrelevant to the case, madam.

It matters not how rich they may be, or how poor you are: the law must take its unbending course. There can be no exceptions made, no mischievous precedents set up."

Widow. — "An' you sind me away impty-handed, whin I'm in sickniss an' throuble, and little Patsy thritened wid a continuenze, wid no hat on 'is hed, an' no money to buy any wid; wid no shoes fur 'is feet, an' no money to buy any wid; wid no med'cine in 'is stummick, an' no money to buy any wid. Oh, jidge! I don't likes to be oncivil and spiteful, but may the Lord chastise you wid a *continuenze*, punish you wid *poverty*, and afflict you wid the *widdy's law!*"

The judge fairly bristled with rage at this unexpected outburst from a poor starveling of a woman. His long head was erect; his eyes glistened and gleamed through his spectacles like two red-hot coals of fire. Ah! what eyes to *see* widows! a patient, patronizing eye for peaceful, quiescent, abnegating widows; a sublime eye for rich, clinging-vine widows; a stormy, uncompromising eye for poverty-stricken widows; a wrathful, unforgiving eye for refractory, hot-headed widows, who dare ask the "whys" and "wherefores" of things.

His mouth worked nervously. Such a mouth to *talk* to widows! — a wise mouth, full to overflowing with wisdom; a pompous mouth, that knows the value and circumstance of ermine; a decided mouth, that, when it says no, means no, a final "no," which admits of no appeal. In this particular case, however, that mouth was silent; but he — the judge — turned upon his deputy an *awful* look, a thousand times more eloquent with meaning than words, at which the servitor placed himself alongside of the little-long-fiery-eyed widow, and whispered something in her ear that made her start back with a look of blank horror. But she instantly recovered herself, and turning slowly around, face door-ward, she edged herself out, between smiling lawyers with "fat" cases, and between grim lawyers with "*lean*" cases. She went as noiselessly as the "ghosts came," — that shadow of a woman, a widow and mother, — followed closely by the mongrel boy Patsy, with his "*thritened continuenze.*"

As the last tatter disappeared through the doorway, the judge moved nervously upon his soft-cushioned revolving seat, turning first to the right, then to the left, then faced (red-faced) about front; which was, I took it, a dignified way of shaking himself out, after a disagreeable wordy combat. After an instant's repose, to lay the last ruffled feather, he exclaimed in his usual melodious key, "What case comes up first this morning?" In the momentary pause which ensued, I chipped in, and said, "Judge Myrick, how much longer is the estate of J. W. Stow to remain undistributed? I heard you give orders six weeks ago to have it distributed at once. Have you no more power in your official position than this? Why don't you enforce the carrying out of your orders? Here is this estate being entirely consumed by the daily accumulation of interest on approved claims. Call you this administering *justice*, or fair dealing? *I don't.*" Without letting a perceptible ripple cross the benevolent expression which he had, with no little effort, moulded into his face for the day, after the first feminine tussle was ended, he made answer, —

"Send your lawyer, Mrs. Stow, send your lawyer. This is a legal question which you do not understand. Send your lawyer." And without waiting a reply he called, with a gustatorial smack of the lips, that echoed through the court-room like a pistol-crack, "The case of the widow *Peaceful* is in order." Ah! this was one of the "*fat*" cases "*with money in it;*" and the widow was a lovely "*clinging-vine widow*," covered with rare buds of helplessness and sweet blossoms of dependence. Charming creature! What a relief to come upon fallow ground after the stones and thistles! The judge waved his majestic right hand to me as a final dismissal. I made my way "*fast*" out of that court-room, fearing I might do some one bodily harm; for what was I to do? I had no lawyer, and San Francisco lawyers are not to be had for the asking, not even during leap-year; and when I put in a legal document praying the court and the judge of the court *to show cause* "*why*" there is no notice taken of it, beyond its being filed, buried out of sight and out of mind forever.

I was out of that *just* court, down the stairs, and

in the second hall-way, ere I knew what I was doing; the sting of outrage, wrong, and injustice which I had witnessed that morning had struck so deep. Hearing a suppressed sob, I turned quickly to learn what there was worth crying about outside of that abominable court, and saw the little long woman crouching in the angle of the wall, holding fast by one hand the "*thritened continuenze*," while with the other she wiped her eyes (from which all the fire was quenched by her fast-flowing tears) with one end of the mangy-black shawl. Going up to where she was, I laid my hand upon her arm, and said, "I am so sorry for you! Have you really nothing left? Has it come to that?"

"Nothin' at all, at all," she sobbed. "Ye see, Pathrick had two best frins, an' they allus wus togither in bizniz. He got in det to wun uv 'em, an' munny a long day it tuck for Pathrick an' ma to pay it; but 'twus all paid at last, an' thin we begun to put muny in the bank to by a hum wid, a cow an' pig, an' we had a'most enuf whin the guid Lard tuck 'im away, — pace to 'is ashes, — an' now 'is two buzzum frins taks it all, all the hard arnins and savins uv mysel' an' dear dead Pathrick, an' laves ma an' the pure leetle craythurs that Pathrick luvd so much to stharve.

"Oh, what shall I do? what shall I do?" she continued, swaying her thin body to and fro in her bitter distress, "whin it taks all ma time to cuck the males an' make the cloze of the five uv us, let alone the arnin. What kin I do? I'm not sthrong, an' the baby, the wee todlin' thing, is allus alin. Oh, dear! Oh, dear, my pure heart will brake!"

"If he paid this debt which he owed his friend, where are the receipts for it?" I questioned.

"Indade, mum! yez'll hev to ask the executioners: they be the wuns that knows all about it, an' they be the two frins apinted by his *Honor* to sarve. Pathrick didn't lay out to dy till the last minit, and thin there was no time fur the makin uv wills. An' whin he was under the sod they — the frins — cum an' ran-seck'd me hous and tuck all there wus uv any vally; an' it's themselves that's got all the muny an' the resates — more's the sorrer fur Bridget MacGee an' her pure distitute darlints!"

CHAPTER XVIII.

HUSBANDS *vs.* PIN-MONEY.

Audire est operæ pretium.

How is it that marriage acts as such an astringent upon purse-strings? In many cases they seem to have got so closely entangled in the hymeneal knot that they never have been set free, but have remained in this vexed and vexatious condition during the entire marriage probation.

During courtship Charles Augustus's money flows like clear water at high tide; but there is a perceptible ebb at the first quarter of the honeymoon, and it keeps at low tide ever afterwards. The husband provides no stated income for the wife, and when she has any money she has to ask for it like a child. At the time of solicitation there may not be the required sum in the purse-carrier's pocket, and that will necessitate another humiliating appeal ere the money is obtained. It is a very hard thing for a young wife — or an old one, as to that matter — to beg for money — that which she feels is hers by right. For does not the husband pledge her at the altar, "With all my worldly goods I thee endow"?

He may think that "worldly goods" do not include money. Many husbands act upon this principle all their lives. I venture to assert that there are more heart-aches, in the marriage relation, over this one question of pin-money than any other.

Most husbands are fashioned in the same mould as Caudle: if they lose money at cards, or upon a bet on their favorite horse at the races, or in some more disreputable way, the wife has to do penance for their sins by being cut down in her pin-money. If she is keeping house, the cupboard must pay for the masculine folly of an hour, or a day, as the case may be. Besides, the poor wife — like Mrs. Caudle number two — usually gets a lesson thrown in, on the sin of wastefulness, and the necessity of hoarding up against a rainy day or a bad day of any sort, instead of spending money for perishable gewgaws, such as silks, velvets, and loves of bonnets; while he, the righteous judge, puffs his royal Havana, and thinks of the sumptuous *male*-banquet ordered, at his expense, at the *Maison Dorée*, at fifty or a hundred dollars the cover, for himself and a few of his dear friends, his jovial pot-house companions, —

("O, Willie brewed a peck o' maut,
And Rob and Allen came to see:
Three blither hearts, that leelang night,
Ye wad na find in Christendie")

while the wife mopes at home, new-lining his coat-sleeves, and sewing on shirt-buttons. Men never waste any money. Oh, no! 'Tis the weaker vessel which has a leak that no tinkering seems to stop. What a pity it is, that it is so! for all men declare mentally, if not orally, with the above-mentioned martyr, "that it is a woman's place to save, — particularly a woman's place — to *save*. Women" — not men — "were designed for it. Economy is one of the noblest virtues bound up with matrimony." However, as it is, and as it has been from the beginning, it is a misshapen, one-sided bundle, because the economy is expected to be all on one side, — the wife's side. This throws every thing out of balance, and consequently there is eternal friction and jarring where, were it otherwise, all might be harmony and long life.

I believe that we should all live out our allotted time — a hundred years — on earth, and most women would, if it were not for this perpetual, intestine, hearthstone warfare about pin-money. This old, hereditary, matrimonial cancer is what has eaten out the hearts of thousands of wives since the advent of fig-leaves.

Custom and law, for the most part, put all the money of the marriage-firm in the hands of the husband. The wife lives as an ignoble dependent. She has only what is given her, cheerfully or grudgingly, as the case may be, — probably the latter, — after asking for it. But she inevitably learns to hate her position, and to grow away from the man who only gives the money she has richly earned, when he is asked for it. This is certain to create discontent and a sense of humiliation; and that most rare and beautiful thing, particularly in wedlock, trust and affection, is gradually lost sight of, while scheming calculation too often takes its place.

The old, moss-grown absurdity, that wives earn no money, is yet cherished in the hearts of husbands, and will continue to be until women are emancipated from political bondage. They look upon wives as dependents upon their bounty; and dependents are always unfortunate. They belong to the unfortunate class.

"Before marriage, a woman's income flows into her own pocket; after, into that of the man she marries. She may have earned it by teaching a few hours a day, and she had all the rest of her time for study and pleasure; but after marriage all her time is consumed in making a pleasant home. She has neither money nor leisure; and she feels just like the pauper and beggar she is, and turns a wistful, retrospective glance back to the old happy days ere she yoked herself to humiliation and dependence."

Is it surprising that she grows old and faded before her prime? When I hear a man boasting that he has had three or four wives, I feel to a certainty that chronic pin-money has been a constant guest in his household. Those wives were all carried off by the continuous or epidemic plague of pin-money. They died of pin-money! It should be engraven upon the headstone of each: Number one, two, or three, wives of Jonathan Grubb, Esq.; died of pin-money. *Requiescat in pace.*

Life ought to be sweet and enjoyable to every one. It is our duty to see to it that it is made to flow healthfully forward, up into the nineties at least. The lower species of the animal kingdom live to the age of five times the period of their growth. The same law would fix man's allotted pilgrimage to be a hundred years. From recent statistics, it would seem that we are yet to enjoy our full complement of decades; women in particular — those that have lived natural and temperate lives, and have not been subjected to a daily crucifixion for the want of pin-money. When woman is properly educated, and thoroughly understands the wonderfully beautiful mechanism of the human form divine, she will no longer torture it out of all proportions for effect. And such an effect! a hideous deformity that pains the eye of all cultivated and æsthetic taste, stifles health in the germ, dams its bounding current at its source. Educate her to aspire to be something above the mere physical plaything of man, and she will cease to incase her body in a strait-jacket, her feet in a vice, and her soul in vapidity.

What is the offering which the average man brings to a woman before marriage? A little chalk-and-water sentiment, administered with a good deal of flattery of this sort: "What a dear little foot you've got! — sure sign of good blood (most likely every toe has a corn and every joint a bunion, where the good blood makes a telling assertion), and such lovely snowflake hands! I can always tell a genuine lady by the size and fit of her glove. What charming eyes, complexion, and teeth like pearls! (hope they're not false), and hair, if black, that puts to shame the raven's wing; if tawny, it is spun gold — a fleece of morning light; if red, it is bewitchingly auburn, Venetian-bronze, incomparably beautiful." And then she sings like an angel (as though a man could tell how an angel sings), and waltzes like a sylph (who ever saw a sylph waltz?).

He never sounds the real depths of her heart, and never asks what there is hidden in the more subtle chambers of the brain. These are unexplored regions before marriage, and after there is no time for such things. He may learn too late, however, that snowflake hands are not the most useful hands, that they are often unhandy hands.

What if she does prefer the opera, *salon*, or rout, to her own dull hearth? Has she not been educated for that? Educate a boy at the faro-table, and then punish him for gambling. Consistency is a rare jewel!

Men create and multiply lucrative offices, and elect men to fill them whose salaries in part come directly and indirectly from the unrepresented and proscribed class; and, if there is a dissenting voice raised, then the daring ones are called naughty names, and dubbed Amazonian agitators, hybridous invaders of masculine territory, etc., etc.

Give woman the same free start in life ere you cast one stone, O most wise, upright man! Put yourself in her place ere you condemn wholesale; before you declare that we are trying to be men, while born women. Therein, most dearly beloved brethren, you err. What right have you to pass judgment? You have, from the beginning, drawn life from first principles; you have not been compelled to be content with a parasitic growth. as women have; and now that they are outgrowing the slavishness of ignoble dependence, are you to hurl them back to the old standpoint by sarcasm, innuendoes, and scorn? No, no! the good time coming will secure pin-money without begging for it.

When a wife's education and political position will warrant, she will be likely to say to the husband, "If you furnish me with the necessary amount of pin-money, very well: if not, I shall be obliged to earn it." And she will be able to earn it. At that time all the lucrative business in the world will not be absorbed by men. Cities, states, and nation will have found out that women are quite as capable, efficient, and honest public servants as men. Then women will not be forced into the trade of prostitution for a livelihood, "dealing in shame for a morsel of bread."

Protection and prohibition have walked hand in hand long enough. Give woman an equal footing before the laws made by man, and God's laws will adjust themselves accordingly. They have always, when unperverted, been in equipoise, and will continue to remain so. Woman will retain her attributes, as woman, without any wish or desire to exchange her finer nature for that of the coarser man.

The most of husbands have yet to learn that the wife requires a fixed income, the same as the housemaid, hostler, scullion, and boot-black, and that if she is denied this right she is an unhappy and discontented wife. I know wives in San Francisco that have the most meagre sums grudgingly doled out to them for the payment of board or the household expenses, and out of this craven pittance they have to manage to clothe themselves as best they may. Such wives are not happy wives, nor contented with their lot, and who would be? They are careful, economical housekeepers; and yet, for all their painstaking, they get no thanks, no pay, no appreciation. They are mentally and physically crushed by such thankless servitude, and the heavy, galling chains that bind them to this Promethean rock. The vulture of discontent is at their vitals. What wonder that they grow narrow and prematurely old, in such a pinching, grinding life, with no door of escape? Driven to desperation, should they even attempt to obtain a situation where they could earn money, they are refused with scorn, and the impertinent query, "What do you mean? Your husband is a man of means and position in the community; he would feel it an everlasting disgrace to have his wife enter an office to earn money." But he does not feel it an "everlasting disgrace" to have her existence clouded, imbittered, and shortened by the sad consciousness that she is but a cipher to the integral figure, — the husband, — and that every dollar she has to clothe herself with must be pinched out of the servants' hire and butcher's bill in two-bit pieces. This style of husband — to keep himself in equilibrium, evidently — is generally most prodigal of money outside of his own hearthstone. He wears the finest cloth, and latest cut; and neighbors wonder how he happened to marry such a commonplace-looking woman for a wife, who has no taste in dress; for dress, to superficial observers, oft makes the *woman* as well as the man. He refuses her a stated income, because it would place her on the same plane as a mistress. Mistresses and servants enjoy stated incomes — not wives. Wifehood is a continuous apprenticeship for board and clothes; and the getting of the latter is a never-ceasing bone of contention, — a consuming matrimonial fire that never lacks fuel.

When the wife of one of these money despots dies of chronic pin-money, she has a sumptuous coffin and a grand funeral, with a free ride for all — the first expensive thing for her exclusive benefit since her marriage. Then all the anxious matable women stand on tiptoe of expectation, and moralize over the sad and lonely condition of Mr. *Save-at-home*. They are all ready to step into the vacant shoes of wife number one. But when some doll-faced, lily-fingered miss in her teens comes into possession, the husband's name changes to Mr. *Spend-at-home;*

and then the money flies, and there is no help for it. Wife number two, like a sensible woman, runs up bills, and leaves them to be collected, when and how she cares not; and there is no use in Caudle-lecturing her. She is totally indifferent and impervious to impending ruin. Didn't she marry the ancient and frisky fossil for pin-money, and nothing else? Love him! the stupid bundle of conceit, old enough to be her father, and ugly enough to be her grandfather; an old boy who apes younger men, and mistakes the premonitory twinges of gout and rheumatism for youthful fire in the blood; who ambles through the giddy mazes of the ball-room like an animated skeleton in a white vest and claw-hammer! Such specimens of humanity are always boys. You can always pick them out wherever you find them. They are filled top-full of folly, vanity, and all manner of conceit. They imagine themselves the centre of the universe wherein they dwell, — the observed of all observers. Your old boy is generally a society boy, — a weak imitation of a Beau Brummel. He wears a wig, or parts his sparse and waning growth of back-hair in the middle, combing it into a scant fringe for the embellishment of each ear, which gives to his countenance a fierce and asinine expression — particularly when he sports a Napoleonic moustache, and goes forth in search of fresh prey to conquer. Marriage with such "boys" is simply a convenience. They are too mean and penurious to pay a housekeeper, button-fastener, and stocking-mender, a salary: so they marry the trinity, and become masters of the situation, and their hearts — if they have any, which is doubtful — remain in the highlands.

Your old boy is to be found in full feather at *matinées*, and, if his pliant conscience takes on a serious complexion, in church festivals and sabbath-school conventions. He is to be met with in every walk of life. He roams at will, fancy-free. The silken bonds impose no restraint upon him.

When such an addle-pate possesses the requisite amount of means, he is sent to the legislature, to make wicked and oppressive laws to govern intelligent women (money, not brains, too often make the laws); and the wife is left at home, to keep the fire-dogs bright, and the hearth swept and garnished, while his time is divided, when out of the "Chamber," between fast horses and faster women.

There has been blown a clarion blast from the four quarters of the globe, about the folly and extravagance of feather-brained women. It is penned and shouted from every desk and rostrum in the land. Pharisaical men have croaked themselves hoarse on the subject. It is high time the tables were turned, and the follies of the dominant sex as thoroughly ventilated.

Until women are admitted to the highest educational institutions in the land, on an equality with men, and until they have a like position in Church and State, I will not blame any one of them for all manner of folly, extravagance, or sin. I have entered the field as a champion for my sex, in whatever circumstances they may be placed, high or low, rich or poor, pure or defiled. They all belong to the great oppressed sisterhood of this nation and of the world at large. I take my stand fearlessly, and will lead where any will dare to follow, or follow where any will dare to lead; and I will not lay aside my armor or sheathe the sword till this wrong is righted. I come not with a "soothing poultice" for this gangrene ulcer, but with the probe which reaches the core hidden beneath proud flesh, — *very proud flesh!* I know not which is the lower down in the scale of morals, in the two extremes of society, fashionable women, or courtesans. Each lead a sensuous, voluptuous, worthless life; and at the harvest of death — in either case — there is nothing left but chaff and stubble. They appear to stand, in the economy of Nature, at opposite ends of the same stick. "Dress, dissipation, and flirting make up the questionable lines which enclose the life of the fashionable woman, and which enclose nothing useful, nothing good, nothing deep or true or holy."

What is wrong? Who is to blame? Who will rise up in judgment against them? Who will cast the first stone? The ambitious fashionable woman is a being of untiring energy, else she could never accomplish what she does. And, were this energy diverted into healthful and productive channels, what a source of happiness and wealth would flow from it into the world's treasury, created by her active brain and artistic fingers!

There are rare specimens of this class of graceful producers to be met with everywhere in society, and their numbers are daily increasing — women who dare to be ignorant in many things, in order to be potential in one or two. Said a proud husband of one of these to me, "My wife paints and practises from eight o'clock A.M. till ten P.M., unless interrupted by the exigencies of housekeeping or society." "And how do you like being tied to such a business-woman?" I inquired. "Oh," he quickly replied, "I glory in her ambition!" "So do I," I continued: "she is one of the successful pioneers in work for women, on a higher plane than the scrub-brush and sewing-machine."

Such women are the beacon-lights to timid feet: they enrich and adorn the times in which they live, by the precept of example, and glorify God by the use of the talent he has given them. They have not despised the day of small things, the patient study and persistent drill, which brings its own exceeding great reward. They have dug *deep*, and laid the foundations of their individuality upon a rock basis, and from this rises the structure of beautiful and symmetrical character; and character is destiny.

Create a sentiment, by properly educating women, that it is more honorable to labor at something that produces valuable results than to be idle, and they will no longer sell themselves, for a permanent home, to one man whom they do not love, or to the promiscuous throng for the transient and evanescent abode of the courtesan.

Women are educated for dolls and spare-hours playthings; and then because they are apt scholars — as they are pretty sure to be — they are blamed for being proficient in the art of doll-pleasures. The old trite saying, "Just as the twig is bent the tree's inclined," is unheeded.

CHAPTER XIX.

PHILISTINES *vs.* WIDOWS.

Væ victis.

AND behold the Philistines — the great and impregnable army of Litigites, whose chief is the high and mighty Myrick the Just — pitched their tents over against San Francisco; a city that goes up to the sea on the west, and down to the bay on the east; a city of great renown, far famed for its palatial residences, its hospitality, its magnificent hotels, its Mint, its City-hall expectations, and its Second-street Bridge. Nevertheless it has its fogs, its damps, its winds, its Chinese odors, and municipal government. And they, the host of Litigites, sent forth a proclamation throughout the length and breadth of the land, from the borders of San Frantisco to Oakland, from Oakland to Red Dog, from Red Dog to Youbedam, from Youbedam to Whisky Station, from Whisky Station to Cut-Throat Gulch; and the proclamation had the great seal of Myrick the Just upon it; and the proclamation read thus: "Be it enacted that all widows be despoiled of their substance, their houses, their lands, their cattle, their minor children, and all they possess of value of worldly goods, in order to enrich the Court of Myrick the Just, the City Treasury, and the great army of Litigites, the whole tribe of Creditorites, the half-tribe of Myrick the Just, the Jiggerites, and the quarter-tribe of Myrick the Just, the Posterites; and let every widow that rebels and kicks against this proclamation have a millstone hung about her neck, and let her be cast into the midst of the sea."

And thereupon the widows lifted up their voices, with an exceeding great cry of wailing and lamentation, saying, "Woe to us! Who shall deliver us from the hand of this mighty high priest, Myrick the Just, and his twelve tribes of Litigites and Creditorites? These be the plagues that afflict widows throughout all the land of *Freedom*. These be the cunning foxes that spoil the vines."

And the wailing widows pitched their tents over against Despair, in the Valley of Desolation. And all the region round about was watered by the river Despair and the Fountain and Torrent of Tears. The fountain and torrent never ran dry by day or by night, for they were perpetually replenished by the tears of the widows and orphans, which are continually falling like rain because of the persecutions of the Philistines and their chief, Myrick the Just. And over against the Torrent of Tears was the Field of Sighs, which bordered upon the Valley of Desolation.

And there was a perpetual war waged by the "fat and lean" Philistines of the city of San Francisco, against the widows whose tents were pitched over against Despair, in the Valley of Desolation, which was by the Field of Sighs and the Torrent of Tears.

And the twelve tribes of Myrick the Just — the Samites, the Eddites, the Cobboreans, the Haightites, the Johnoreans, the Creditorites, and the half-tribe of Myrick the Just, the Jiggerites, and the remainder of the whole tribes of Myrick the Just, which went to make up the great body of Litigites which composed the twelve tribes of Myrick the Just — waxed fat on the spoils of the slain. For Death, with sword, fire, and pestilence, was continually swooping down upon the goodly city of San Francisco, and carrying off the husbands and fathers out of their beautiful homes, which homes at once became the prey of the spoilers; and the widows and orphans were driven forth naked, at the point of the two-edged sword of the law, out of their earthly paradise into the Valley and Shadow of Desolation, which valley did lie alongside the Field of Sighs.

And, behold, in those days it came to pass that one Joseph was gathered to his last home, and slept with his fathers; and his wife Lizzie was in a far country beyond the sea. And this wife Lizzie belonged to the tribe Strong-minded. As soon as Joseph was buried out of sight, in Lone Mountain — the burial-place of the dead of San Francisco — lo, and behold! the bosom friends of Joseph gathered themselves together, and parted his garments. They cast lots between them before the court of Myrick the Just in

San Francisco, and divided the possessions of Joseph into many parts, — to the Creditorites a fiftieth part; to the Litigites a thirtieth part; to the great high priest, Myrick the Just, a tenth part; and to the Posterites, the Pressites, and the Auctioneerites the remainder.

And the Executorites despised the absent widow, the widow belonging to the tribe Strong-minded; and they wagged their heads, and said, "We will publish, in the paper called 'Alta,' that we sent her a despatch telling her of the death of her husband Joseph, and also of the mailing of a notice to the said Lizzie, of the tribe Strong-minded, — who was absent in a far country, in the city called Geneva, at the time of the death of the said Joseph, — of the proving of his will;" all of which the said Lizzie, of the tribe Strong-minded, never received, because the postal system is "*bad*" in the country called France, and the country alongside, called Switzerland, in which is situate the city called Geneva. After many weeks, the widow Lizzie heard of the death of her husband Joseph, through a letter written by her sister called Gertie. Then the widow — the strong-minded Lizzie — rose up and fled out of the far country, and travelled by land and by sea, by day and by night, until she came to the city by the bay, the city of San Francisco, even to the inner court of Myrick the Just; and said she to him, "Great and upright judge, behold, mine enemies have gotten possession of all my goods, the things that were mine and the things that were Joseph's — who is resting from his labors, in Lone Mountain. Give me that which belongeth unto me. What right have these men to sit in judgment over my estate? They are usurpers — and I pray you, mighty judge of the quick and the *will* of the dead, to cast them out from their ill-gotten power."

Then Myrick the Just opened his mouth, and spake thus to the widow of Joseph: "If thou be a strong-minded woman, as I hear thou art, go up with the tribe of the strong-minded sisterhood, and storm the walls of the city of Sacramento, which city lieth upon the banks of the great river which hath its tail in the mountains, its body in the valleys, and its mouth in the bay. Go up and besiege the temple in which assembleth the chosen and anointed of the people, the two branches of Legislature called and known throughout the land as Senate and Representative. They alone are to blame. We are weak, and they are mighty. Go up, thou strong-minded, and besiege their outer walls, and pull down their stronghold, and compel them to deal justly with widows and the female tribe 'Strong-minded.'"

Thereupon the widow of Joseph made answer, and said unto Myrick the Just: "Behold, O mighty judge, we cannot go up to Sacramento; for the Philistines have despoiled us of our lands, our houses, our cattle, and our poultry. We have no money wherewithal to buy beautiful apparel to please the eye of those lawgivers, no frankincense and myrrh to tickle their nostrils, no shekels of gold nor shekels of silver to purchase their friendship; without which we are as stubble before the flame. A look consumes us. Besides, O mighty judge! we have no money nor lands to pay the tribe of Charleyites for the privilege of riding in their chariots of wood and iron. Sacramento is a far city. We cannot walk; for our sandals are worn, our staff broken, and ourselves growing old and gray, and stiff-jointed as well as stiff-necked."

Then Myrick the Just bade the widow of Joseph depart in peace, and trouble him no more—*forever.*

Now, it came to pass that the widow of Joseph waxed very wroth at this, for she had no money to buy meal and oil, and San Francisco ravens had forgotten their cunning; and she said, as she made good her escape out of the Inner Court, "We'll see if there's a God in Israel;" and she went forth, and prayed one Albert, a Philistine, to come up to battle with her. But lo, and behold! when they came before the court of Myrick the Just, the friends of Joseph, "a great cloud of witnesses," were brought up out of the highways, byways, and hedges, to testify that Joseph died a pauper, or rather that all his possessions went by natural entail to his bosom friends. There was the high priest Horatio, the ironmonger Ira, the Philistine Smut, the quill-driver Bell, the porter Dick, the baby-tender Hardy, and the boot-black Pil. And they all swore as with one voice, and the voice was like unto the voice of the beast that one Balaam rode. And they said, —

"In life our brother Joseph had an ever-open palm: what was his belonged to his friends also. And now that he is dead, what he has left of worldly goods, shall it be taken from his friends and neighbors, — lawful inheritors under probate rule, — and given to a woman who by some kind of enchantment, legerdemain, or other influence known to the female tribe Strong-minded, possessed herself of Joseph our neighbor? Yes, she, the strong-minded Lizzie, captured and married our brother Joseph without our knowledge or consent. Shall we suffer the goods of our friend to fall into her hands?" And they — priest, pill-man, pot-hook, and all — lifted up their voices with a great shout, and cried to a man, "No, never!" And the Scribe wrote it down in a big book, for which he was paid, out of the estate of Joseph, two hundred and fifty pieces of money in gold, called dollars. And the three Philistines that fought against her one Philistine beat him; and they waxed exceeding merry over their triumph, and skipped about on their right ear, and made faces at the Philistine Albert, because he was one "lean" Philistine, while they were three "fat" Philistines because they had their hands in the dead man's pocket. They were paid a great price to fight the widow of Joseph, and the widow of Joseph's estate paid the great price; and she had nothing but her groans to pay the Philistine Albert, and those were bad pay, not marketable on 'Change. The Executorites and their three Philistines had stolen her weapons to fight her with, which swelled them out on all sides like unto the small animal which once upon a time sought to rival the proportions of the ox.

And it came to pass, after this defeat of the widow of Joseph and the one Philistine, that the widows and orphans in the Valley and Shadow of Desolation rose up out of their sackcloth and ashes, and clothed themselves in the stanch armor of the true faith and exceeding great wrath, and crossed over the Torrent of Tears and the River Despair, and camped over against the Philistines. And, behold, the Philistines were very drunk with their ill-gotten spoils, and did not see the vanguard nor rearguard of the approaching enemy. And they did not hear their steps round about the city, for they came as softly as a thief in the night.

And lo, and behold! while the Philistines yet slept, the widows from out the Valley of Desolation fell upon the tents of the Haightites, the Cobbereans, the Eddites, the Samites, the Creditorites, and the tents of the half-tribe of Myrick the Just, — the Jiggerites, — and slew them all to a man with the jawbone of a woman. And, behold! the number of slain was beyond computation. And, when the last Philistine was vanquished, there went up a great shout from the victors; and the compassionate bowels of the earth opened, and swallowed up the great host of slain, together with the Valley of Desolation, the Field of Sighs, and the River Despair; and the Fountain and Torrent of Tears were dried up, and a great peace fell upon the earth. Selah!

CHAPTER XX.

THE MERCANTILE LIBRARY.

Non quis, sed quid.

To further demonstrate, in my own experience, the disabilities that pertain to sex, I will give a history of Mr. Stow's life-membership in the Mercantile Library Association. That organization was very much embarrassed financially, at the time he became a life-member ; and it continued in that unhappy condition for many years thereafter, in spite of the generosity of its numerous friends, and the series of concerts that the gifted Camilla Urso inaugurated and carried forward with so much credit to herself — she being only a woman — and such universal satisfaction to all concerned.

At last a crisis came, when a very large sum of money had to be raised. Then the sages, the wise men and fathers of the library, laid their heads together, and spread their wings over the financial nest, and brooded for weeks; and the incubation brought forth a lottery chicken. Lucky for those bookish fathers that the Rev. Dr. Talmage was not one of their number, to uncork his vial of lottery wrath upon their unregenerate heads!

Not a dissenting voice was raised loud enough to be heard; and soon every one was possessed with the fallacious idea that he or *she* was to be the fortunate winner of the magic $100,000 prize. Everybody and everybody's wife and everybody's mother-in-law bought tickets. Men went without drinks, and women without "loves of bonnets," to buy coupons. Ministers were robbed of their donations, the heathen of their flannel, the ungodly went without tracts, and babies without bibs, all to enable some one to become modestly rich at one turn of a wheel. Thus a large mass of the people, at home and abroad, were made participants in the great lottery scheme to free a noble institution from ignominious debt. It was maliciously hinted that some poor people sold all they had to possess themselves of the wherewithal to secure the captivating $100,000. But "*hearsay*" is a scandal-monger; and what if they did sell their little homestead? Is that an unusual or remarkable circumstance? Whenever there is a *corner* in the stock-market, is not this same thing repeated again and again? What of it? Everybody, excepting wives and widows, has a right to do as everybody pleases in a free country.

On the day of the drawing, there were about six thousand people assembled within the old Pavilion, — a building that was an eyesore for years to the tender-eyed Union-square people. There was a motley crowd gathered together in that transitory edifice, — a seething, bellowing, heaving multitude. The elegant, in fine, sweet-scented raiment, hobnobbed with the unwashed, uncombed, and unkempt. The millionnaire and Barbary-Coaster sat down together, awaiting the turn of Fortune's wheel. On the stage and in the gallery were reserved seats for the managers, their wives, sweethearts, and lady friends. Upon the stage was the wheel, and within the wheel was the $100,000 prize, with some lesser prizes and many blanks. The prizes were all shut up in little, long finger-boxes, the size and shape of a whistle, which suggested to the loser the consoling privilege that he could whistle down his disappointment. Three blind mice from the Deaf and Dumb Asylum officiated at the drawing, thus symbolizing the idea that justice is blind. One turned the wheel; one thrust in his hand, and seized the first paper whistle that came in contact with his delicate fingers, which paper whistle he instantly gave to the third assistant; who opened it, and drew forth the check upon which was stamped in large letters the number and value of the prize; and this check he held up in full view of the eager crowd, while Mr. Stow, standing behind him, called off the lucky number and the amount of the prize. Three times was each number and the amount shouted from the stage, and taken up and repeated three times by the mass inside, for the benefit of the mass outside. There were nearly as many without as within the building. "Ten thousand" was called; "thirty thousand;" "one thousand;" "twenty thousand;" "fifty thousand;" "two thousand:" then the wheel refused to go round. It evidently was filled with compassion, as well as tickets, for the grief and bitter disappointment that its revolutions were bringing to so many hearts. At this interruption a sound like the groan before a tempest surged through the immense building. Some cried out "*Fraud!*" Others with wild eyes pressed forward with muttered curses, bent upon taking things into their own hands; babies screamed, and women fainted. At this painful crisis Mr. Stow stepped to the front of the platform, and said, "Be patient, my friends: it is but a momentary interruption. A little oil will allay the friction, and then all will work well again."

"Where's the $100,000?" broke out many voices, — "where's the $100,000? Show us that, and we'll be quiet; but not till we've seen that will we believe it's all right. Hurry up! no foolin'!"

By this time the wheel was in motion again, and the $100,000 was soon turned out, which caused many hearts to drop way down to the soles of their shoes, and there they remained for many a day — perhaps.

Immediately after the drawing of the last prize, Mr. Stow beckoned to me (I was near the stage in the gallery) to join him. As soon as we could free ourselves from the throng, we got into the carriage, and drove with all speed to the Occidental, where we were boarding at the time. I said to him, "What made you look so pale while you were speaking? were you ill?" "*Pale!*" he replied: "do you see this and this?" and he took from his pockets two revolvers; "why, my child, every one of us, to a man, was armed to the teeth; and I thank God it's over! I would not pass through another such ordeal for the price of my life, and I'm no coward. But I assure you, it's not a pleasant thing to talk to plug-uglies when you know they are armed, and bent on mischief if all does not go according to their peculiar code of honor."

Several of the managers called that evening to congratulate Mr. Stow on his happy escape out of the threatened difficulty; and among them was the late R. B. Swain, who had been one of the most active and efficient agents in perfecting the enterprise, and bringing it to a successful termination. Said he, "Well, Stow, you have done more than all of us put together. I would not have stood in your shoes when that outbreak came for all the money drawn to-day. That was an ugly crowd. An unguarded word would have sent the bullets flying, and the roughs would have taken possession of the stage, wheel and all, making short work of such as resisted."

At the death of R. B. Swain, his Mercantile Library mantle gracefully descended, without remonstrance of any sort, upon the shoulders of his son, then about fifteen years of age. Of course his widow was left out in the cold, the same as I am; but I have no son, so the grateful library has my husband's and my money (fifty dollars paid for the life-membership was mine by law) all for nothing. I have written two letters to two sets of officers, begging that high-minded chivalric body, or those bodies rather, in remembrance of the unusual services rendered that institution by my husband in its hour of need, to grant me the use of his membership as long as I should be held in durance vile on this coast by the Probate Court. An ominous silence has been maintained. Not one scratch of a goose-quill have these momentarily great officials accorded me. That library has no time, pen, ink, or stomach, to waste on a poverty-stricken widow. It wants a dollar a month if I quench my thirst at its fountain; but it won't get it. No! nor would it were I worth a million. If any one in the city of San Francisco has a right to read the books in the Mercantile Library without further pay, it is the widow of J. W. Stow.

The librarian said that Mrs. Swain paid her *dollar* a month without making a FUSS about it. But I am neither subdued nor quieted by precedent. Rebellion, under such treatment, is Godlike. What right has that library to take away that life-membership from me? I repeat, fifty dollars of the purchase money was mine by law; for Mr. Stow became a life-member after we were married. There is no honor nor justice in an institution that robs a widow of any privilege enjoyed by her as a wife. If I had had a son, there would not have been a hand raised to strike off his head. Why? Because he would have belonged to the unquestionable gender.

When a man dies without male issue, his mantle of membership is wrapped around him with his burial clothes, and put into his coffin, and the lid screwed down, and the earth heaped upon it so high that the mantle can never have a resurrection under any circumstances. His wife and daughters must live in ignorance of books, if they cannot afford to pay the price of membership over again. What a sublime, enlightened, humanizing age we live in! How fatherly, brotherly, Christianly! how noble, how dignified, how absolute! how pretty, how polite, how refined! how lovely, how sweet, how charming! how gallant, how chivalric, how sublime! how dutiful, how greedful, how *pitiful!*

I go every week to that library, and get books, and read the papers, and sit in the perpetual twilight of the room "exclusively for ladies," where there has not been a fire all winter, or, at any rate, the days that I have been there. Coals are very *dear* in San Francisco. I have longed, when I have heard the ladies sneezing, as they refreshed the "inner woman" —mentally—on the *magazine literature* of that or those rooms, to get a peep into the chess-room for men, believing that there was sunlight and firelight both there. There is neither on the ladies' side. We are compelled to "see by a glass, darkly." Good enough for women, who live so much of their time in a reflected light that they ought to be used to it by this time. I expect, every time I ask for a book or books, to get the long-looked-for information from the polite young gentlemen who officiate behind the railing, that the "committee-men" have decided that Mrs. J. W. Stow has been accommodated with books long enough without pay. But for this *denoûment*, I, like Antonio, "am armed and fully prepared" for the blow, and when it comes I intend to take up my daily residence in the magazine-room (not powder), for it is warm and light up there. I think it was designed exclusively for men; but women have invaded the sacred territory, and it would take bullets the size of cannon-balls to drive them out now.

I feel almost certain that the time draws nigh when I shall be refused books down stairs; for, when I go to the library, those polite young men aforementioned look at each other, and whisper, "There's Mrs. Stow," which reminds me of the wisdom of a follower of the renowned and amiable Dogberry, who had knowledge of one "*Deformed*," knew him by sight, etc., etc.

CHAPTER XXI.

UNJUST TAXATION.

Dum vivimus, vivamus.

I HERE and now, on the twenty-eighth day of the month of December, in the year of our Lord eighteen hundred and seventy-six, and for all time to come, make and place on file in the Tax Collector's office in the City and County of San Francisco, State of California, in the Federal Republic known as the United States of America, the blazing star of freedom and equality among the civilized nations of the earth, a perpetual *protest* against paying taxes for the support of a government in which I am denied all voice or hearing of any name or nature, — a government professedly claiming to be free and equal.

I claim, as every other woman in the land has a right to claim, that no subsidy, charge, tax, impost, or duties ought to be established, fixed, laid or levied, under any pretext whatsoever, without the consent of the people so taxed.

So long as the entire government of the State and Nation, in all its various branches, executive, legislative, and judicial, is masculine, — or, in other words, so long as the entire power of making, interpreting, and executing all the laws which are to affect the property of every woman in the State and Nation is exclusively vested in male citizens, — the government is a fraud ; and under it women are deprived of safety and protection in their property-rights, their wages, and their freedom of action. Under it the noble language of the Declaration of

Independence becomes as sounding brass and tinkling cymbals. What is the meaning of these words? "We hold these truths to be *self-evident:* that all men are created equal, and endowed *by their Creator* with certain *inalienable rights;* that among these are life, liberty, and the pursuit of happiness. That, *to secure these rights*, governments are instituted among men, deriving their just powers from *the* CONSENT of the *governed;* and that, whenever any form of government becomes destructive of these ends, it is the right of *the* PEOPLE to alter or abolish it."

We women-"PEOPLE" claim this inestimable right, the right to claim our just prerogative, — representation and recognition as "*people.*" We would be free! Take away the rank political injustice which forms the ground-work of all proscription, tyranny, and absolutism!

The keynote of the Declaration of Independence is, that governments derive their just powers from the *consent* of the governed; a beautiful theory which has never come into practice. I am taxed, with every other woman in the land, without my consent. Taxation without representation is tyranny; taxation without representation is unconstitutional: taxation and representation are inseparable correlatives.

MARIETTA L. B. STOW.

The right of protest and criticism is an inalienable inheritance. No usurping power can stop up the escape-valve of speech, prayer, and supplication, while it steals the contents of purse, lands, live-stock, or personal effects, to support a *free* government which holds half of its adult population in legal bondage worse than serfdom — for serfs are not the educated social companions of their masters.

A hundred years ago men, aided and abetted by women, freed themselves from the ignoble bondage of a forced taxation without representation. They fought bravely for their rights. Now, when women are roused to the same zeal for personal protection against criminal oppression, how do the mass of men view the movement? Do they rush to the rescue as our foremothers did, when they moulded their spoons into bullets and their love into heroic deeds? Do they come to the front with brave words of cheer, or sneak behind the high wall of prejudice, and hurl the poisoned arrows of ridicule, malice, hatred, and scorn, at the undaunted leaders of the "Unterrified Sisterhood"? Women are taxed every year by Congress millions of dollars, without their consent. Our forefathers risked death rather than pay a tax of threepence a pound on tea. The gallant sons of those heroic rebels compel the daughters to pay a tax of twenty-five cents (two bits) on every pound of tea they consume. They — the sons — sell their — the daughters' — lands, live stock, and personal effects, to pay taxes which have been levied without their consent, and in the face of the most vehement protest.

Every farthing thus wrested from a disfranchised class is in direct violation of the fundamental laws of the nation. We deny the constitutional right to tax any person without his or her consent. A hundred years ago taxation without representation was deemed well worth a war of seven years. Blood and treasure were freely given to gain what is now denied to women. It is not strange that *brave* men fought for such rights: it is only strange that *brave* men to-day inflict such WRONGS upon woman, and that so many women meekly endure it. What will rouse them to the consciousness that they are living under an oligarchy or absolute despotism from which they have no appeal?

Taxes, to the last decimal, are wrung from widows and unmarried women, while usurers go free — or pay but a moiety of what a true assessment of their possessions requires that they should pay. The cry comes from every State and Territory, "Taxation without representation is tyranny." Here is what the Sisters Smith of Glastonbury, Conn., say: "We have paid our tax at the point of the bayonet. When you fall into the hands of banditti, and have turned every way, and done all in your power to escape, and find no escape for you, you must yield to their demands. Our case, taking the literal meaning, is perfectly parallel to the account given in the Bible of Naboth the Jezreelite.

"We have had our valuable cows seized and sold at the auction-block, our whole meadow-land attached, and eleven acres sold, for a tax of not quite fifty dollars, worth more than two thousand dollars. We seem to be left without a country, and we cannot see but we should fare better under a king; for King George himself never attached woman's property in so unfeeling and cowardly a manner as has been done to us."

Abby Kelly Foster, of Worcester, Mass., has had property sold to the amount of thousands of dollars for a tax of less than a hundred. Mrs. Foster gave more than thirty years of her life to secure the personal rights of slaves. Now she is doing battle for the personal rights of all women. She says, "When I am free, as men are, to help make and unmake or alter the condition of organized society, I will cheerfully bear my share of its expenses." By resisting the payment of taxes just as they do, Mrs. Foster and the Sisters Smith show the same spirit which John Hancock and Samuel Adams did a century ago.

Women, as a class, are excluded from any part in the governmental organization of society. Men of all nations, color, and creed are admitted to it. The male minor only waits to reach majority. At twenty-one he is a voter. The foreigner has only to conform to naturalization laws, and he is a voter. All men, rich and poor, who are not imbecile or criminal, have only these easy conditions of admission to the body politic, and to their full influence in making, unmaking, or altering the conditions of organized society. Even the reservation Indians in Massachusetts, while under guardianship, are allowed to vote if they pay poll-tax. In what does the difference of poll-tax and land-tax consist? I, for one, desire to pay poll-tax if I can vote by so doing.

Indians under guardianship are like the wives of this State, with the exception of suffrage: they cannot sue or be sued without being joined in the suit by their protectors; they cannot receive wages for a voyage, if payment is forbidden by their guardians. And yet, though subject to these disqualifications, the rights of citizenship are conceded when they own property, and consent to be taxed.

All women in Massachusetts who own property are taxed without representation, while the more favored Punkapogs and Nipmugs who scalped their ancestors are relieved from the burden if they refuse to pay taxes. Their cows and wigwams do not fall under the hammer. Ah, no! the humane Massachusetts voter protects his masculine ward. Lo, the poor Indian, is of far more consequence than Abby Foster or Abby Smith. William I. Bowditch of Boston, in his admirable work on "Taxation," says, "There is another fact connected with the taxation of women, which, being a man, I am ashamed to point out, but which yet cannot be passed over in silence; and that is the inexpressible *meanness* of the thing. We men save at least two millions of dollars every year from our own burdens by this act of injustice.

"The cities and towns pay more than half the taxes levied in the State, and the women pay more than one-ninth of the whole; so that one-half the men of property in the State save every year more than one-ninth of their taxes, by compelling the women who have no votes with which to protect themselves to pay the amount.

"Do the women of this Commonwealth consent to such taxation? Under the Constitution, 'no tax,

&c., ought to be levied, &c., under any pretext whatsoever, without the consent of the people or their representatives in the Legislature.' This consent may be, and, as we shall see, has been in several instances, individually given by the person who is taxed; but, for the mass, such consent can only be given in the way pointed out by the law for the mass of the people to use, — that is, by voting. So long as a citizen can vote in open town-meeting for or against his own taxation; so long as a citizen of any city can vote for members of the city government to whom he has, under the law, intrusted the power to levy taxes on his estate; and so long as a citizen can vote for governor, senators, and representatives, to whom, under the Constitution, he has intrusted the power to lay State taxes, — he has no reasonable ground for complaint. Nor can he object to being taxed by either of these bodies, if, thus possessing the power by his vote to assent or dissent, he refrains from exercising the right. In all cases, therefore, where a citizen has the right to vote, no matter whether he exercises the right or not, he virtually consents to all the state, county, city, and town taxes which may be levied upon him or his estate. When the Constitution declares that no tax can be levied without the consent of the people, it is to be understood as referring to the people who are thus taxed, and nobody else. It was of no sort of consequence to our fathers, that the people of England consented to tax America. And when our Constitution says that no tax ought to be laid without the consent of the representatives of the people, it is to be understood as referring to the representatives whom the people who are to be taxed have the right to vote for or against, and which representatives, in this way, become authorized to consent to such taxation.

"But the Constitution is to be construed in a reasonable manner. The consent of every one who may be taxed cannot possibly be obtained. A citizen may become insane, and therefore incapable of contracting. His consent to being taxed would be nothing, even if it could be obtained; and he surely ought not to be allowed to vote. Therefore, although the Constitution requires the consent of every citizen to his taxation before he can be legally taxed, it must be understood to refer only to those who are recognized by the law as capable of giving such consent, or those who are deemed capable of contracting, of earning, holding, and conveying the property which is to be taxed. The Constitution does not, therefore, require the consent of minors to their taxation, because, being under the age of consent, they may avoid any contract they may make (except for actual necessaries), when they come of age, no matter how fair and honest the contract may have been. Nor does it require the consent of persons under guardianship, — as insane or spendthrifts, — for they have no greater power to contract than minors possess. But it does require the consent of every other citizen in the way above stated, before he or she may be lawfully taxed, except only paupers and convicts. A citizen who is a pauper has nothing to be taxed for, and is not allowed to vote. A citizen who becomes a convict, as part of his punishment, is deprived of the right of suffrage. An alien who resides here knows that his property is liable to be taxed. Having no natural right to remain here, if he continues to remain, by such act he consents to be taxed, within the meaning of the Constitution.

"This disposes of all the inhabitants or residents who can possibly be taxed under our laws, except only male and female citizens of full age, none of whom are paupers, convicts, insane, or spendthrift, and all of whom have equal right to contract, to acquire, buy, and sell the property which is to be taxed, or, in other words, precisely the same qualifications for voting, except merely sex; and the larger number of these citizens are women. Everybody else in the State, of full age, who can be taxed, either consents to such taxation, or, being legally incapable of contracting, cannot consent, or is excluded from suffrage, on grounds entirely disconnected with sex; that is, for want of property, or for ignorance, insufficient residence, or as a punishment for crime, &c.

"Here, then, are two classes of citizens, each possessing equal qualifications for voting; and the right of suffrage is confined to males, but both males and females are taxed.

"Can any female citizen who is thus denied the right to vote be constitutionally taxed?

"In the opinion of the judges of our Supreme Court, the taxation of male citizens must go hand in hand with his right to representation; and, if he is denied the right to vote, he cannot constitutionally be taxed.

"If, under our Constitution, a minority of the citizens can deprive the majority of the right of representation, and still retain the right to tax them, then our fathers fought to save their pockets, and not their principles. If we male citizens of Massachusetts can rightfully do this, then the Declaration of Independence and our Bill of Rights are a mere tissue of glittering generalities, and wholly incapable of any practical resistance to oppression.

"That the right to tax male citizens is based entirely on their right to vote, is also clear from the fact that, whenever we have deprived them of the right to vote in the place where they reside, we have also relieved them from taxation in such place."

The republics of the Old World gave the franchise first to the patricians, then to the peòple, and lastly to the helots, always degrading womanhood. What was the result? Is this nation to drift into the same vortex of ruin and anarchy? The election portals are thrown wide open to the felon from prison, the pauper from the almshouse, to all ignorance, all vice; but to the high-born American woman, cultured, refined, rich, and pure, those *free* portals are doubly locked, doubly barred, by man's prejudice and power. The power of might! We claim that this political right to vote belongs as much to a woman citizen as does the land for which she is taxed.

Men make laws, and they should be chivalric enough to pay for the support of the same. They compel me to pay enormous taxes and street assessments to support a wasteful, extravagant government, in which I am denied all voice and under which I have no fat clerical position. My taxes in 1874 in San Francisco were $158.50; in 1875, $121.24; in 1876, $171.06. What caused the variation in the amount in two years' time? Did the real estate suddenly depreciate in value, and then as suddenly appreciate? Each time these fluctuating taxes became due, I had no money to meet the urgent demand, because I was caught in the relentless jaws of Probate.

Two wrongs do not make a right! I am wronged and outraged by being thrust into Probate against my will. I am wronged and outraged by being taxed against my will.

Tax number one, during Probate seizure, was paid, as heretofore narrated in these pages, by the sale of my silver; number two, by the sale of tickets for lectures — which very few felt inclined to attend — perhaps it was the rain that dampened their ardor: it poured each night. Number three was paid on the 28th of this month, by the proceeds of the sale of tickets for a handsome ring, — opal set round with brilliants, — one of the Christmas presents made me by my husband in 1873.

Ticket number forty-eight drew the silver in 1874, and ticket number sixty-seven drew the ring in 1876.

A sewer has been dug in front of my house, and the street McAdamized, which cost me several hundred dollars. And yet I had no intimation that such improvements were in progress (I do not live in the house), until the bills were presented for payment. The excuse was that they could not find me. But when money is wanted I am found as quickly as a man is found, and, judging from experience, oftentimes much quicker.

What did it matter to high masculine potentates whether I could raise the money to pay for the work, or not? They were secure. They could lien my property, and sell me out.

It is said that men hate to transact business with women. Some of them do not hate to possess themselves of their money, however; but they hate to refund it, or render an exchange of courtesy in any form. Several of the savings banks of this city hated to loan me money, — hated so strong that they refused altogether. When I asked for $10,000, they said the sum was too large, — that they were not at that particular year, month, week, day, hour, minute, and second, loaning so *large* a sum to one individual (woman); and when I asked for $2,000, they said that they were not at that particular year, month, week, day, hour, minute, and second, lending so *small* a sum to one individual (woman).

These banks hated to lend me money, but they loved to have the use of my money for nothing. I bought pass-books, — $2.50 apiece, — from two of these sensitive banks, and have had from time to time money on deposit to the amount of several thousand dollars, taken as a whole, which money has rarely paid interest because it was not on deposit long enough at a time. I asked the president of one of them if he would have refused my husband a loan upon my property if he had applied for one during his life. He — the president — maintained a golden silence, leaving me to uncertain conjecture as to that fact.

One handsome, portly director, to whom I mentioned the matter, said to me, "I voted against you when your application came before the board."

"How could you be guilty of such a wicked deed?" I exclaimed.

"Because I did not want to see you lose your property by a forced sale. It is very hard to sell a widow's estate," he made answer in the most amiable and dignified manner possible. All handsome men are dignified towards the weaker sex in San Francisco.

"How very considerate!" I continued. "But never fear. The bank you help steer shall never foreclose on a rood of my land, nor shall any sister savings institution be shocked and pained by such a sale. I never intend to suffer strangulation by a banker's noose."

CHAPTER XXII.

MARRIAGE A COPARTNERSHIP.

Cavendo tutus.

WHY do men marry? There must be some method in their madness. Is it for love? Rarely, I think. They may swear it by the moon; but usually, the stronger they swear, the more ephemeral the "ethereal fluid." Sam Johnson gives "*proximity*" as the reason. But Sam evidently argued from a personal standpoint; and that is bad logic, with "Hetty" in his eye. There are many reasons why a man marries, the principal one being *selfishness*. He will not admit the fact, however, because he does not take the trouble to analyze his feelings. He construes his personal necessities into love. One might commit a greater error. A true man wants to perpetuate himself in his *legitimate* children, therefore a wife is indispensable; besides, he needs a housekeeper or a companion, and it is cheaper to marry the necessity than to hire it.

A young man often marries for money and position. He secures the money by taking a wife, as a necessary evil, to cement the contract. Another marries to have a home of his own. He is tired of hotels and boarding-houses, tired of buttonless shirts and toeless stockings, tired of being a fraction among the common herd: he sighs for warm slippers and the absolutism of his own hearthstone. He would be a general: rank and file have become distasteful to him.

An old man turns into a human vampire, and marries a young girl in order to eke out his life upon the youthful vigor and animal magnetism of his — too often — unsuspecting victim, who yields her life a living sacrifice upon the pestilential altar of decay and mammon. But, in her case, the romance of being an old man's darling is soon dissipated.

Then, again, others marry because they are *fascinated* — this is claimed to be the age of fascination — they are caught "in the magical trap of an auburn curl," a saucy lip, a little foot, a pretty hand, a merry eye — any thing that tickles the fancy; and the enamoured swain is wretched until he secures his enchantress.

These are among the most baneful marriages extant. The woman may be as beautiful as Aurora, and yet not know how to order a dinner or superintend a nursery. A husband of this kind of a wife soon learns that, —

"A man may live without poetry, music, or art;
He may live without conscience; he may live without heart;
He may live without friends; he may live without books;
But civilized man cannot live without *cooks*.

He may live without books — what is knowledge but grieving,
He may live without hope — what is hope but deceiving?
He may live without love — what is passion but pining?
But where is the man who can live without *dining?*"

A wife's beauty may be as short-lived as the dew upon the blossom, and when that is gone what is left? A faded flower — nothing more. Yet if a man will dance he must needs pay the fiddler. It is claimed by large authority, that physical beauty, with men in search of wives, carries all before it. This demonstrates the sober fact that we have not yet entered upon the golden age of wedlock. I don't think we have! The heart must not be divorced from the intellect. Matrimony must rise to the higher plain of intellectual reciprocity ere we shall understand all the capabilities for good that are embraced in the marriage relation.

When a man marries a woman, he says, "With all my worldly goods I thee endow." This it appears is *only appearance;* for the property which he has at this time is considered his separate estate, and at his death he can by testamentary law take it all away from the woman whom he endowed with it. Here is a mystery which no feminine sounding-line is long enough to fathom. Wherever in the deep sea of masculine inconsistency you may sink it, no answer comes up. But the essential conclusion upon which woman may rest is, that it is the "*will of man.*"

They may live years together, and yet apparently add nothing to the estate: although it has increased in value all the time, still it is the husband's property, in which the wife has no community of interest that the law respects. I am familiar with one such case in this city. An acquaintance of mine married a lawyer who ostensibly owned a large amount of real estate, and has, so he tells her, added nothing to his possessions since the marriage; and how is she to know whether his statements are true or otherwise? He treats her as most husbands do their wives — in a confidential, business point of view — like a fool; never lets the left hand, the wife, know what the right hand — the husband — doeth.

Now, to keep this wife in proper subjection, this amiable husband tells her that he can will his property in case he dies first, so that she cannot get an iota of it. At the time he married her she was a teacher on good pay, making a handsome living by her accomplished industry; well dressed, and a stranger to pots and kettles, as much a stranger as her subjugator was and is to the boot-black kit. Since her marriage, she has occupied the position of upper servant in his house, because he is too mean to provide her money enough for household expenses, and to pay a good servant a fair price. Her life has been tormented out of her almost, for the want of pin-money. He thinks, if she has the magnificent sum of $100 a year, it ought to clothe her in purple and fine wool. They have no children, and what he is hoarding for, he alone can tell. Probably he intends to build a posthumous monument to perpetuate the name of "*Skinner*" — *no tellin'*. Horace Haws tried to make a "spread-eagle" institute of some sort, to go sounding down the ages to his glory; but the flickering flame went out with his life. James Lick did the same thing over again, but on a loftier basis, because he had more money. Time alone will demonstrate the upshot of all his calculations. Lawyers generally get the lion's share in the legal tussles over colossal estates. They rub the ears of relatives, brothers and sisters, uncles and aunts, mothers and mothers-in-law, fathers and fathers-in-law, cousins and second cousins, nephews and nieces, grandchildren and great-grandchildren, thirty-second cousins and grand-nephews, the ramifications of whose family-tree are past finding out, whose branches go out in every direction, and then begin over again. Every ear, and every pair of ears, along the whole line, tingles from the excoriation caused by the itching palms of lawyers. They, the ancestors and descendants, to the fourth and fifth generation, are ready to risk all they have in this court-game of chance — miscalled "*justice*."

If the wife were a partner in any true sense, this farce in many acts could not be played. The moment a man marries, the half of his entire possessions should belong to his wife, even though he lived but an hour or a day after he had perpetrated the deed, or if he were divorced from her the week after. The ring should deed, mortgage, and convey away irrevocably the half of all that which a man was seized at the moment of wedlock. No Benedict should escape. Then the reading of the marriage service could be changed from a pleasing fiction to a substantial fact, which would read thus: "Beloved Seraphina, I take thee for better or for worse, and with *half* my worldly goods I thee endow."

You may ask, "Should not this rule apply to the bride as well?" No. "But why not?" Because a woman who is self-supporting usually abandons her occupation when she marries, and it is very difficult to resume it when she becomes a widow, especially if she has children to care for. Then, again, a woman's wages are nearly always far below the price paid to men in a like department of labor. But the most arbitrary rule of all is that a woman of society is not allowed to earn money; if she does, she is ostracized at once, while a man is looked upon as a species of vagabond if he does not turn his money in business or speculation often enough to keep it bright.

You may say, again, that a widow can manipulate her fortune through an agent, a "middle-man." That is very true; but it is also very true, — sad to say, — that, when she does this proxy business, she generally loses all she has. Agency speculation, carried on by the subjectors for the benefit of the subdued, is a risky business. It don't pay. When women have had the years of experience that men have had, when they have confidence in their individual strength and capacity, and when the burden of child-bearing and child-rearing is equally divided, — then, and not till then, will the "separate property" rule work well in both cases.

All marriages should have a material basis. Lovers should not forget, while in the ecstasy of sipping nectar and ambrosia, that it takes bread and butter — lots of it too — to make bone and muscle; and they should bear in mind the old saw, that "When poverty comes in at the door, love flies out of the window." People who mate like the birds, but, unlike the birds, have no summer-lands to migrate to when the winter of adversity overtakes them, are the ones whom the fickle god soonest deserts. Hence comes the necessity for the easy divorce-law. And from this class of divorced women, the loathsome ranks of professional prostitutes are filled. Dr. Sayers of New York City says that two-thirds of all that class of women who lead a life of shame for a livelihood have been married and divorced, or have separated from their husbands. This is a sad commentary on injudicious marriages.

In Germany, when a man and woman have decided to marry each other, they go before a notary public, and make a sworn statement of what they individually possess. This affidavit is entered on the great register of the town and county where they reside. Thus the separate estate is secured to the survivors without cavil. If a girl brings to the marriage contract no more than twenty-five dollars in money, furniture, or live stock, it is legally set to her credit; and should she become widowed, no crafty creditors of her husband's or thieving court can wrest this much from her to pay "*honest* debts." When there is no evidence but the widow's, she stands a small chance to get any thing; for she is not allowed, in this country, to testify to the fact that she owned any thing, even herself, at the time she married her dear departed. And if she had any money at that most important moment of her life, which she had placed in his hands for safe keeping, that would be a transaction between husband and wife, — a sacred transaction, — which no just law would profane its equitable fingers by touching. She might have misplaced her confidence as well as her money: the law cannot remedy the evil. She would still have the same consolation, however, that the little boy had when he lost his father: he said to his mother, upon that sad occasion, "Well, mother, there's no great loss without some small gain: we shall get rid of Katy." This Katy was a most unlovely nurse, whom the now powerless subjugator had persisted in keeping against the wishes of his wife and children. A widow thus robbed of her separate inheritance by a deceased husband could learn wisdom thereby, and practise her acquirements on husband number two. No great loss without some small gain! Still it is far better to obtain such important information before the knot is irrevocably tied. As a usual thing, the marital state is far more material than spiritual. On this account common sense should find its way into courtship before the question was hot enough to "pop."

If marriage were looked upon more in the light of a business partnership, where two people could be of mutual benefit to each other morally, socially, and financially, much of the sickly sentimentality which afflicts our daughters would be done away with. The lives which are emasculated by fictitious reading year by year is something appalling. Would that some *réveille* might marshal this mighty host in solid ranks, before women supine, careless, and indifferent, believing that the fearful sight might stir the latent spark of energy within her to action! There is no happiness for an idle woman. She is imprisoned in the dungeon of discontent. Trashy novels and society gossip cannot minister to the needs of diseased and crippled faculties which are covered with rust, and creaking at every joint for the want of proper exercise.

It was considered honorable for women to labor in olden times. Alexander the Great exhibited, in his palace, garments made by his own mother. The finest tapestries of Bayeux were made by the queen of William the Conqueror. Augustus the emperor would not wear any garments except those that were fashioned by some member of his royal family.

Labor is pure gold; idleness, dross.

It is a withering thing for a man or woman to have nothing to do; and the first lesson taught should be how to earn an honest living. Hand and brain should be educated for that purpose. Many women are boastfully proud that they are ignorant of all financial, money-making employments. Not so was the accomplished Madame de Staël. She said, "It is not these writings that I am proud of, but the fact that I have facility in ten occupations, in any one of which I could make a livelihood."

A girl should be educated with the thought that at a suitable age she was to marry, if she could find a good man for a husband; that the marriage relation is the most natural when it is entered upon freely and independently by both parties to the contract. But, if the right man should never be met with, then she should still strive to become a worthy factor in the economy of life; assuming her place with a quiet self-assertion, and maintaining it with a firm purpose. Woman must be made to feel her individual importance in the drama of life. She must be made conscious of the power which she possesses, but has never wielded. She should be taught self-dependence. This ought to be first and paramount. Then she will have no need to marry solely to be maintained. If she does this, then she is a deception and a fraud, and not the noble woman that she appeared to be. It is a weak woman who marries because she is tired of self-support. But cruel custom is the source of her weaknesses, her follies, and her vices. It compels her to overlook the depravity of her male associates, and to cultivate in herself the lowest and most selfish traits of her nature. She must be pleasing to men; and few men are pleased with learned women, self-poised and independent. It is an echo of their own oracular wisdom which men seek in women. Sparkle, not substance, is most in demand. What an error, and how wide-spread the evil!

When marriage arrives at that standard of excellency which is recognized as a legal copartnership, and which restrains the husband from undersigning notes, mortgaging and selling community estate, without the signature of the wife; in short, when a husband and wife stand to each other in the same position that two business partners stand to each other, — then, and not till then, will a wife occupy a true position in the household and before the world. Then will be developed her highest capacity for doing good. The power of a wife thus poised and supported cannot be estimated. Free to act and develop the strong, brave, pure womanhood within her, she will throw to the winds the weak, vapid life which has chained her so long, and mount up on wings of high resolve and noble purpose, like eagles. Then, with true recognition and reverence, she will meet the royalty of manhood with the royalty of womanhood, saying, "If thou art the world's king, I am the world's queen." Then man will test all his relations with woman by the same code of impartial honor which makes him honorable among men; then a husband will cease to say, "I will absorb, rule over, possess, this creature of God." It will be then that each will seek in the other their noblest friend, their truest and dearest companion, their bulwark of defence in times of danger; when the wife shall revere the husband because he is worthy of such honor, and the husband revere the wife because she commands his reverence, while she wins and retains his love.

But until the law is changed which controls wedlock, and those of the so-called "weaker sex" under its bonds, this best condition of wifehood can never be reached. Under the law as it now stands, there is no such thing as a partnership relation in the marriage union. The man and woman become one, but that one is the man; for the rights of the married woman are still nearly all suspended during coverture, while all the rights of the married man remain established and protected by law, just as they were before marriage. In spite of our boasted progress and civilization, in wedlock woman is still a slave, because she is not a free agent. She cannot use a dollar of the common property which she has helped to earn, without the husband's consent; she cannot prosecute a physician for malpractice, nor a druggist for carelessly poisoning her, without the co-operation of her husband; she cannot recover damages for defamation of character, without the husband joins in the suit; she is obliged to live wherever the husband pitches his tent, no matter how repulsive the spot: she has no power to resist the will of her subjugator. But what is to be done when a husband wishes to live on one side of the river, and the wife on the other? Sit in a boat in the middle of the stream, and test the power of muscle against will?

No: I would exhaust arguments, and then "draw cuts." That is easy and convenient where there is a match-box, or two sticks; and people generally abide by the decision of so simple a measure.

You may say that making the wife a legal partner will embarrass and cripple the business transactions of the husband, that a wife's indorsement would occasion a ruinous delay, &c., &c. Sometimes delay is salvation with men who act upon impulse. Nothing but this recognition of the importance of the wife's consent will lift her out of the position of a legal nonentity. No brother can treat his sister in the cavalier manner that he does his wife. If he transacts business for his sister, she must put her name to the voucher, unless she has constituted him her attorney. A husband can get the same permit to act for his wife, in case of absence, or a desire on her part to maintain her old position still as a "*nonentity.*"

In 1877 it is proven in a court of justice, that a married woman in the State of Massachusetts does not own her own clothes. Here are the comments of "The Boston Daily Advertiser" upon the subject: "The old common law still reigns a despot in Massachusetts! The gift of a husband to his wife is void. The great majority of married women in this State have no legal title to the clothes they wear. I do not wonder that married ladies are shocked to find that this relic of their ancient subjugation and inferiority still survives in spite of all the modern enactments made in their favor. If the husband makes the wife a present of jewels, furniture, wearing-apparel, or any other gift of real or personal property, the gift is void in law. But, worse than this, if the wife lend the husband her own money, and he give her an express written promise to pay, the promise cannot be enforced, either in his lifetime against him, nor after his death against his estate. The amount of injustice perpetrated in this way cannot be estimated. A married woman, by the repeal of the old law, having now become capable of holding property and making contracts, what reason remains that husband and wife should not make gifts and sales to, and all sorts of contracts with, one another *directly*, thus simply effecting what they can now do as completely *indirectly?*"

It is alleged that such a change in law would aid husbands to defraud creditors. It is true that husbands do sometimes defraud creditors by placing property in their wives' hands; but the law does not sanction such frauds, and would not tolerate them if conveyances were made directly, any more than it does now when they are required to be made indirectly; and the means of detecting such frauds would be quite as easy as under the present system, and probably more so. It is further argued that to allow a wedded pair to enter into contracts together would necessarily give them power to prosecute suits in court against each other, a consummation so awful as not to be thought of for a moment. It is not a pleasant sight, I agree, to see persons who have been friends — and especially near relatives — pursuing one another in court. Yet no court has ever thought of making a law to prevent a daughter from suing father or mother, or a sister her brother. And why is there no such statute? Simply because every one ought to have power to obtain justice from the courts. The same reason applies to those united by wedlock as to those united by blood. The effect of authorizing such suits would never make them common; suits at law between near relations are never common: between husband and wife they would be less frequent. But the wife, like the sister or daughter, ought to be left to her own judgment whom and when to sue."

CHAPTER XXIII.

THE SUBJUGATION OF WIVES, AND MARTYRDOM.

Sic semper tyrannis.

THERE was a time when the careful burghers neglected no method of strengthing the defences of their towns. They increased the thickness of their walls when the cannon superseded the catapult. In the same manner have husbands, from time to time, changed their mode of procedure in their coercion of wives.

Wives, bend your necks to your husbands, has been rung on every change.

From the remotest period of our history, men set a great value upon women. A wife was far more profitable than an ordinary slave. Yet the man in quest of a wife did not stoop to win her affection with cunning speech and subtle device: he went forth upon his amatory expedition like a thief in the night, and captured her by brute-force if she refused to follow him, like any other beast of prey. He needed her services, and that was enough; she should be his slave, and do his bidding like a dog. Such a wife knew no law but the will of her master;

in him she lived (if such an abject existence can be called living), moved, and had her being.

After a time fathers became so impressed in regard to the value of their daughters, that they classed them with other merchandise, and sold them to the highest bidder in the open market-place, in the same manner as slaves have been knocked down from time immemorial. Often an avaricious father would sell an unusually attractive daughter half a dozen times, to as many different suitors, and, by making some plausible excuse for not delivering the commodity at the time of sale, at last hand her over to another on the receipt of an extortionate sum.

With a quiver full of handsome daughters those old chivalric reprobates had a good thing of it: they bartered their own flesh and blood, and that of their wives into the bargain, if they could find purchasers, with as little compunction as Charles Surface did his ancestors.

It never occurred to the slaveholder, that a daughter might have a predilection for "natural selection" in obtaining a husband. If it did, he scouted the idea that a woman should presume to have a like or a dislike in the matter of being wived. It was simply the transference of a right from one master to another. But this woman chattel was never to rise above her place, which was under the foot of her lord. To fitly symbolize her condition, a shoe was given the bridegroom by the father-in-law to mark the transfer of degrading power. A fallen foe was thus degraded by the heel of the conqueror. Assuming his newly acquired prerogative, the husband playfully tapped his bride upon the head with the ensign of power, which said plainer than words could express, "You are now mine, body and soul; to obey my lightest wish with fear and trembling; to bear my warrior sons, but to have no rule over them; to rear my slave-daughters; to be the veriest household drudge, and never complain; to have no wish in your heart but to serve me till death breaks the fetters which bind you."

Those wives were in a delightful (to the husbands) state of subjugation. If by any insanity they should rise in rebellion to such abject slavery, the husband could beat them with a pliant stick, the size and thickness of his thumb, into subjection or into their coffins; it mattered little which. For it seems that these old-time subjectors exercised the power of life and death over their wives, from the sickly record of the fate of a bride of a week. Here is the condensed extract of husband-power contained in eight lines of blood-curdling doggerel, —

"*Bought* a wife on Sunday,
Brought her home on Monday,
Beat her well on Tuesday,
Sick she was on Wednesday,
Dead she was on Thursday,
Buried she was on Friday,
Glad was I on Saturday,
And now I'll *buy* another."[1]

[1] Man is the only animal that maltreats or kills the female of his own species.

When the domestic rod of correction had somewhat lost its terrors, and the husband sighed for a more public recognition of his marital prowess, the bridle, or brank, was invented. This instrument of torture was a frightful cage made of hoops of iron, and fastened at the back of the neck with a padlock. This brank was placed over the head of a refractory spouse, and securely locked, while an iron gag was pressed into the mouth at the front. In this manner a wife and mother was led through the streets of the town by the beadle, to the exultation of her protector, and the hilarious merriment of the primitive hoodlum, and as a wholesome admonition to all perverse wives.

For the most trifling offences they were stripped to the waist, and flogged at the cart's-tail by the common hangman, sometimes for a distance of five miles in the dead of winter, while the surging rabble shouted after. They also adorned the whipping-post while a subjugator laid on the stripes.

The ducking-stool was another amusing instrument of husband-torture. This was invented for the special benefit of scolding wives. It is said that thousands of people would assemble to enjoy the delightful and ennobling spectacle of seeing a wife ducked in the Thames. Sometimes she died from the combined effect of the chilling bath, shame, and disgrace; but what of that, if the subjector's wrath was appeased, and the great unwashed tickled? Surely no one ought to grumble: still her sucking babe might miss her; who can tell?

Secular punishment for wives having grown alarmingly tame, some blessed genius immortalized himself by inventing the divine cutty-stool of repentance, which was a prominent seat in the house of God. Here the culprit was obliged to sit in full view of the congregation for three consecutive sabbaths. If the sinner happened to be young and pretty, it must have had a most demoralizing effect upon the masculine worshippers; and if old and ugly every aggressive, waspish husband worked himself into a violent perspiration because it was neighbor Jones's wife who was doing penance instead of his, who needed to be perpetually seated upon a cutty-stool if she had her just deserts. However, in those days of fire and brimstone punishment, after death had relieved the "cutty," the husband — even under such trying circumstances — ought to have been able to pray in serenity, with the consolations of the retributive hereafter before his mind's eye.

What a keen edge it must have given the sermon on the power of evil, with such a palpable witness! enough to sharpen the dullest clerical blade, and tip with asperity a featherless arrow — let fly in either High or Low Church, even though it were almost dead with respectability.

In 1876, under the head of "The Cutty-Stool Revived," appeared this notice in an English paper: "In a church in Black Isle, Ross-shire, on a recent Sunday, a woman who had been guilty of transgressing the seventh commandment was condemned to the cutty-stool, and sat during the whole service with a black shawl over her head." The record does not state where her partner in iniquity sat, or under what he hid his shamefacedness — if he had any to hide.

An English husband brought a prostitute into his house, and confined his wife to her room under pretence of her insanity; but the court held this to be insufficient cause for the wife to desert him. Would the verdict have been the same, think you, if the wife had thus confined her husband, and installed her paramour in his place? and why not?

Newspapers are literally filled with horrors, of which men are the authors, and women the victims. Wife-beating, wife-murder, rape, and bigamy are becoming so common as scarcely to excite remark. Here is one among the latest: "Patrick Tooley of New York, a laborer, last night poured a can of kerosene over his wife, because she said he was hard to please. She screamed and prayed to him not to set her alight; but he exclaimed, 'By G——, you shall burn, you she-devil!' Suiting the action to his word, he struck a match, and ignited the oil. Her piercing screams roused the neighborhood. When Officer Raleigh found her she was a pitiable sight, great pieces of flesh hanging from her breasts and arms. Her face and hands were burned as black as jet. She died before morning in the most heart-rending agony."

The alarming increase of insults and personal outrages inflicted upon women must be attributed to a public sentiment hostile to their individuality and equality of rights; and to the subjection and disfranchisement of women, which is so injurious to society, destructive of morals, corrupting to politics, and a reproach to Christianity.

Husbands still in some instances, as of old, hold the power of life and death over their wives. This power is more indirectly exercised, perhaps, but the results are the same. To substantiate these premises, I will state two cases in the land of the free; one North, one South. First — in 1860, in the town of Manteno, Kankakee County, Ill., a sane Christian wife and mother was torn from her babe eighteen months old, and her five other children, by the order of her husband, the Right Rev. Theophilus Packard, and taken by brute force to the Jacksonville Insane Asylum, Illinois, and there shut in with howling maniacs for three terrible years. Nothing more conclusive is needed to show that the woman was in the vigor of sanity, than that she kept her wits about her during such a fearful ordeal, which was enough to cloud the brightest intellect and wreck the most robust constitutions.

Only sixteen years ago, in broad daylight, this kidnapping of a perfectly sane woman was permitted. Why? Because there was no law to restrain the hand of her legal subjector, human — and it is claimed — divine. This modern husband hid his Satanic wolfship under the pure lawn of the Church militant.

Did he succeed in killing her? No. But that was

no fault of his, for that appears to have been his intention. The record shows that he tried by every available means to kill both body and soul. Why did this expounder of Christ's doctrines thus treat a good wife and a tender mother? why? Because he could not come out of their wordy combats on religious subjects, first best. He could not yield his prerogative. He would resort to other more potent means to subjugate the "woman." He was a true disciple of Paul, a stanch standard-bearer of his faith.

O Paul, Paul! what mountains of iniquity are laid at your door! what seas of wormwood and gall your words have engendered among the enlightened peoples of the earth!

Why are not modern husbands as tenacious about the "good old way" in every thing else? Why don't they clothe themselves in skins instead of fine linen? Why don't they live in tents, instead of sumptuous palaces? Why don't they plough with a crooked stick, instead of a gang? Why don't they eat with their fingers, and lick off the platter, instead of using knives and dishcloths? Why don't they worship in God's first temples, instead of behind bronze church doors, under fretted roof with pillared aisles, where the poor — God help them — dare not enter? Sweet, loving, gentle, protecting subjugators, you are not consistent. That most rare jewel is not set like a flaming brand in your foreheads.

But to return to the exemplary Theophilus, the

divine wife-tamer, the mundane God-head of the household.

When his wife asked him why he did such a wicked deed as to separate her from all she held most dear, to incarcerate her in a living tomb, — a madhouse, — he made answer, —

"I am doing as the laws of Illinois allow me to do. You have no protection in law but myself, and I am protecting you now. It is for your good I am doing this. I want to save your soul. You don't believe in total depravity" (what a marvel, with such an incarnate embodiment before her!) "and I want to make you right."

Then she continued, "Does not the Constitution defend the right of private judgment to all American citizens?"

"Yes, to all citizens it does defend the right. But you are not a citizen; while a married woman, you are a legal nonentity, without even a soul in law. In short, you are dead as to any legal existence while a married woman, and therefore have no legal protection as a married woman." I have taken these facts from Mrs. Packard's able work, "Modern Persecution."

Under the head of "Charities," there was a law passed in Illinois, in 1851, which reads thus: 'Married women and infants who, in the judgment of the medical superintendent (meaning the superintendent of the Insane Asylum), are evidently insane or distracted, may be entered or detained in the hospital on the request of the husband of the woman or the guardian of the child, *without* the evidence of insanity required in other cases."

Hon. S. S. Jones of St. Charles, Ill., thus remarks upon this act: "A corrupt husband, with money enough to corrupt a superintendent, can get rid of a wife as effectually as was ever done in a more barbarous age. The superintendent may be corrupted either with money or influence, that he thinks will give him position, place, or emoluments. Is not this a pretty law to incorporate into our statutes? Why not confine the husband at the instance of the wife, as well as the wife at the instance of the husband? The wife had no voice in making such a monstrous law.

"Who, being a man, and seeing this section in the Statute Book of Illinois, under the general head of '*Charities*,' does not blush and hang his head for very shame at legislative perversion of so holy a term? I have no doubt, if the truth of the matter were known, this act was passed at the special instance of the superintendent. A desire for power! What is a married woman's protection under such a statute law? Is she not allowed counter testimony from a physician of her own choice, or can she not demand a trial of some kind, to show whether the charge of insanity brought against her is true or false?

"Nay, verily. The statute expressly states that the judgment of the medical superintendent, to whom the husband's request is made, is *all* that is required for him to incarcerate his wife for any indefinite period of time. Neither she, her children, nor her relatives, have any voice at all in the matter. Her imprisonment may be life-long, for any thing she or her friends can do for her to prevent it. If the husband has money or influence enough to corrupt the officials, he can carry out his single wishes concerning her life destiny." It is due to the citizens of the State of Illinois to say, that through the indefatigable labors of Mrs. Packard, aided and abetted by able legislators and the governor, the cruel law of 1851 was repealed in 1866, and the "Personal Liberty Bill" took its place upon the Statute-Books of Illinois.

I am told that there are sane wives to-day dragging out an utterly hopeless existence at Stockton Insane Asylum, California, kept there by moneyed subjugators; that these husbands have become weary of legitimate life, and have taken this easy method of bringing about the change that is so desirable. Forbidden fruit is sweet: yet when purchased at such a price, I should think it would turn to dust within the grasp. This brings me to my —

Second, "*Dishonor and Death.*" — In the month of June, 1876, at Beaufort, S.C., the lovely young wife of a government officer was discovered by her husband to have a too ardent friend in the person of a brother officer. Her protector intercepted letters which passed between the friends, and with these weapons charged home upon his victim. She confessed, in the presence of a mutual friend, that she had broken her marriage vow. Upon this statement, the husband at once separated from her, taking their only child, a little girl, a mere infant, with him. The wretched mother was too polluted, with her *one* error, her *one* lover, to touch the hem of his PURE and undefiled garment, or to caress her darling child.

Whose palm, husband's or wife's, think you, was the cleanest, purest, whitest, in this respect? Why did not he too make a confession before that mutual friend? Perhaps *he* had none to make. Perhaps? Public Opinion, that equitable criterion, was loud-mouthed in its sympathy for the dishonored husband, while it rolled the follies of the wife as a sweet morsel under its tongue.

But she, dishonored, deserted, forlorn, preferred an ounce of laudanum and a navy revolver to the world's cold scorn, — the virtuous world, and its virtuous subjugators.

The record states that probably the gallant officer will abandon his position, and "seek new scenes." If he possessed a spark of manhood, let alone gallantry, he would have taken his erring (no knowing what caused her to err: his history is not given) wife by the hand, and said to her, "I too have sinned, I too have broken my marriage vow; but in new scenes we will forgive and forget — *the past*, and be true to ourselves, and therefore to each other, in the future. We will not part, because we have taken each the other for better or for worse. We will go on together."

That would have been honest, brave, and true, worthy of an officer, a man, a husband, a father. But as it was, he played the fool and the coward; and his wife's blood is upon his craven soul, and cries to Heaven for revenge, as much as though he had shed it with his own hand. He drove her forth to death. But the great eye of the pitiless world, and the brotherhood of subjugators, was upon him. Public opinion must not go to the wall. The order of the day is to reason from without, and not from within. Consult "folks," and not "heart." Starve if need be, but keep up appearances. Bury dead hopes under a wreath of smiles, and weave fresh garlands over the crater of despair. But do no natural, spontaneous act, lest it be "vulgar."

Question no act of a husband, however diabolical, for it is in the breast of every man to be master. No matter how inferior he may be to the woman who bears his name, and suckles his "fools," he is *dignior persona*, and runs his little race with many a grotesque antic, — a living embodiment of Darwin's theory.

Absolutism is one of the original sins inwrought in man's nature, and it has never been uprooted by the harrow of civilization.

As we have seen, our remote subjugators held wives as only fit for beasts of burden, and "breeders of sinners." When woman came timidly forward, and slaked her thirst at the fountain of knowledge. the legal cannon took the place of the murderous social and legal catapult. Although woman has risen from the position of a favorite slave to that of an enslaved favorite, still she is not a freeman under the law, but a bondman. Marriage as it now exists is another species of bondage, irreconcilable with the spirit and enlightenment of the present age. Wedlock should leave each party to the contract equally free; it should be for the mutual benefit of both parties, in reality as well as in name. The relation of husband and wife is, like every thing else in nature, twofold. The husband is head of his business outside, while the wife *should* be the head of the domestic department. A man is as much out of place lording it over the intricate machinery of the household as a bull in a china-shop, or as his wife would be in his office down town, dictating to his clerks.

There must be two heads to the marriage firm instead of one, if we would arrive at the best results of marriage. The theory that one head is better than two heads should have been exploded long ago. The old saw bluntly argues that two heads are better than one, if one is a sheep-head.

When men come down from their stilts, they will be astonished to see how often the sheep-head is on the masculine shoulders.

The husband holds undisputed sway in his legitimate realm. So the wife should be the sovereign queen in hers. It is only a sneak who interferes with her prerogative.

A lover obeys his Dulcinia's slightest wish; but the moment the "shoe is plucked off" there is a transfer of power. "A man will sigh and fawn around a woman for months, perhaps years, celebrate her unparalleled *wisdom* in bad rhymes, lose flesh and spirit if she frowns, kneel to her as the Hindoo to his idol, and grovel in utter abasement before her conceded *superiority;* and then when he is permitted to put the circlet of power upon her finger — as if by magic — she grows imbecile, *idiotic*, unable to act and judge for herself; loses her power to control her own property and earnings, even when the law permits her to do so."

The common law recognizes the inability of the wife to judge of what is best for her to eat, drink, and wear; and will punish, by damages awarded the husband, any one who takes advantage of her idiocy in that respect. The husband, under this law, can recover damages of the vender of an article which he did not approve. Thus, if a greengrocer sell a wife colicky cabbage instead of mild squash, the husband can make him smart for it. But the wife has no corresponding action against a rumseller, a confidence operator, or swindler of any name or nature, for throwing her husband into bankruptcy by dishonest manipulation.

A drunken husband, whom the wife supports, can beat her, steal her wages, and beggar her children, and she has no legal protection against him; and, if she has separate property, she is liable for his debts. Why should a wife answer for the indigence of one whose lawful privilege it is to strip her of her own means of support without her consent? But the old law expressly says, "All that a woman hath appertained to her husband. The will of the wife is subject to the will of the husband."

The theory of the common law is that a woman needs to know nothing but how to get a husband — he knows it all. She becomes like an infant, utterly irresponsible for every thing she does. No, not every thing: if she has done any thing worthy of prison or hanging, the law deems her of sufficient mental capacity to answer for that, but adjudges the subjector the vicarious sufferer for all else. What a fall from

> "A perfect woman, nobly planned,
> To warn, to comfort, and command"!

All women are still under subjugation to the arbitrary rule of some man, at the hearthstone, in the Church, and in the State. Woman is still a slave. The manacles which bind her may be wound with golden thread, and padded with velvet: nevertheless they are manacles still. But too often they are neither wound, padded, nor concealed; and then they sink deep into the galled and quivering flesh of the powerless sufferer.

If a wife does not live under the rod and slipper, as of old, she is still wed with a ring, another symbol of fetters and bondage. She is made to promise to obey with her lips, when her heart — it is to be hoped — is far from it. One should obey the voice of God within. — their own conscience, — and not be subjected to the will of another. Each soul should walk by its own light.

Man has been a usurper since the day he was driven out of the Garden. He has walled himself about and sentinelled the outposts with might, not right. But when women rouse themselves from the Lethean apathy of ages, the situation will become more and more untenable, until at last the walls of masculine power will crumble, and adult humanity will go forth unfettered and free. To learn what women have suffered at the hands of men, we have only to turn over the pages of ancient and modern history, and read what the martyrdom of the daring ones has been.

What was the fate of the Maid of Orleans, the fearless heroine who redeemed France? Did not the young king whom she crowned at Rheims abandon her to the justice of the enemies' courts, and to the righteous judges of those courts, — to priest and prelate? Did he ever speak a word, lift a finger, stir a foot, to rescue this young and lovely woman, to whom he owed his throne and kingdom, from the fagots and the stake?

Oh the base ingratitude which abandoned her to the brutal, blind wickedness of men whose poignant animosities proclaimed her as God-forsaken and

Devil-inspired! — who vehemently accused her of heinous crimes savoring of heresy; whose malignant spite would be avenged on a *woman* who had brought their pride to the dust by her marvellous victories won by her bravery and the pure lightning of her enthusiasm, which had kindled a flame that flashed like a meteor above the midnight of conflict and despair! Where lies the blackest shame of *Jeanne d'Arc's* cruel tragedy? with Charles VII., who abandoned her? with the Duke of Burgundy and Jean of Luxembourg, who sold her? with the English council, who delivered her up to the Church? or with her ecclesiastical judges, who condemned her?

O damning truth! Princes of her own nation betrayed her to death, and priests of her own nation accomplished her death. Of the English lords, on whom recoiled the deep dishonor of it, the English sage might have been speaking when he said, —

> "How oft the sight of means to do
> Ill deeds, makes ill deeds done!"

At the opening of the trial of this girl of seventeen, there sat on the tribunal, as counsellors or as assessors, fifteen doctors of divinity, four doctors of canon law, seven bachelors of divinity, twelve bachelors of canon law, four licentiates of civil law, and forty-two ecclesiastics, of whom all but eight belonged to the body of secular clergy. Eighty-four long-robed, erudite braves arrayed against an unlettered child that could not write her own name:

what a spectacle! She felt the bad atmosphere of their malice, hatred, and revenge pressing all round her; but she stood valiantly on her own defence, showing to those heavenly judges as intrepid a countenance as ever she had shown to her enemies on the *secular* battle-field.

She was neither suffered by her holy condemners to hear mass, receive the sacrament of the altar, nor to go to confession, which was a grievous trial; for she was eminently devout. When the justice of the Church laid hold on a victim, woe betide the wretch who dared venture to impugn her motives or her tender mercies! It suffered no interference with its pious hatreds.

For five months this child, with the stigma of woman upon her, languished in her prison-house, — the castle of Beaurevois, — suffering every indignity from her men-jailers. She was chained by her feet to a log — a ponderous log — of wood while walking; sleeping, she was ironed by the legs with two pieces of heavy fetters locked to the bed. She slept in her prison clothes, as she had slept on the march with the army, while three English guards kept vigil. A royal equerry was her chief keeper. Besides these three shut in with her at night, two other subjugators sentinelled her prison door outside. It took five stalwart men and two pairs of strong iron fetters to guard this prize, whose price was above a king's ransom.

There was *one* man called to take part in this

disgraceful farce, misnamed a trial, who was noble enough to condemn the illegality of the whole proceedings; a famous Norman lawyer by the name of Lohier. Said he, "In the first place, it has not the form of an ordinary trial; in the second, you are carrying it on with closed doors, where the council and assistants have not full and free liberty to speak; in the third, you treat in it of things concerning the honor of the king of France, of whose party the Maid is, without calling him, or any in his name; and, in the last, neither bill nor articles have been given to the accused, as the law in trials for the faith requires, nor any council to direct her, who is but a simple girl and a minor, in answering the masters and doctors in such great and delicate matters as those she calls her '*revelations*.' For each and all of these reasons, your trial seems to me invalid: they will catch her in her own words. She says of her '*voices*,' *I am certain*, instead of, *It seems to me*. The latter would not condemn her. They are impelled by hatred to destroy her."

She prayed in vain to see the Pope, or to be allowed a military trial. All was denied her, although she was a person of such high chivalry that there was no knight in Christendom whose fame overshadowed hers. By all the ordinary courtesy of war, she was entitled to the privileges of a prisoner of war. She had been a generous foe, if a resolute and successful foe. Neither cruelty nor treachery could be laid to her charge. Her life was stainless, her brief career most glorious. But her persecutors never rested until the ascending smoke of her torment blessed their vision; until the red-tongued flames licked up her blood, and her fair young face was scorched and blackened by the fires of martyrdom; until the freed spirit, that no manacles of man could chain, burst through the tortured cinders, upward, upward, to realms of peace and rest.

> "Oh, change! oh, wondrous change!
> Burst are the prison-bars:
> This moment there so low,
> So agonized, and now — beyond the stars.

CHAPTER XXIV.

THE HISTORY OF A PET DOG.

Parvum parva decent.

I GIVE the history of Jack, not because he differs materially from any other well-bred dog, but to show what men — who call themselves *honorable* — will do to persecute a woman who dares to claim her own property wherever she can find it, in spite of masculine pomposity and time-honored subjectors.

Some time during the summer of 1870, Mr. Stow purchased Jack of a stable-man, paying five dollars for him. My husband was very fond of dogs, and he had taken a great fancy to this one, a large-sized black-and-tan terrier. We were summering in Oakland at the time of the purchase. He said to me when he brought him home, "I have found one of the finest dogs of his kind I ever saw." I replied, "Why did you get another dog while we are broken up housekeeping?" We were living in a furnished house, and had one black-and-tan already, which was quite care enough for me, particularly when we were boarding at a hotel; and besides, we never went anywhere to be gone over night, but that the little dog

"Gyp" went too. Car and steamboat porters were always on the alert for him. It mattered not how deftly he was smuggled out of the carriage into cabin or car: they knew he was there among the wraps somewhere. But little Gyp's doggish dignity was never outraged by a moment's stay in baggage-car or porter's berth.

Mr. Stow replied to my question, "Jack is to be an office-dog. I only brought him home to let you see what a beauty he is." But, as "the best-laid plans of mice and men gang aft aglee," so did my husband's plans in regard to Jack. He had not been in the office more than three weeks, before he was set upon by a canine subjugator several times larger than himself, — might, not right, — and nearly killed.

Mr. Stow with much difficulty, and with the aid of a carriage to and from the depots, got the badly maimed dog home; and, for several weeks thereafter, Jack remained at the house, an interesting invalid. And, like all other male invalids, he was very exacting. Blankets were arranged in a Turkish chair in my chamber for a suitable bed for the sufferer; for on no account would Mr. Stow listen to the idea that the dog could be accommodated with a room by himself. He argued that Jack was very much attached to him, and that a separation at night would retard the recovery of his pet. Therefore I had his company both day and night. He could not move at first without assistance; and my servants considered it somewhat out of their line to carry a dog that weighed twenty-four pounds up and down stairs several times a day. It was done, however; and when he was quite well again, and went back to the office during the day, the night generally found him in Oakland. Why? Because Mr. Stow said it would break the poor old fellow's heart if he could not see me every day, and that I had entirely usurped his place in the heart of the affectionate creature. However, I suspect that it was the nice dinner taken from off the family roast, which he was sure to get with Gyp, and Poll the cat. From that time forward, he never lost his position as an honorable member of the Stow family, until his master's death. At that time all things were changed.

It is claimed that Mr. Stow, when he was dying, gave Jack to Dr. Howard of Los Angeles, although my husband had given the dog to me, in the presence of my sister and another person, soon after he came into his possession. I had complained of the extra care of having a sick dog to nurse; and Mr. Stow replied, "Well, my dear, I will make you a present of Jack; and when you get tired of him, Howard (a former employee of Mr. Stow's) can have him."

Sister Gertie, at whose house my husband lived and died in my absence in Europe, was very much attached to Jack, and greatly surprised that Mr. Stow should have given him to any one, under any circumstances, and particularly when he was no longer his to give. When I learned that Howard claimed the dog, I at once wrote and requested him (Howard) to leave Jack at my sister's until my return. He complied with my wishes on the subject, and the dog did not go to Los Angeles until my sister broke up housekeeping.

At the time I sent Jack to the doctor, I said to Gertie, "Whenever you want Jack, you shall have him; for he is my dog. I have a prior claim of ownership. He was given to me, as you know; besides, my care of him evidently saved his life at the time he was so badly hurt." Last June I paid a visit to Los Angeles, with the intention of bringing Jack home with me. I called upon Mrs. Howard, and found, to my regret, that the doctor was absent. I said to her, "I am very sorry the doctor is from home, because I wish to take Jack to San Francisco. You are blessed with three little ones, and that should fill your cup of domestic happiness without Jack. I have lost all the fortune which belonged to my husband and myself, and I would like to have the dog back. I am going East whenever I can get free from the Probate Court, and wish to give him to my sister. She loves Jack very much. She was never paid one farthing by the honorable executors for taking care of my husband during his last illness, and I think this much she ought to have." Mrs. Howard replied, "Mrs. Stow, if you want the dog, you shall certainly take him; for no one has as strong a claim upon him as you have. I will stand between you and all harm. The doctor will certainly respect my decision." I then said, "Write to him, and get his consent." She complied with my request, but there came no answer to her letter; and, as silence gives consent, I brought away the dog, saying, "I will take him up on a visit; and, when the doctor is in San Francisco, he can see me in person about the matter."

At that time it was not my intention to raise the question of ownership, or to keep the dog unless Howard was perfectly willing to have me. I had said nothing to my sister upon the subject, But I never, for a moment, doubted that if I told Howard that *I* wanted Jack, but that he would at once relinquish all claims to him. Ere that time I had looked upon the man as an honorable gentleman.

Very soon after my return from Los Angeles he came to the city, and remained several weeks. He did not call upon me, but contented himself with various and sundry notes, in which he requested me to send Jack to the office of the Consolidated Tobacco Company. I urged him, by letter, to come and see me. But no: he was ashamed—I suppose—to face me about the matter. At last he sent a man to get Jack; and I said to the messenger, "If Dr. Howard had been the gentleman I once took him to be, he would have been polite enough to have seen me in person about the dog. If he had shown the widow of his '*dead friend*' the least consideration in this proceeding, he could have had him. Howard claims that Mr. Stow gave Jack to him when he was dying. That I do not believe, because, if my husband was in his right mind — and all the physicians say that he was — he would not have taken the liberty of making a gift of my property without the qualifying clause, 'with my wife's consent.' He was too honorable for that.

"When Jack lived with me or my sister he was as carefully groomed as a thoroughbred every day. When I brought him to my sister's house from Los Angeles, she exclaimed, 'What *cur* have you got there?' He did not look as though he had been washed or brushed once since he left San Francisco. His coat was filled with dirt and fleas. People said to me on the steamer, 'What is the matter with that dog? he is biting his back all the time.' I should never have allowed him to be taken from here if I had not thought he would have had different care from what he has received. He has been kept out on Freeman's ranch, and housed in a stable or kennel, I should think, instead of being taken care of by Howard. Mr. Stow took him out of a stable to save him from the horrors of a life of fleas, kicks, and dirt. He knew nothing but affectionate care with us; and judging from his appearance when I got him back (for he acted like an old dog), he has had little since. A man with three babies to tend has not much time to bestow upon a dog. Better leave him with those who are not thus blessed, and to those that have a prior claim of ownership."

"Ain't you goin' to let me take Jack to the doctor?" said the diminutive specimen of a woman subjugator.

"Take him? No," I replied. "Dr. Howard shall never have him after the course he has pursued, unless the equitable law gives him to him. Give the doctor my compliments with this message."

Then commenced a petty persecution — worthy of the Pygmies — in which the small malice evoked showed the true proportion of this Esculapian subjugator. He got out a writ of replevin, and deputy sheriffs and private detectives had a lively time of it for about two weeks. They waited upon my landlady at all hours — when I wasn't in. They followed every big woman that left the house but me — and I am not physically *small.* One poor woman carrying a bundle, which they evidently thought was Jack in his swaddling-clothes, was pursued so furiously that she fell down and nearly killed herself in her fright. At last they came when I was in, but Jack was out. Still I wished them to think I had him with me. I locked my door inside, and stood with one foot in my room and the other on the balcony, as uncertain as man — who is represented with —

> "One foot on land, and one on sea,
> To one thing constant never."

Still it is not a perfect simile in my case, for I was most constant in my determination to protect Jack. I did not intend to see the officers, and I didn't. While they were thundering at my door, I stepped into the next house through the balcony window. After they were gone, I went down to the City Hall, and, calling upon the sheriff, said to him, "Ain't you in pretty small business persecuting a 'poor, lorn creetur' about a pet dog?" He replied, "I cannot help it: I must do my duty as an officer. I admit that it is very small business, Mrs. Stow, but it's law nevertheless." "Well," I continued, "I hold no malice against you for doing your duty; but I shall give you all the trouble I can, and in the end you won't have the dog. You have woman's wit to outwit; and that you'll not be able to do with all your deputies." And it was no idle boast, for they did not get Jack.

When Howard failed to take him from me through legal chicanery in one form, he resorted to the shuttle-cockery of courts.

Then I was sued. "*Sued for a dog!*" some will exclaim, with an extra turn of a nose that was *retroussé* enough before. Some people have no fellowship with dogs: I have. I have found them faithful friends. They never turned on me with a viper's fang, in payment for kindnesses rendered, as some human creatures have; they never have sought to heat my enemies, or cool my friends, as some human creatures have; they never have been summer friends, and turned a cold shoulder during the winter of adversity, as some human creatures have. They are true till death: they are not human. Dr. Stone of this city once gave a lecture, the subject of which was "The Intelligence of Animals." Mr. Stow wrote him a note the next day, in which he said, "Bravo for you, my boy! The more I know of dogs, the less I think of men."

The case was tried in the Justice Court, before Judge Joachimsen, a handsome, dark man, with no very strong predilection for dogs.

The party of the first part had brought suit against the party of the second part to recover the sum of $250 in gold coin, in case a certain black-and-tan dog that answers to the name of Jack is not produced in court—*bodily*. When I saw the price set upon poor Jack's head, I argued in this wise: "Cannot I get an offset, a kind of rebuttal, against the $250 claimed by the party of the first part, by bringing in a counter claim for services rendered as sick-nurse by the party of the second part?" I have paid $20 a week for sick-nursing,—not within the last two years, however, for when I was sick unto death the just Probate would not allow me one extra sixpence for medical attendance and nursing. There is no encouragement held out to probating widows to be interesting invalids. They must keep themselves in robust health, or suffer the penalty of their folly.

The court-room on this particular morning presented a curious appearance. The subjugating plaintiff, with a long line of subjugating witnesses, headed by his beardless, youthful,—but doubtless MOST LEARNED,—attorney, sat on the left of "*his Honor;*" while poor little me, with my one witness—sister Gertie—and my attorney, sat on his right.

Then began the squabble in dead earnest. Witnesses were examined all the way from Los Angeles to San Francisco — that is, they had travelled that distance, braving the perils of sea and land, to aid a man in robbing a woman. Freeman, of Temple and Worrell collapsed-bank fame, tall and dauntless, declared that Jack was worth $200 to catch rats on his ranch; at which statement the judge questioned, "Cannot any cur catch rats?" A very perceptible wave of disgust flowed over the broad face of Freeman, and he said no more, but slunk away through the open door — somewhere. Then the heroic plaintiff took the stand, and testified that he was a physician and surgeon, was a graduate of the Royal College of Physicians, London, England, and of the Royal College of Surgeons, Edinburgh, Scotland; that he was out of practice at the present moment, but was liable to commence again at any time: no tellin'. He further deposed and said, "On or near the 1st of August, 1874, I was called in consultation with Drs. Keney and Holland of this city, by the request of the late J. W. Stow, whom, on arriving here, I found in a dying condition. He said to me, 'I wish to make you a present of Jack. Keep him, for my sake, as long as he lives; and on no account let another person have him, particularly *my wife.*'" When Howard said this, it was so amusingly absurd that I burst out laughing. [I] might have been fined for this breach of court etiquette, but I wasn't. The firing of that gun, like

Charles Lamb's chicken-wing, "did the job for him;" he hadn't another word to say. The other evidence taken is too trivial to mention — "*in a standard work.*" When all the chaff had been winnowed by the legal zephyrs, a letter which I had written the doctor was read by the aforementioned youthful antagonist, in a very insinuating voice. Then he opened a volume of my first edition of "Probate Confiscation," and with great consideration for my feelings said, "Mrs. Stow, I believe you are the author of this work." I modestly confessed that "I did the deed:" after which he read various and sundry passages therefrom, evidently charmed with the music of his own voice; then he argued the case at length, how that "*we* were in peaceful possession of the dog, and that defendant had fraudulently possessed herself of the dog; that it was not the value of the dog which they sought, but the *bona fide* dog." As he warmed and glowed in his youthful ardor, and brilliant display of legal fire-works, every hair on the judge's bald head bristled with amazement: he was not prepared for such a whirlwind of eloquence.

At last the adolescent aspirant for forensic honors sat down, amidst a burst of perspiration, from sheer exhaustion.

During the breathless silence which followed, my attorney turned to me, and said, "Mrs. Stow, I am unable to respond to the dazzling effort on the part of our opponent." To which I gaspingly replied,

"You have my profoundest sympathy, if that will assuage your embarrassment." He looked the gratitude which he could not speak.

The judge began to open his mouth at this desperate moment, and when the feat was accomplished said, "The defendant must pay the costs of court, and produce the dog Jack, or pay five dollars, the value I set upon him."

As soon as the judge had rendered his decision, the long line of witnesses, headed by the plaintiff and the youthful attorney, tore out of that court-room in their wrath, down the stairs, and into the street, where they were lost to sight, if not to memory dear, in the twinkling of an eye. They melted away like a beautiful dream, or like dissolving views. But why were they wrathy? they had won their case, judgment was in their favor; why or wherefore, I know not. That is one of the things which will ever remain "past findin' out." My attorney said it was because I had spoken of Jack in my letter as being Howard's dog, and that my letter had killed my case. I shall never be quite clear on the subject: that is, because I'm not versed in the ways that are dark and the tricks that are vain, no doubt. But there is one thing which I am perfectly clear about; and that is, that if they did win they have not got possession yet, and the case was decided months ago.

Jack is safe among admiring friends, enjoying a ripe doghood — if I may use the expression; and why not? He is far more worthy of the compound than many a cur that goes on two legs instead of four; he is brave, honest, and true, and would *talk* if he could; he tells me every time I go to see him how much he loves me, and how much he would like to go home with me, in his own eloquent dog-language; he is a tried friend that I am proud of. Mr. Stow used to say that he understood the English language perfectly. To those who are fond of dumb animals, and study their ways, many things concerning them are perfectly explainable that may appear very absurd to those that have no love for the lower order of beings.

Returning to my room late one afternoon, I found Jack upon the rug outside my door, and discovered at the same time that my dead latch was inside. I wrote on a card that I was out without my key, and attached the card to Jack's collar, and then explained the situation to him, and told him to go to his master's office with the message. My husband was speaking with a friend in front of the office when Jack made his appearance. Mr. Stow remarked, when he saw him, "There comes Jack with a message from his mistress." He soon came back to me with Mr. Stow's key in place of the card. Do you think Jack Stow understands English?

Howard has not accepted the five dollars which I placed on deposit at the clerk's office for him: he says it is only a question of time, that he will have him in the end.

Now I call upon all justice, all humanity, and ask,

"Who has the best right to Jack, Dr. F. P. Howard, or Mrs. J. W. Stow?" She has taken care of him for three years, and her sister one, making four years of care; she has saved his life by careful nursing; she has never for a moment relinquished her right to claim him at any moment; she has possession of him in spite of courts, sheriffs, deputy-sheriffs, and sneaks; and possession is nine points of law.

Perhaps they will get him: I don't say but that they will. The law gives them five years to wage their guerilla warfare in; Jack will be verging towards the sere and yellow leaf by that time, for he is ten years old now.

The only live stock that Mr. Stow and I possessed was Jack; and the only real estate which we owned together is the cemetery lot. That Mr. Pringle has asked me to set a price upon, — *a small price at that* — "For," said he, "you would not expect to get a fancy price for it, for there are three bodies there already. It is natural that the man who has a mother and a child buried there should want to own the lot." But of course it is *unnatural* that a wife should want to own the last resting-place of a husband. Then, again, "Where am I to be hidden when I die? in the Potter's Field? What shall I do with the money paid for my husband's bones, and the few feet of earth that surrounds them? Shall I buy a love of a bonnet with it, or bank it with the hope that I may live long enough so that the principal and interest may, in the dim future, amount to enough to pay for cremation?" This, like many another solution in the problem of wresting every thing from a widow by male subjugators, is a vexed question. I have not as yet set a price on the coveted lot; that is the only thing the just law has not taken from me; and I have not a doubt, if these shameless executors were to bring this into court, but that the upright Myrick would decide against the non-voter, and for the voters. He has a hawk's eye for votes and the extinguishment of widows; yet he is an "*upright judge*," so say the people who have not felt the weight of his ermine upon their shoulders. True, I have Jack yet, and would have kept him if the law had imprisoned me because I did not produce him. I would have eaten bread and water behind bars to have defied it, and protected him; and yet wherever right is maintained I am a law-abiding — what? not a citizen — A NON-ENTITY!

I beg to ask the legal *savants* and all the other absolute rulers, if it isn't a little rough, to say the least, that one full-grown body — I cannot call myself an individual under the law, for individual rights are protected, and mine are not — cannot reasonably hope to maintain peaceful profession of a pet hedgehog, weasel, or tarantula, that one has tamed and cared for for years, and learned to love? for it is a law of every true nature to love that which one daily cares for. If one can be protected in the ownership of a hedgehog, he or she ought to be protected in the ownership of a dog. A dog is more affectionate than a hedgehog; that is, we are in greater sympathy with its demonstrations. When I was a little girl, and lived in the blessed country, and not the wicked city, I had a pet toad that I named Billy. Now, Billy knew his little mistress's voice, and would come hopping out of his dark corner in the garden-wall when she called, "Billy, Billy," for he was sure of getting a fly or two; and after he had swallowed the flies with a duck of the head and a great relish, he would suffer her to pat him on his back. Now, no one ever thought of robbing this little girl of her pet Billy. Why? Because she wasn't a *widow* in a court of *justice*.

Is it not a reproach and a shame that the law permits a husband when he is dying to give away a household pet? No one but a base wretch would do such a despicable deed in his sane moments; and no one can accuse my late husband of so vile a deed with impunity: he never did it.

When I was in Rome I visited the studio of Harriet Hosmer, only to find the genius of the place absent. It was a very warm day; and wearied and disappointed I sat down to rest for a few moments among the beautiful productions fashioned and perfected by the cunning of the absent hand. Suddenly, while speaking to the person who accompanied me, I heard a bumping upon the naked floor, and looking down at my feet I saw a little mud-turtle, with its head, so suggestive of the first tempter's, stretched far out of its shell, and its gleaming eyes fixed on my face. I stooped down, and picking it up placed it on my lap, and, patting its uneasy head with my gloved hand, said, "Poor little lonesome thing! did you mistake the sound of my voice for that of your mistress's? You understand the difference between the English language and that of the Italian evidently."

Do you suppose that any Italian court of justice ever sought to rob my fair compatriot of her pet mud-turtle? Single women can live in peace with their pets, without a fear of their being legally stolen from them; but not so with married women and widows. Their pets, with every thing else, are shipwrecked upon this legal Gibraltar called JUSTICE.

CHAPTER XXV.

GILROY CONSOLIDATED TOBACCO COMPANY.

Cui bono?

CHRISTMAS of 1873 Mr. Stow made me a present of a hundred shares of tobacco stock, saying, "This little piece of paper looks like a small gift, and yet in the near future it will be worth par, — ten thousand dollars." Three weeks from that date I started for Europe. But before I left home I placed in a savings bank in San Francisco, where I had money on deposit, this stock, together with my will and other valuable papers, for safe keeping.

At my husband's death great was the consternation of the usurping powers because they could not lay their itching fingers upon my stock, as they had done upon every thing else of value belonging to me and mine. But the double convex lens of executors and creditors — real or imaginary — failed to discover its whereabouts, although every drawer in bureau and desk was ransacked, and every pigeon-hole in the bookcase dug out. Books were shaken from their bindings, and plethoric envelopes rent asunder; old stockings were unravelled, and old shoes burnt, in the frenzy of despair; work-boxes were upset, and patch-baskets capsized; pillows and pincushions, mattresses and door-mats, were disembowelled to find it - but all in vain. The key of my moth-proof chest was then demanded, but my sister "thought" I had taken it with me. At last they got scent of the papers at the bank; and hither they hied in a body, to be met by the bold cashier, who told them that I had a box there, — "contents unknown" to the defendant, but said to contain "*valuable papers*" which he had promised to retain until I called for them in person, or until called for by my sister with proofs that I was dead. Now, as I was still living and not dead, he refused to break the trust.

Baffled, but not discouraged, they struck out on a new lead: they laid a mine to unearth it or create new paper by assessing the capital stock at the rate of five dollars per share. The attorney who managed my affairs before my return from abroad, after Mr. Stow's death, called upon the president of a savings bank, and requested him to bid in my stock at the delinquent sale, as I had the amount of the assessment on deposit at his bank. He complied with the request; but without the knowledge of the attorney, and at the instigation of a creditor and one of the executors, he signed a paper, prepared by them, which virtually robbed me of my stock, and for several months this honorable trio withheld it from me. It was assessed again, in the mean time, for ten dollars a share. I took the thousand dollars to the president, and demanded the surrender of my stock. But he declined to deliver it unless I produced the all-important paper, and that my husband's loving friends refused to surrender. When I asked the creditor for it, he referred me to the executor; and when I interviewed the executor, he disclaimed all knowledge of any transaction of the kind, and referred me to the executive lawyer.

Thus I beat about the bush for months, but the snared bird could not fly. At last, when the brilliant managers of this consolidated *fiasco* discovered that it would be a good thing to levy a third assessment, these magnanimous friends of my dead husband decided that it would be a stroke of financial policy to deliver the stock to the rightful owner. They argued from the standpoint of greed in this wise: "We will permit this woman to have her stock, for by so doing we shall be enabled to get a part, and perhaps the whole, of her personal property, in assessments; and in that way we will beggar our dear friend's widow, and in the end we shall have the stock besides."

They proved themselves wise logicians. They have fleeced me out of five thousand dollars in assessments, and carrying the value of these assessments at a usurer's ruinous per cent and commissions; and they have got my stock. It was sold on the 6th of October, 1876, with the stock of other victims, to the amount of three thousand shares, — so the auctioneer, Gen. Cobb, informed me at the sale. If my private property had not been tied up in Probate, I should not have paid the last assessment, that I did pay, of a thousand dollars; but I was compelled to do so, having no other property to give as security to my note of twelve hundred dollars, which was held by a usurer with the stock as collateral security. The holder of the note would have again paid the thousand dollars assessment, only that I had freed my private estate from Probate, and therefore could mortgage it for enough — $2,000 — to pay the amount that I then owed him, and take up my note.

I look upon the whole transaction, from beginning to end, as more reprehensible, yes, a thousand times more, than the operations of highwaymen. A professed thief takes only your purse and jewels; but legalized thieving takes the food out of your mouth, the clothes off your back, the bed from under your body, the roof from over your head, — *every thing!* Rich men are all powerful. They can do any thing, hold out all sorts of inducements to get people's money, when they know from the beginning, and that is what it is done for, that in the end this same money falls indirectly into their pockets. What do they care if the poor plucked victim does blow his brains out in despair at his ruin? They are bloodless!

What is the matter with the Gilroy Consolidated Tobacco Company? Why have they found it necessary to water the stock to the tune of twenty-five hundred shares, and levy assessments at the rate of forty-five dollars a share in a fraction over two years? Criminal mismanagement is the answer to this question, if all have paid their assessments, which I very much doubt. One of the officers told me, that, if a fourth assessment was levied, he was a ruined man, that the accumulation of thirty years was irrecoverably lost. And yet he voted for the fourth and fifth assessments. This is a game of chance which I do not understand.

Forty-five dollars per share on 10,000 shares is some money to squander in the short space of two years, without a more substantial showing than this company is able to furnish forth. When the last delinquent three thousand shares were sold for assessments, there was not one bid.

In a few days after the sale there was a fire at the seat of operation, Gilroy. The building and tobacco destroyed by the conflagration was insured for $63,-000. I hope the company may get it. It takes money to carry on such a spread-eagle enterprise. Big salaries, bombastic displays at fairs and expositions, flamingo advertisements, and princely gifts, draw heavily upon the treasury. What does a close corporation of five care, if it can get money out of confiding victims to splurge with, if it does ruin a few men and women? What do the great in purse — and nothing else — care about the *canaille* who are low and mean in nothing but poverty? Honesty counts for nought with a class of men who must have money at all hazard and at any price. These are the successful financiers who are at the head of corporate bodies, whose heads are stall-fed until their eyes stand out with fatness, but whose bodies are emaciated to skeletons.

Let me warn women, now and here, to beware of corporations; for the history of corporate waste reveals something akin to the bottomless gulf. The enormous sums of money that are squandered by the plethoric heads of these lean bodies is something fabulous. Avoid both secular and religious stock companies, — that is, organizations whose members are of the *pious* sort. Here is what Rev. Dr. Talmage says of this kind of serious speculation: "Some elder or deacon of our churches may get up an oil company, or some sort of religious enterprise sanctioned by the church, and induce the sisters to put their money into a hole in Venango County; and if, by the most skilful derricks, the sunken money cannot be pumped up again, prove to them that it was eternally decreed that that was the way they were to lose it, and that it went in the most orthodox and heavenly style.

"Oh the damnable schemes that professed Christians will engage in — until God puts his finger into the collar of the hypocrite's robe, and rips it clear down to the bottom!"

I do not think he often puts his finger into the collar of secular thieves, for they seem to thrive on their ill-gotten gains with whole robes.

Individual enterprise is far more certain of profitable results than to risk money in the pool of speculation or in corporate-pools and company-pools of any name or nature.

I took up my stock in time to attend the annual meeting for the election of officers. I had never been present at a meeting; and, as this was my last opportunity, I meant to embrace it, although I was advised by a friend not to go, as it would do no good, that there would probably be no other woman there, and that I would feel like a cat in a strange garret.

I indignantly protested against ever having such a feline feeling, and, buckling on my armor of determination, went. The "important meeting," as it was called, was to open at three, P.M., rather a late hour to transact very much weighty business. I was the first one there; and many a wondering stare came from the greater and lesser tobacco-lights, as they filed in one after another, and took their seats, and waited in unspeakable dignity the advent of the president. He entered sharp on the stroke of three, and, taking the chair, proclaimed the meeting open, by calling for the report of the investigating committee of five, which had been previously appointed to learn why the assessments had trodden upon each other's heels so fast.

There was one out of the five, it seems, that had not been fitly chosen; for he got up, — as soon as the four others had declared every thing "lovely" and sat down, — and after properly adjusting his necktie, and pulling down his white vest, said, "Mr. President, I don't wish to censure or condemn, but I don't approve of some things I saw while at Gilroy. I don't think it financial policy to pay a man two hundred dollars a month, as overseer, that is not out of his bed before noon." Thereupon the superintendent, the physically smallest man of the five which compose the very close board of directors, sprang to his feet, and said the speaker was mistaken, — or something to that effect, — and cut such a hot figure that I expected every moment to see him run his little fist down the investigator's throat, as he plunged head foremost into the daring dissenter's bosom, — *à la* Miles Standish and the savage.

At this moment there was a cry of "Order, order!" and that speeches — and, it would appear, conflicting reports — were not in *order;* and the president said his time was "*up*" at four o'clock. A brief period for transacting "important business," — one hour. After Mr. Investigator was choked off, Mr. Bell, one of the close five, rose and rung some charming chimes on the "princely generosity of the president, the masterly ability of the superintendent, and applauded the '*dewins*' of the polite man of many tongues, who had done the honors in the 'pagoda' at the Centennial," — which pagoda should have been topped off with an ass's head, as symbolical of the wisdom of the managers of the Gilroy Consolidated Tobacco Company.

At this point the unruly investigator kicked over the traces again, by jumping up and saying, "As speeches appear to be in order *just now*, I have something further to say." "*Sit down!*" shouted the pugilistic little superintendent. "I have the floor, and I *will* be heard," replied the determined investigator. Then there was an uprising and an uproar. Nearly every one sprang to his feet, madly gesticulating, and let fly a wordy missile. Not knowing how it would all end, and fearing some stray fist might come my way, I eagerly measured the distance — with my eye — from the open window where I sat to the roof below, and wondered which would come off first best in case I was forced to jump out, the glass skylight or my legs. However, I was spared the trial by the polite Centennial man. He came mildly to the rescue, and poured soothing sirup into the blazing bowl of contention, in the form of "gentle words and loving smiles," said it was only a slight mistake, that the investigator was right and the superintendent was right, and that every thing was "lovely," &c.

Seeing by the disgusted looks of the investigator that he needed a sugar-plum to make him *feel* right, he — the speaker — proposed his name to fill a chair among the close five which was not vacant, which seat the investigator promptly declined, not choosing to sit double, and remembering the old adage, that "if two ride one donkey, one must needs ride behind."

Order having come out of chaos, a long-winded annual report was read through the nose of the secretary, eulogizing the deeds of the immaculate "*five;*" "how they had bravely fought difficulties which had enveloped them like a tempest; how the other tobacco companies had all set their teeth upon them, and would not coalesce, calling the new process of curing the weed a 'mongrel process,' and thereby injuring its sale; how their finest Havana cigars had been returned upon their hands as unmarketable" (because the Gilroy ass was recognized under the skin of the Havana lion); "how the proceeds of what was sold fell into another's pocket than theirs; how this year's crop would overtop all other crops; how the cantankerous tobacco-worm had decreased longitudinally, and increased proportionately diametrically, but that its capacity for green Gilroy tobacco, weight, habits, and complexion, were unchanged; how the heathen setters had abandoned the *un*beautiful style of shaving their heads, and adopted the '*Melican*' mode of dispensing with tails; how the president, like a prodigal, had lavished untold gold to keep the company's financial wheels greased, and that Parrott was but another name for Napoleon; how the superintendent was a man of rare parts, a genuine genius, an improver upon nature; how their polite Centennial brother had clothed himself in a flowing pair of cardinal-red Turkish pants, and sat under a turban adorned with a crimson and gold tassel, in the doorway of the Gilroy Consolidated Pagoda, smoking a chibouque filled with Gilroy tobacco, the incense of which rose, and hung like a pillar of cloud over the City of Brotherly Love, thereby causing great destruction among the birds of the air; how each masculine pilgrim who visited the Grand Exposition was presented with a box of Gilroy

Havana-flavored cigars, without money and without price — as samples; how every snuffy old pilgrimess's heart was made glad with a half-pound box, filled to bursting with pulverized Gilroy tobacco scented with bergamot; how foreign ambassadors of all nations, kingdoms, tongues, and complexions, had *condescended* to acknowledge the receipt of 'Gilroy Extra Fine Cut;' how his Excellency, the President of the United States of America, had turned his short nose into a chimney-pot for the express accommodation of 'finest Havana-flavored' Gilroy cigar smoke; how there had been some mistakes made in the management, but that mistakes were human; how, if the weed was bitter and unpalatable in its undoctored state, it was the fault of the soil and not of the company; how the company might congratulate itself on its fine tobacco-sheds and manufactories builded out of moneys wrung out of malcontents who stupidly preferred dividends to assessments; how the fame of Gilroy tobacco had gone up and down the earth, and then come back again — on its own strength; how it would be wise to chop up the returned cigars into vermin exterminator, that no perambulating cockroach, marauding moth, persistent pismire, pestiferous flea, or scented bedbug, would roam within cannon-shot of Gilroy tobacco — it being too strong for them; how the company were growing potatoes instead of tobacco, at the present moment, on the Gilroy Tobacco Rancho, because the demand for Gilroy '*spuds*' was greater than that for Gilroy tobacco; how the princely *liberality* of the Gilroy Consolidated Tobacco Company was wide-spread," &c., &c. But never a word was spoken of how the money that furnished forth this lavish expenditure of "*liberality*" and wasteful *splurge* was obtained; how it had been wrung out of confiding victims with such as the following promises: "This is the very *last* assessment that will be levied. The stock is really worth par," and kindred truthful statements.

During Mr. Stow's life he claimed that the chief excellence of the Gilroy tobacco consisted in the leaf as a cigar wrap; but since his death it has cost the company several hundred thousand dollars, so I was told by Maurice Dore, one of the largest shareholders, to purchase Havana wrappers.

Did the small shareholders — who paid their assessments in ready gold — vote for that grandiflora tobacco blossom on a dry stalk at Philadelphia, which, it is alleged, was the most expensive thing of its kind on the grounds? No! I, for one, knew nothing about it until I read of its magnificence in the papers. I wonder if the specimens tested, on which it is trumpeted a premium was granted, were not by accident entirely manufactured out of those Havana wraps, instead of being merely bound up in them? It might have happened by a sly trick of those "heathen Chinee." If not, those judges must have queer taste. Perhaps they had recently tested the merits of California wine, and the two "*native*" productions had got a little tangle-footed in their brains.

The small shareholders paid for every leaf and fibre of those premium cigars as the Sultan pays for the Turkish tapestry beside his throne. The money of men and women, widows and orphans, who could ill afford it, has been sunk in this bottomless pit of invisible absorption; and it will never have a resurrection for their benefit. The hidden hands that carry off the plunder are not perceptible to the mortal ken of small shareholders, so ingeniously have they been contrived. But the frost-bitten fingers of the "frozen outs" will not be able to touch a farthing. It takes a great many little fish to fill the maw of a big one. We, the little netted fish, are hurt very much worse than we should have been if some one had slit up our pockets and taken our purses. The difference is only in the way of doing it.

But to return to the winding-up of the "important meeting." When the curious annual report was ended (the best of things must end somewhere), the right party made a motion that the old Board keep its seat — and it was not unseated. Just as I was about to rise, for I had gone there for the express purpose of telling those men what I thought of such management, Mr. President adjourned the meeting *sine die*, after which he crossed over, and patted Mr. Investigator on the back, and Mr. Investigator patted Mr. President on the back, and locking arms they walked down stairs a reconciled pair. But not so with me: I was full of wrathful indignation, probably because I had not been able to speak my "little piece" — of mind. Speech is a great safety-valve. Besides, no one offered to pat my back because I was offended.

I was telling a friend what I thought of the whole cut and dried (beforehand) proceedings, and the unseemly haste that strangled every thing antagonistic to the wishes of the all-powerful "five." He laughed at my simplicity, and said, "A much more important annual meeting that was held a short time ago not 'ten thousand miles away,' which involves hundreds of millions of capital, instead of hundreds of thousands, was of much shorter duration. Some disagreeable stockholders were bent upon being present, and arrived at the appointed place for the meeting in grand good time. Soon the 'powers that be' entered, and said to these inquisitive bores, 'Friends, you are too early: you will have time to step round the corner, and get a *damper*.' Feeling rather desiccated by the warmth of their zeal, they put their heads into the trap by embracing the opportunity, — and stepped round the corner. But, lo! when they returned, the meeting had just adjourned. During that brief space of time the knowing old heads had voted themselves into office for another year. What could these now thoroughly moist shareholders do? Nothing, unless it was to console each other by saying, 'Well, it would have done no earthly good if we had been here. It would have been all the same: heads I win, tails you lose.' "

Such is power and misplaced confidence; and when there is an ostensible showing of fair play, what does it amount to? A stockholder is thrown into an ecstasy one day by getting a dividend, and thrown out of it the next by getting an assessment twice the amount of the dividend, and he can only wonder at the capers of stocks.

I believe there is a new process for curing tobacco, known as the "Culp Process." I was speaking to one of the oldest tobacconists in San Francisco about this process. Said he, "Mrs. Stow, if you wish to enjoy the perfume of a flower, do you pluck off the petals, and put them in a heap where they will heat and ferment? Will that improve the aroma? Would not this packing destroy all the delicate fragrance? Now, this is all the Culp Process amounts to; and it leaves the tobacco bitter and odorless, and the perfume has to be supplied by foreign substances. Here are two samples which I wish you to smell of. One is cured the old way, one the new." I did as he desired me to do; but, as tobacco in any form is most offensive to me, I was unable to judge of the merits or demerits of either specimen. Mr. Tobacconist continued, "The company will have to abandon that process before they will realize any thing but costs." I wonder who will pay the bills, now that the directors have got possession of nearly all the stock.

In my peregrinations about San Francisco with books and tickets, I have asked at least a thousand smokers if they liked Gilroy cigars, particularly those that "take on the flavor of the finest Havanas;" and the answer has been "No!" with but one solitary exception, and that was an old Irish laborer. The universal complaint was, "They are bitter. I had a box given to me to try, but I could not smoke them myself, so I handed them over to the clerks to battle with."

At the last delinquent assessment "*bid in*," I said to one of the directors, "I have lost $5,000 in this leaky ship; and I feel most bitterly about it, for it has gone to further enrich the executors of my estate. I have suffered enough in that direction without this additional loss." He smilingly made answer, "*I*, Mrs. Stow, have lost all I have. I risked all my worldly wealth in this same ship, and it went down to-day along with yours; and I have a family to support." "How cheerful you are under such a sweeping disaster!" I replied. "Men are so much more philosophical than women under great afflictions. How I envy you your equanimity and self-poise!" I shall watch, with just five thousand dollars worth of interest, the upshot of this little game.

The same day I asked Mr. Dore what the stock was valued at. "Twenty dollars a share, at a very low estimate," he made reply. "Well," I continued, "I shall ever hold this company responsible for the present value of my stock, $2,000. You have all my husband's stock that did not disappear at the time of his death, and you have all the money of paid-up assessments on it, and mine, which the company bid in to-day. You took the price of assessments on his stock out of my estate when you knew what the end was to be as well as you do at this moment. If the estate had been closed, as it should have been, a year and a half ago, the amount of assessments paid on Mr. Stow's stock would have remained for the benefit of the estate instead of the Tobacco Company. Therefore I hold you individually accountable for *my* $2,000." "How can we reimburse every one for his lost stock?" he rejoined. "Every one has not been such a loser through your manipulations as I have. Mine is an exceptionally cruel case. You got control of all I have in my absence, and have kept control of it in spite of every effort of mine, thus tying me hand and foot until I am *legally* plundered of nearly every thing I possess; and you are one of the choice friends who my husband said would treat me like a brother in case of his death." Heaven defend me from such friends!

CHAPTER XXVI.

IN TRANSITU UNDER DIFFICULTIES.

In extremis.

FASTIDIOUS people had better omit this chapter.

On the eighth day of January, 1877, I left San Francisco *en route* for the East. Having a few unsold copies of the first edition of "Probate Confiscation" left, I stopped off a week in Sacramento, and sold them.

Before leaving San Francisco I went to the owners and managers of the Central Pacific Railroad and begged them to give me a pass over the road, urging, as a plea, that I had been such a financial sufferer — for the last going on three years — through the manipulations of man courts and men thieves; and further, that Mr. Charles Crocker had given my husband and me a pass over the road for a whole year when it was first opened, which pass we did not find time to use but very little; that I was going to return to public life, and wished to conserve every farthing saved from the wreck of my fortune to aid in the establishment of horticultural schools for women in this country; and that if I did not get a pass or a half-fare ticket I should be compelled to go on the emigrant train.

Then these gentlemen made answer, and said, "We cannot aid you. Should we give you a pass, or reduce the fare in any way, it might cost us $10,-000. It is not our fault: the 'powers that be' at Washington have done the deed. They have cut off all dead-heads on the road." "But how will they know it?" I pleaded. "They do not employ spies, do they?" "No; but we are discharging conductors and other employees, at different times, who would be sure to report any transgression of enforced law on our part."

When I came to buy my ticket, I learned that I could not stop off a week or a day on an emigrant ticket. Therefore I had to pay my fare to Sacramento, and then pay full price for my ticket there; thus realizing by personal experience that the curse of the poor is their poverty. None but the rich can have stop-over accommodations; none but the rich can worship God in elegance. "Not for the *poor* swingeth wide open the bronze church-door." I never knew what it was to want for a dollar in my life until I was J. W. Stow's widow; and none who knew him will ever believe that he died a poor man.

If my separate property had not been tangled up in Probate, I should never have known the value of money as I now know it. People will never believe that I suffered for the common necessaries of life, because I was comfortably clad. When we see a well-dressed person we never stop to think that in spite of his good clothes he may be starving. I have not spent a hundred dollars for wearing-apparel in nearly three years, including every thing, — shoes, gloves, and loves of bonnets. The latter has cost me two dollars for a straw in San Francisco, which I trimmed myself with odds and ends of silk, ribbon, and feather, which I had on hand. I paid forty-five cents for a frame since I came to Boston, which I covered with '73 silk and velvet. The garniture consists of an old feather and a new ribbon — cost ninety cents. I do not count the cost of making, as woman's time is of "no value."

I should have gone hungry many a day in San Francisco, or lived upon charity, if it had not been for the money obtained by the sale of my book. For the four hundred copies which I sold in that city I realized nearly a thousand dollars, many having given five dollars a copy for it, although the price is but two. Why did they do this? Because I was such a sufferer under the law.

Some said to me, "Why don't you sell your unproductive real estate, and live comfortably? What do you go back to public life for? Who will thank you for the gift of money or labor? The income of twenty-five or thirty thousand dollars, the value of your property, will support you in elegance;" to all of which I made answer, "I cannot sit down with folded hands, when I have health, time, means, and ability to save one and perhaps many of my less fortunate sisters to lives of usefulness and honor, that might otherwise go down in ruin and death. Somewhere it is said, 'He who is the means of saving one human soul shall be counted worthy of eternal life.'"

Perhaps the scathing lesson which I have been forced to learn, so much against my will, may prove a salutary one; for I know how to sympathize with the poor as I never could without just such an experience. An eminent divine says, "You cannot lie on a sofa in your sumptuous parlor, and read sentimental stories of misery, and want, and suffering, taking misery as a pinch of salt to make something else taste better, — and understand what it means."

I tried to get something to do to earn a comfortable living, as the Christian Probate Court refused me a support after the first year, while it held all I had in its iron grip; but I could not. It is a difficult matter for a stranded woman to earn a *temporary* livelihood in San Francisco. Why? Because every avocation, with a few exceptions, open to women is invaded by the Chinese; and they reduce the price paid for labor to a minimum low standard, or to almost starvation prices.

When I left Sacramento, a trunk which had travelled with me more than a hundred thousand miles, and upon which I had never once paid an extra pound of baggage either in this country or in Europe, was weighed. I don't believe it would have been put upon the scales if I had had a first-class ticket. I said to the baggage-man, "Why do you weigh that trunk? I have never paid extra baggage upon it." He replied, "Well, I just thought I'd weigh 'er." He charged me nine dollars to Omaha for sixty pounds over-weight. I begged a man who had no baggage but a valise to assist me out of the dilemma. He consented at once, and presented his ticket; but the baggage-man said, "You have nothing in that trunk, have you?" "No," he replied, "nothing." "Well, then, you can't help her any." "What a shame!" I said: "our tickets are over the same route, and if we had come together in the first place you would not have refused." Then the man of weight said, "If you will take out part of the things, and put them in a bag, I will check them off on his ticket." The bare proposition nearly took my breath away. My good bonnet and best gown in a bag on a fast train, checked off to a strange man. "If he had a collar or handkerchief, any thing however small, in that trunk," continued the baggage-man, "I could pass it; but you both say he hasn't." A toothpick or a dicky-band in the right place would have saved me nine dollars. Several of the male passengers told me afterwards that their trunks weighed as much as or more than mine. But they were not of the proscribed class: so they were allowed the benefit of the doubt.

I was so indignant that I waited over six hours to see the superintendent, who was up the road, and then took the express to catch up with my precious emigrant. It availed nothing, however, for I had the nine dollars to pay. I was told by some of the conductors on the road that excess of emigrant baggage to Omaha was ten cents a pound, and not fifteen, and that I had been overcharged. It is a most surprising arrangement if third-class passengers have to send their baggage first-class, thus making their dry goods and traps superior to themselves. However, it is good clothes, and not merit, that commands respect. It is a most humiliating confession which I make when I say that my friends, even, bow lower to my silks, laces, jewels, and fine wool than they do to me — both men and women. Let me go down street looking like a shop-woman or upper maid-servant, and nearly *all* my acquaintance whom I may chance to meet suddenly become near-sighted, or they are searching for the little cloud no bigger than a man's hand in the streak of sky above the street. But let me go down elegantly clad, with powdered face, — I powder, — crimped hair, and light kids, and the hats of my male friends fly off so suddenly that I am in an agony for fear they have taken off their heads in their haste to recognize me.

A lovely lady of refinement and social position in New York City, whose charming home was always open to me for a long or a short sojourn in years agone, said, in speaking of this matter of the superiority of dry goods to "folks," "When I go to market with Bridget in the morning, dressed plainly, I nearly always *stand up* in the cars. The gentlemen are so much absorbed in the digest of the daily news that they do not see me. But in the afternoon, when I am returning from making calls or shopping, handsomely dressed, these same gentlemen, wearied with the toil of counting-room and desk, spring up out of their places as though they were seated on a powder-keg with a blazing lucifer-match inside of it, and beg me to *sit down* by all means." Now, this beautiful woman was a true lady at all times. Apparel had nothing to do with her ladylike bearing and refined manners.

But to return to Sacramento and my journey. I was very warm, although the weather was very cold, the twenty miles I rode in the express-train to overtake the emigrant. If that conductor had asked me extra fare, I should have told him to "put me off the train." But he deigned no word of comment when he saw my ticket, which I found too soon was a badge of dishonor and disgrace. I learned, if possible, a stronger lesson than I had been learning for the past — verging on three years — that poverty is a crime, and that a poor person, if she be a woman, is to suffer as a criminal; that with a certain class of people she is entitled to no respect whatever.

The emigrant cars were switched off on a side track, at the twenty miles station, awaiting our arrival. They were quickly coupled to the fast train, and we all sped on together. Here was a conglomeration and gradation of quality. The head of the train, minus the locomotive and feeder, was a sumptuous palace sleeper, which represented the aristocracy of money, and perhaps something of more intrinsic value, — brains and personal worth, — for they are not always divorced. The second coach was a first-class open carriage, for the accommodation of way-passengers, such as wanted to stop off at Cape Horn or the Devil's Slide. The third carriage was for second-class passengers. Here the male quality came, and vilified the air with poisonous tobacco-smoke, and converted the floor into a vast spittoon which soon became a reeking puddle of filth. What mattered it to them if there were delicate women and tender babes in this car, to whom every inhalation of the Bacchanalian wreath was strangulation? Had they not paid a price which entitled them to seats in *two* cars instead of one? What if every first-class woman passenger had come into this car, and brought a little pot of assafœtida or skunk's cabbage, and set fire to it, and then held her nose over it until her mouth was filled with saliva, which she at once proceeded to squirt out over the floor and back of the seat in front of her? What would be said of such a performance? Would it be tolerated? No! and yet the burning assafœtida and skunk's cabbage would not be half so nasty, stinking, and unwholesome as tobacco-smoke is to some sensitive women and helpless children.

Ah, men and brothers and protectors! do you ever consider what liberties you take, and how many more indulgences you accord yourselves than you accord the dear creatures that you so gallantly protect?

Then came the two emigrant cars. They formed the tail. What a fall was there — from head to tail! Yet we, the occupants of the last named, felt to rejoice greatly that we were accounted worthy to occupy the position, and be whirled along at express rate. Our short-lived joy melted into grief at Ogden, for there we were attached — a misplaced attachment — to the plodding freight-train. Previous to this transfer, I had begged of the polite conductors the privilege of riding in the first-class coach, because tobacco-smoke was so offensive to me; and after the emigrants had exchanged their inseparable companion — the pipe — for the pillow, I noiselessly crept in, and arranged my two seats into a kind of bed, and vainly courted the god of slumber; but the air was so vitiated, so foul, that it could have been cut in slices, and hung on a line. Those emigrant smokers hate pure air. Poison could not be more distasteful to them. If I raised my window an inch high, some one of them would manage to sneeze — most likely he had tickled his nose with a straw to produce the admonition. Then there would be a chorus of voices exclaiming, "You are catching cold, friend: there is a draught. There must be a window *histed* somewhere;" at which they all looked in my direction, and the other woman (there were but two of us) would call out, "Madame, will you pleze schud de winda? I'z throubled wid de rumetizm." What was I to do? I did not dare sleep in the first-class car, even should the conductor consent to such a violation of rules, for fear that he might forget to tell me should he switch off the tail in the night; for I had some valuable baggage in it that I had paid no extra price upon.

What was the atmosphere of those cars composed of? The individual odor of all nationalities mingled with the smell of food peculiar to each, and tobacco-smoke. In the one where I was, there was a Swede and a Norwegian, Americans, Englishmen, Irishmen, Dutchmen, Germans, Polish Jews, and what other extractions of the human family I know not. The perfume and habits of the "faderland" clung to each one of them like dew to a flower. Each man smoked a pipe, and such phthisicky pipes! The air as it was sucked through them struggled, groaned, and gurgled like a drowning man. It seemed to protest, and say, "Do I not smell badly enough as I am? Am I not made loathsome enough with the odor of Stilton cheese, onions, garlics, soiled clothing, and not over-clean bodies, without being drawn through such a nasty conduit, and decaying teeth, to be emitted in putrid breath?" Every particle of life was scorched out of the air by two stoves in either end of the car, which were kept at a white heat day and night.

Looking over their sleeping forms at night, I marvelled that they did not rise up and slay each other in a mad frenzy of suffocation, as the eighteen hundred prisoners in the Black Hole of Calcutta did. They were confined in a dungeon without an adequate supply of fresh air, only for one night; and all that survived the infernal ordeal were a hundred and forty-six, and nearly all of these came out in a high state of putrid fever. Knowing as I did the ills that blood-poisoning is heir to, I dared not think what I was taking into my clean lungs, that have such a capacity for fresh air. But they were in an active state of rebellion: I coughed constantly, not from a cold, but from nicotine and other poisons. Never did I feel the pangs of poverty so sharply as I did then, when I was denied enough of the pure air of heaven to breathe. I could feel the burning eyes of the *zymotic* fiend upon me. For a day and a night I was very sick, and many of the others were ill also; but I could not persuade them that they were suffering from the poison of their own contaminations, — carbonic acid gas, and the secretions from the skin and pulmonary mucous surfaces, — which proper ventilation would remedy.

The emigrant cars west of Omaha are nothing but boxes with windows and doors in them, but no ventilators. They are very low: a tall man can barely stand upright in them. In every way they are a disgrace to the company, and should be remanded back to their original use, — lumber cars. I wonder how many of those victims are sick or dead from the effects of inhaling the fœtid, deadly combination of impurities which took the place of air in those cars. I, for one, was sick unto death for months after my arrival in Boston, from blood-poisoning.

At Ogden I changed into the rear car. It contained fewer passengers, and I knew if they smoked all the time there would be some chance for me to have my window open. Then, again, the larger number in that car were Americans, — artisans, I think, who, having failed in their expectations on the Golden Shores, were returning home.

I was comparatively comfortable during the day. The gentleman who had so politely tried to assist me in getting my baggage through had the seats in front of mine. I had no idea that these men, any one of them, would consider me an intruder upon their masculine rights; but subsequent developments showed me my error.

Every thing passed off quietly during the day; but at night some little girls came in at one of the stations, vending cider and apples, — girls not over a dozen years of age. To these children I heard language expressed which I could never have believed would have been spoken outside of a bawd-house. This language came out of the mouths of four young men that I took to be American-born at least. From their conversation I learned that they were educated for mechanics, but that they had taken a hand as conductors and drivers on street-cars, &c., &c.; that they were ready as "Jacks at all trades" where there was a chance to "*knock down*," as they termed putting their employers' money in the wrong pocket.

When it was time to arrange for sleeping, one of

these young desperadoes was detailed to look after the fires during the first watches. For the short space of an hour, perhaps, all was quiet, like the lull before the tempest; and then the pent-up Satan within them, that had been somewhat exorcised by my presence, burst forth in all its frenzy. They fought a mimic battle with their broom (they owned a broom: whether they had "knocked it down" or paid for it, they alone can tell), the poker, and the slat-bottomed seats; using such oaths and such obscene language as I could not believe would be allowed in the lowest brothel in the civilized world. They indulged in every relief of nature excepting one; using the zinc at the back of the stove for a *pissoir*, until the fluid-excrement ran in a vile flood through the car. Not a word of reproof was spoken by any one, although there must have been from ten to fifteen respectable men in the car.

As this night of horrors wore slowly away, and it was nearing daybreak, one of the youthful villains was narrating his individual experience in a San Francisco brothel; at which another of them felt that it was wise to check him on my account. Then this young male bawd raised his voice to a higher key, and with the vilest oaths and execrations and personalities cried out, "If she didn't want to hear and see such things, why did she come amongst us? What business has *she* in this car?"

Forbearance had ceased with me: I rose to my feet, and faced these PROTECTORS, saying, "Young man, I have just as good a right to occupy this car as you have; and I have the same right to expect courteous treatment from you as you have from me. I came into this car because the people in it were mostly my countrymen, and it was reasonable to expect civil treatment from them: I received it at the hands of foreigners in the other car. It is my misfortune that poverty compels me to cross the continent in this way: still I have the same right to be poor that you have. In Europe I have rode at all hours of the day and night in a third-class coach, but I never saw an obscene act, or heard an oath or a vulgar word. If you, each one of you who have made this night hideous with all sin, all folly, if you have mothers, sisters, or sweethearts, it is a marvel how you can ever again look them in the face without a blush, when you remember the ruffianism of the past night during which you have sought to outrage a fellow-passenger, and that one a woman. You have undertaken to drive me out of this car, but you will not: I shall remain here unless I am forcibly ejected."

Not a word was spoken in answer to my reproof; and from that time until they abandoned the situation, I heard and saw nothing to offend the most fastidious. They had a roll-call, in which they dubbed each other Shadrack, Meshack, and Abednego; but it would take a furnace heated seven times hotter to purify these dastards in the form and semblance of men, than it did to test the faith of the illustrious trio of old.

In the morning when they made their coffee one of them brought some of it to me, as a kind of peace-offering, and begged my pardon for his share in the night's orgy. When he came for the cup he found the contents untasted. He exclaimed, "Why didn't you drink the coffee?" I replied, "I did not dare drink it." He looked shocked, whether he felt so or not, as he said, "This is the most cutting rebuke I ever had in my life."

Soon after breakfast was over, and they had swept out the car with their broom, the laid spirit within them began to rouse. If they could not drive me out, they would go themselves like their four-footed brethren of old that ran howling into the sea. So they paid five dollars to have the use of a vacant car to carouse in. This vacant car had cushioned seats; and they brought me two of them, as another peace-offering, for a bed. I hold no malice against them, but make this record to show how the rights of women are respected under peculiar circumstances.

What they did in that other car I know not, with the exception that I was told that they had broken one of the windows; and the broken broomhandle, upon which they had evidently been practising the refined and graceful accomplishments of the mid-night pursuers of the unlucky "Tam," spoke for itself. What else they could have done in there that they did not do in the car that I was in, passes my ken, unless they stood on their heads, and played football with the red-hot stoves, or pig-backed with the deacon. There was one among the passengers, — a Jersey deacon, — so he said. He was as modest as Uriah Heep; confessed to me that he was unlearned, but had a "leanin' that way." However, I noticed that in a discussion on taxation, upon which subject I am almost as tender-footed as I am upon Probate practice, when I chipped in he took not the slightest notice of my remarks, although I perhaps spoke as intelligently upon the subject as he. What were a woman's views worth to a man? Probably women keep silent in the temple where he handles the bread and wine.

One night after all was quiet, I laid down upon my hard pillow, made out of my waterproof and some other things, with my nose to the air-hole smuggled under my veil. I was roused from my fitful sleep by a dream in which I saw my demi-train slowly dragging over the snow after unpolished masculine boots, while the head of the owner of the boots was protected from the storm of snow and sleet by my Chantilly-covered parasol. I started up in a paroxysm of perspiration, to find my nose full of miniature icicles, and to hear my opposite neighbors (there were two lodged together) say, "She groans a two-horse power: she must be sick, or else she has a bad conscience." "No, my friends," I replied as I rubbed my nose to see if it would ever be of any further use to me, "I have not a diseased conscience: it is the want of conscience in other people that troubles me."

At Omaha we were dumped off at the Emigrant House for a night. What is this delay for, in which every one is mulcted of fifty cents for a night's lodging, whether he uses a room or not? Who is benefited by this enforced toll of four bits *per capita* at the emigrant rendezvouz? First and second class passengers are not treated to a stop-off willy-nilly. Getting in at half-past nine, P.M., and going out at five, A.M., gives no one time to go to a comfortable hotel and get washed and a night's rest.

I said to the clerk, "Can I sit here by the stove all night?" "No, but after twelve you can sit out in the men's room. But why don't you go to bed?" he queried. "I prefer to sit up," I replied. The other woman and her husband had gone to their room, and I was beginning to feel very anxious about being alone with strange and very rough-looking men. All the emigrants travelling with me had either gone up town or to their rooms here. Presently I heard very loud talking at the clerk's desk; and looking in that direction I was greatly astonished to see my sister emigrant holding that amiable functionary by the shirt-collar, and vociferating, "He duzzent wear no *pee*-stole. He never draws no *pee*-stole. *It ish one pig* LIE!"

I went over to the scene of conflict, and said, "What's the trouble here? Who's got a pistol?" The clerk replied, as he disengaged himself from his female antagonist, who had reversed the tables, and was heroically protecting her protector, "I hain't goin tew hev no *Jews* run this here shanty."

It seems that these people, who had seen better days, were not satisfied with their accommodations, and desired to pay a larger price to secure a better bed, but the clerk had none to give them; and that in the discussion the poor Pole had unluckily put his hand under his coat-tail after a handkerchief, or to dislodge an imagination caught in the mischievous bed which was as "*hardt as de pords.*" The clerk had taken the movement for a hostile one, and accused the offender of intending to draw a pistol.

I poured some of the sweet-oil of my nature upon the troubled waters—and there was peace established. Then I prevailed upon the discomfited Poles to help me kill the weary hours which kept vigil between that time and daybreak, beside the two-story stove in the men's waiting-room, where the piercing wind dashed in with a whistle under one door, and dashed out with a whistle under the other.

I have watched with the sick as the leaden hours of darkness crept slowly by, counting, meantime, the fitful wave of life as it ebbed to and fro of those I loved; I have sat out the stars alone with the dead, keeping lips that would never smile upon me again moist with perfume, and placed my warm hand throbbing with life upon the white pulseless clay beneath the damp locks, and experienced no fear; I have been high up in the Swiss Alps when the gathering storm has burst in all its fury, with clouds and red lightning, at my feet, and dazzling, lurid electricity all around me, while the mad thunder hurled itself from peak tc peak with a thousand deafening reverberations as I rushed up and up the zigzag path until I arrived breathless and exhausted at the little *châlet* set like an eagle's nest under the cliff; I have been in a ship that lay all night in the cradle of the deep—stranded in mid-ocean—when the tempest was so fierce that she dared not cope with it; and I have passed other nights of peril and discomfort which I hope I may never be called upon to face their like again: and yet the combination of circumstances which brought me to my present lowly state, the surroundings, the people, all united, conspired to make this night only second, in my experience, to the one spent upon the cars a few nights before amid the fiendish revels of abandoned men.

On leaving Omaha I parted company forever, I trust, with those debauchees. Their course lay over another route than mine, and may it continue in that direction!

The coach delegated to our use was in every way first-class, excepting the tobacco-smoke. There were but a few people, however, in this car, so that the air was much purer than it had been in the others. The conductor told me that I could go into the first-class carriage in welcome as far as he was concerned; but that there would be several different conductors ere we reached Chicago, and that he could not vouch for their leniency. I said, "Three years ago this month I passed over this road *en route* for Europe. I then had a middle section of the palace sleeper all to myself. At every change made, the agent entered, and, calling out my name, said there was a centre section reserved for me by a despatch-order from my husband. When I reached the Everett House, New York, I found a suite of apartments provided for me in the same way. I have travelled many hundreds of thousands of miles, and this is the first time want of money has compelled me to go any way but first-class."

At Dunkirk I was put into a first-class car; and from there to Buffalo, from Buffalo to Binghamton, from Binghamton to Albany, I rode first-class. Not a conductor so much as intimated that I was out of my sphere. I was delayed two nights at Binghamton, and one at Albany. At the latter place I exclaimed, "Well, I'll pay no more hotel bills! I'll stay in this depot all night unless I'm put out of it." And I kept my word. I was feeling very ill; but I arranged myself in two chairs close to the heater, and prepared for another night's watching. Some other passengers in the gentlemen's waiting-room did the same. Several officers were lounging about the rooms all night; men who got good pay, without a doubt, for their night services. At four o'clock in the morning came two horny-handed "*angels*" with mops, scrub-brushes, brooms, and pails, to "rid up" the waiting-rooms. These women were in their true sphere. They did not unite the "softness of the dove to the meddlesomeness of the magpie," as it is claimed that the women who "buzzed politics" in the *salons* which were honored by the presence of the man of destiny did. Ah, no! no imperial autocrat desired to banish them, because they were not troublesome De Staëls nor intriguing De Polignacs. These "angels" were tobacco-spit scrubbresses; and the havoc they made in that direction with hot soapsuds and stiff brooms was something miraculous. The men gathered up their legs and feet into a bow-knot, to prevent them from being parboiled, and sat upon it while they cracked coarse jokes with the "angels." Little dogs ran howling into the street at the first sniff of boiling-hot tobacco-juice. When they — the "angels" — had finished, I said to one of them, "Please excuse me, madam, for it is no idle curiosity that prompts the question; but how much are you paid a month for this two hours work?" "Twenty-five dollars apiece," she replied. For three hundred dollars a year these poor women rise at three o'clock for three hundred and sixty-five mornings, in the heat of summer and the frost of winter; and they are glad and eager to get the opportunity to do it.

As nights are not interminable, day came at last, and with it the train for Boston. I of course seated myself in a first-class carriage, arguing in this wise: "I am so ill from the effects of tobacco-poison, night-watching, and general exhaustion from so long and uncomfortable a journey, that no one but a monster would compel me to ride another inch amid the nausea of tobacco-smoke. Then, again, it takes no more steam, and whistle, and puff, to convey me over the road in one car than it does in another."

I was fast asleep when the conductor came. Half rousing, I mechanically drew out my ticket, and showed it to him. The moment he glanced at it, he put on the front of Jupiter, — as near as such a "missing link" could. He was lean, cadaverous, dyspeptic, and looked as though he had just been taken down from some smoke-house, where he had been forgotten for a century. Said he, "Madam, why did you come into this car where you don't belong?" "I generally belong in this car," I replied; "but misfortunes for which I'm not to blame obliged me to make the transit from San Francisco on a low-grade ticket. I am very ill, as I have had a tedious passage with many delays; and I beg of you to let me remain in this car. There are very few people in it, and I cough nearly every breath where the air is full of tobacco-smoke. I have rode first-class ever since I left Dunkirk, and you are the first conductor that has so much as mentioned that I was in the wrong car." "If you pay me three dollars, you can stay here; otherwise you will have to go into the other car." Having delivered himself of this mandate with all the loftiness which inferior specimens of the *genus homo* assume towards women, he strode out. A little power is a dangerous thing.

I cuddled down under my wraps, hoping that he might forget his victim, and was asleep again, — so sick, so tired, so sleepy, — when I was startled by an authoritative voice, exclaiming, "Madam, you must come out of this car, or pay the extra fare." I started up in time to see the brakeman grasp my portmanteau, obedient to my tormentor's command, "Take out these traps."

The car into which I was taken was in every respect precisely like the one I had left. The only difference was that this one was blue with tobacco-smoke. I said, loud enough for all in the car to hear, "I am sick, and this is an outrage. No one but a man with the instincts of a brute would do such an inhuman act. I have come all the way from California; and this is the first time I have been ejected from a comfortable place, where there was one to be had."

"Yes," said this apology for a man, "you have lived in California, and that accounts for the way you talk. I am obeying the orders of the company, madam." "Is it the rule of this company to compel a sick woman to ride in a car full of poison, because she is too poor to pay first-class price? There are exceptions to all rules. Is a dying child, dying of nicotine poison, to be kept in this car until it is strangled? Can it be possible that the owners and directors of any road in Christian New England are such human fiends and financial Judases? If so, then all honor to the servitor who obeys their rules with such fidelity!"

I claim that I have a right to ride second or third class without being poisoned. Tobacco-smoke is poison to me. I never allowed it in my home when I kept house, nor in my parlors at a hotel. When men said to my husband that he was pretty well domesticated when he did not dare to even light his cigar in the hall, he replied, "The smoke of the weed offends my wife; and if she were to indulge in a pernicious habit which did her no good, and was very objectionable to me, I should lose respect for her, and have a just cause to doubt her love for me — and *vice versa*."

I said to that conductor who was so conscientious in obeying rules, "I would like you to give me your name as a *souvenir*." "Oh, yes, certainly!" he sneeringly replied, "you shall have it if that will do you any good." I made the request three times; and each time he said "Yes," but did "no." I then asked a boy at a station; and he replied, "That conductor's name is Jolly Marsh." *Jolly!* He looked any thing but jolly. His appearance and behavior suggested a pestilential marsh filled with Pandora's plagues. I suppose his jolliness consists in thrusting sick women into a nauseating atmosphere, when they refuse to give him three dollars extra fare.

It was bitter cold; but I raised the window, and sat in the piercing draught, coughing at nearly every inspiration. Did any person in that car abate one puff of smoke? No. What was the life or death of an emigrant woman to them, as weighed against their indulgence of an acquired appetite? One young man with his feet hanging over the arm of the seat said, as he complacently watched the curling poison float over his head, "I always go third class, 'cause I can do just as I" (strong expletive) "please."

Every man who entered the car that day — and there were many exchanges, for it was a way-train — knew at a glance that I was a sick woman: they knew, too, that I was strangled nearly to death by the smoke; for I continually fanned it away from me with my veil, and held a heavy woollen shawl over my mouth. These men — there was no other woman — were the gentlemen of the towns through which we passed. There were but three of us emigrants left, — an old Irish gentleman, a youth who stopped off twenty miles west of Boston, and myself. Not one of those gentlemen would have presumed to smoke in my drawing-room without my consent. Not one of them would have failed to accord me the courtesy which every gentleman accords a lady, if I had met them under any other circumstances.

I accidentally dropped the stopple to my smelling-salts bottle, and asked the newsboy to pick it up for me. He said that he could not reach it. I told him to use the crooked handle of my umbrella, which was lying upon the seat in front of me. He did as directed; but on replacing the umbrella he gave it a dexterous turn known to boys, and threw my lunch-pail which was upon the seat to the floor. It came down with a crash, breaking a little pitcher and a wine-glass, valuable only from association. At the sight of the wreck there rose such a yell of delight behind me, that for a moment I imagined myself in the Black Hills with a scalping-knife over my head.

The boy pretended to be very sorry, and said it was purely accidental, &c. After gathering up the fragments, and tossing the broken pitcher out of the window, I turned round in my seat to see who it was that could imitate Camanches so well, and be so hilarious over the augmented sufferings and discomfort of a sick woman. Each and all of them, old and young, had the outward appearance of gentlemen. I wondered in what particular part of their bodies the hyena slumbered: it was quiet then. I also wondered if it had been a relative of theirs, a mother, wife, sister, or friend even, if they would have yelped with delight at a malicious trick played upon such an one by a perverse boy? That boy took his cue from men.

Some, perhaps many, will ask why I put the revolting facts contained in this chapter upon paper and in a book? They will reason in the same way that a man did in San Francisco, who would not buy my book upon the grounds, that, if the laws were bad, the less that knew it the better. I replied, "Would you condemn a man who signalled an engineer that a bridge was gone, thus saving hundreds of lives, because he did not let the train dash over the precipice to certain destruction?" Will the nausea of reading this chapter parallel the suffering of the one who endured it? I give it to more firmly impress upon your minds the necessity of abolishing this frightful curse to widows and orphans, — this Probate inquisition; I give it that you may judge of its guilt by my sufferings, under all the cruel circumstances through which I have been dragged by it — both directly and indirectly; I give it to show that a disfranchised person cannot travel from one end of this free federation to the other without insult. She can with this qualification: "If she be rich, or can afford first-class tickets, it matters not how obtained."

To what conclusions will such an ordeal as I have passed through bring a person? First — If a woman is poor, she should hide herself under a bushel, and never stir abroad, particularly in an emigrant car. Second — That if she does she should be willing to die of suffocation and nicotine poison unmurmuringly. Third — That none but the rich are protected. The poor are subjugated, snubbed, spit upon, insulted, outraged, scorned, and hated. I was hated instead of being pitied for being in that car. They did not want the window open to let in the cold, and let out a modicum of their fumigation. "Why didn't I pay the extra three dollars, and leave them in peace, instead of being a sitting reproach to their nasty habits?" Fourth — Women with second or third class tickets, in this country, are entitled to no respect while travelling. In Europe second-class passengers are never subjected to the strangulation of tobacco-smoke. I said to one of the conductors on the Central Pacific, "What is the reason that there is not a separate smoking-car, instead of using the second-class?" He replied, "It is to force as many as possible to go first-class." This cruel injustice falls entirely upon women, — people who earn and have the least money. Every man can go second-class or emigrant, because every man nearly uses the "devil's weed" in some form or other. Is not this cruelty to animals, for protectors thus to torture the protected? Where's Bergh?

On some roads there are special cars for the benefit of fumigators. Towards the support of this extra rolling-stock, and the wear and tear of the roads, every woman travelling by these routes pays her *pro rata* of expenses. She does not smoke, but she suffers in pocket by such as do. Every man whose bad habits oblige him to have extra accommodation on a railway-car should be obliged to pay for it. There should be smoke-tickets issued to such persons. What railroad company would run a special car for women to dip and snuff, make tea and gossip in, without making them pay roundly for it? This indirect robbery of women for the benefit of men is on the same principle that underlies the unlawful taxation of women for the benefit of their protectors. They make helpless women assist in paying for their indulgences.

Men and brethren, are you not ashamed of such a prostitution of power?

CHAPTER XXVII.

PROBATE A HIGH COURT OF CHANCERY.

Par nobile fratrum.

THIS chapter is almost entirely made up of extracts from "Bleak House." Mr. Dickens says in the preface of this book, "Every thing set forth in these pages concerning the Court of Chancery is substantially true, and within the truth. The case of Gridley is in no essential altered from one of actual occurrence, made public by a disinterested person who was professionally acquainted with the whole of the monstrous wrong from beginning to end. At the present moment (1853) there is a suit before the court, which was commenced nearly twenty years ago, in which from thirty to forty counsel have been known to appear at one time; in which costs have been incurred to the amount of seventy thousand pounds; which is a *friendly suit*, and which is (I am assured) no nearer to its termination now than when it was begun. There is another well-known suit in Chancery, not yet decided, which was commenced before the close of the last century, and in which more than double the amount of seventy thousand pounds has been swallowed up in costs."

"Hard by Temple Bar, in Lincoln's Inn Hall, at the very heart of the fog, sits the Lord High Chancellor in his High Court of Chancery. Never can there come fog too thick, never can there come mud and mire too deep, to assort with the groping and floundering condition which this High Court of Chancery, most pestilent of hoary sinners, holds this day in the sight of heaven and earth.

"On such an afternoon, if ever, the Lord High Chancellor ought to be sitting here — as here he is — with a foggy glory round his head, softly fenced in with crimson cloth and curtains, addressed by a large advocate with great whiskers, a little voice, and an interminable brief, and outwardly directing his contemplation to the lantern in the roof, where he can see nothing but fog. On such an afternoon some score of members of the High Court of Chancery bar ought to be — as here they are — mistily engaged in one of the ten thousand stages of an endless cause, tripping one another up on slippery precedents, groping knee-deep in technicalities, running their goat-hair and horse-hair warded heads against walls of words, and making a pretence of equity with serious faces — as players might. On such an afternoon the various solicitors in the cause, some two or three of whom have inherited it from their fathers, who made a fortune by it, ought to be — as they are not — ranged in a line, in a long matted well (but you might look in vain for Truth at the bottom of it), between the register's red table and the silk gowns, with bills, cross-bills, answers, rejoinders, injunctions, affidavits, issues, references to masters, masters' reports, mountains of costly nonsense, piled before them. Well may the court be dim, with wasting candles here and there; well may the fog hang heavy in it, as if it would never get out; well may the stained-glass windows lose their color, and admit no light of day into the place; well may the uninitiated from the streets, who peep in through the glass panes in the door, be deterred from entrance by its owlish aspect, and by the drawl languidly echoing to the roof from the padded dais where the Lord High Chancellor looks into the lantern that has no light in it, and where the attendant wigs are all stuck in a fog-bank! This is the Court of Chancery, which has its decaying houses and its blighted lands in every shire; which has its worn-out lunatic in every mad-house, and its dead in every churchyard; which has its ruined suitor with his slipshod heels and threadbare dress, borrowing and begging through the round of every man's acquaintance; which gives to moneyed might the means abundantly of wearying out the right; which so exhausts finances, patience, courage, hope, so overthrows the brain, and breaks the heart, that there is not an honorable man among its practitioners who would not give — who does not often give — the warning, 'Suffer any wrong that can be done you, rather than come here.'

"The Court is yawning — or its members, *attachés*

rather — this murky afternoon, for no crumb of amusement ever falls from *Jarndyce & Jarndyce* (the cause in hand), which was squeezed dry years and years ago. This scarecrow of a suit has in course of time become so complicated, that no man alive knows what it means. Innumerable children have been born into the cause; innumerable young people have married into it; innumerable old people have died out of it. Scores of people have deliriously found themselves made parties in Jarndyce & Jarndyce, without knowing how or why. Whole families have inherited legendary hatreds with the suit. The little plaintiff or defendant, who was promised a new rocking-horse when Jarndyce & Jarndyce should be settled, has grown up, possessed himself of a real horse, and trotted away into the other world. Fair wards of court have faded into mothers and grandmothers; a long procession of Chancellors has come in and gone out; the legion of bills in the suit have been transformed into mere bills of mortality; there are not three Jarndyces left upon the earth perhaps, since old Tom Jarndyce in despair blew his brains out at a coffee-house in Chancery Lane. But Jarndyce & Jarndyce still drags its dreary length before the court, perennially hopeless.

"Jarndyce & Jarndyce has passed into a joke. That is the only good that has ever come of it; it has been death to many, but it is a joke in the profession. Every master in Chancery has had a reference out of it; every Chancellor was 'in it,' for somebody or other, when he was counsel at the bar. Good things have been said about it by blue-nosed, bulbous-shoed old benchers, in select port-wine committee after dinner in hall. Articled clerks have been in the habit of fleshing their legal wit upon it. The last Lord Chancellor handled it neatly, when correcting Mr. Blowers, the eminent silk gown, who said that such a thing might happen when the sky rained potatoes: he observed, 'Or when we get through Jarndyce & Jarndyce, Mr. Blowers,' — a pleasantry that particularly tickled the maces, bags, and purses.

"How many people out of the suit, Jarndyce & Jarndyce has stretched forth its unwholesome hand to spoil and corrupt, would be a very wide question. From the master, upon whose impaling files reams of dusty warrants in Jarndyce & Jarndyce have grimly writhed into fantastic shapes; down to the copying-clerk in the Six Clerks' Office, who has copied his tens of thousands of Chancery-folio pages under that eternal heading, — no man's nature has been made the better by it. In trickery, evasion, procrastination, spoliation, botheration, under false pretences of all sorts, there are influences that can never come to good. The very solicitous boys who have kept the wretched suitors at bay by protesting time out of mind that Mr. Chizzle, Mizzle, or otherwise, was particularly engaged and had appointments until dinner, may have got an extra moral twist and shuffle into themselves out of Jarndyce &

Jarndyce. The receiver in the cause has acquired a goodly sum of money by it, but has acquired, too, a distrust of his own mother, and a contempt for his own kind. Chizzle, Mizzle, and otherwise have lapsed into habits of vaguely promising themselves that they will look into that outstanding matter, and see what can be done for Drizzle, — who was not well used, — when Jarndyce & Jarndyce shall be got out of the office. Shirking and sharking in all their many varieties have been sown broadcast by the ill-fated cause; and even those who have contemplated its history from the outermost circle of such evil, have been insensibly tempted into a loose way of letting bad things alone to take their own bad course, and a loose belief, that, if the world go wrong, it was in some off-handed manner never meant to go right.

"Thus, in the midst of the mud and at the heart of the fog, sits the Lord High Chancellor in his High Court of Chancery.

"The farce having ended for the day, the Chancellor is about to bow to the bar, when a prisoner is presented, — another ruined suitor, who periodically appears from Shropshire, and breaks out into efforts to address the Chancellor at the close of the day's business; and who can by no means be made to understand that the Chancellor is legally ignorant of his existence after making it desolate for a quarter of a century. The man from Shropshire ventures a 'my lord;' but the Chancellor, being aware of the import of the prisoner's conglomeration, has dexterously vanished. Everybody else quickly vanishes too, and the empty court is locked up. If all the injustice it has committed, and all the misery it has caused, could only be locked up with it, and the whole burnt away in a great funereal pyre, — why, so much the better for other parties than the parties in Jarndyce & Jarndyce!"

John Jarndyce, a ward in Chancery, and guardian of two minor wards in the same weary suit, said, in speaking of the hopeless cause, "The lawyers have twisted it into such a state of bedevilment that the original merits of the case have long disappeared from the face of the earth. It's about a Will, and the trusts under a Will — or it was once. It's about nothing but Costs now. We are always appearing, and disappearing, and swearing, and interrogating, and filing, and cross-filing, and arguing, and sealing, and motioning, and referring, and reporting, and revolving about the Lord High Chancellor and all his satellites, and equitably waltzing ourselves off to dusty death, about Costs. That's the great question. All the rest, by some extraordinary means, has melted away. A certain Jarndyce, in an evil hour, made a great fortune, and made a great Will. In the question how the trusts under the Will are to be administered, the fortune left by the Will is squandered away; the legatees under the Will are reduced to such a miserable condition that they would be sufficiently punished, if they had committed an enormous crime in having money left them; and the Will itself is made a dead letter. All through the deplorable cause, every thing that everybody in it, except one man, knows already, is referred to that only one man who don't know it, to find out; all through the deplorable cause, everybody must have copies, over and over again, of every thing that has accumulated about it in the way of cartloads of papers (or must pay for them without having them, which is the usual course, for nobody wants them), and must go down the middle and up again, through such an infernal contra-dance of costs and fees, and nonsense, and corruption, as was never dreamed of in the wildest visions of a witch's sabbath. Equity sends questions to Law, Law sends questions back to Equity; Law finds it can't do this, Equity finds it can't do that; neither can so much as say it can't do any thing, without this solicitor's instructing and this counsel appearing for A, and that solicitor instructing and that counsel appearing for B, and so on through the whole alphabet. Through years and years, and lives and lives, every thing goes on, constantly beginning over and over again, and nothing ever ends. And we can't get out of the suit on any terms; for we are made parties to it, and *must be* parties to it, whether we like it or not. But it won't do to think of it. When my uncle, poor Tom Jarndyce, began to think of it, it was the beginning of the end.

"I was his heir, and this was his house, Bleak

House. When I came here, it was bleak indeed. He had left the signs of his misery upon it. Here he lived shut up, day and night poring over the wicked heaps of papers in the suit, and hoping against hope to disentangle it from its mystification, and bring it to a close. In the mean time the place became dilapidated, the wind whistled through the cracked walls, the rain fell through the broken roof, the weeds choked the passage to the rotting doors. When I brought what remained of him home here, the brains seemed to me to have been blown out of the house too, it was so shattered and ruined.

"There is in the city of London, some property of ours — I say property of ours, meaning of the suits, but I ought to call it the property of Costs; for Costs is the only power on earth that will ever get any thing out of it now, or will ever know it for any thing but an eyesore and a heartsore. It is a street of perishing, blind houses, with their eyes stoned out; without a pane of glass, without so much as a window-frame; with the bare blank shutters tumbling from their hinges, and falling asunder; the iron rails peeling away in flakes of rust, the chimneys sinking in, the stone steps to every door (and every door might be Death's door) turning stagnant green, the very crutches on which the ruins are propped decaying. Although Bleak House was not in Chancery, its master was; and it was stamped with the same seal. These are the Great Seal's impressions all over England, — and the children know them.

"Here's my ward Rick, a fine young fellow, full of promise. He must have a profession. Kenge and Carboy will have something to say about it; Master Somebody — a sort of ridiculous sexton, digging graves for the merits of causes in a back room at the end of Quality Court, Chancery Lane — will have something to say about it; counsel will have something to say about it; the Chancellor will have something to say about it; the Satellites will have something to say about it; they will have to be handsomely feed all round, about it; the whole thing will be vastly ceremonious, wordy, unsatisfactory, and expensive; and I call it, in general, Wiglomeration. How mankind ever come to be afflicted with Wiglomeration, or for whose sins these young people, Rick and Ada, wards in Jarndyce & Jarndyce, ever fell into a pit of it, I don't know: so it is."

"By my soul, Jarndyce," said Mr. Boythorn, "If I were in your place, I would seize every Master in Chancery by the throat to-morrow morning, and shake him until his money rolled out of his pockets, and his bones rattled in his skin. I would have a settlement out of somebody, by fair means or by foul. If you would empower me to do it, I would do it for you with the greatest satisfaction. There never was such an infernal caldron as that chancery, on the face of the earth! Nothing but a mine below it on a busy day in term-time, with all its records, rules, and precedents collected in it, and every functionary belonging to it also, high and low, upward and downward, from its son the Accountant-General to its father the Devil, and the whole blown to atoms with ten thousand hundred-weight of gunpowder, could reform it in the least."

While visiting some orphan children in miserable lodgings, Mr. Jarndyce and his wards met for the first time "the man from Shropshire,—a tall sallow man, with a careworn head, on which but little hair remained, a deeply lined face, and prominent eyes. He had a combative look, and a chafing irritable manner, which associated with his figure—still large and powerful, though evidently in its decline—was rather alarming. He entered the room where they were sitting, evidently in great displeasure at the sight of strangers, and said, 'I don't know what you may be doing here, ladies and gentlemen, but you'll excuse my coming in. I don't come in to stare about me.' 'No one, surely, would come here to stare about him,' said Mr. Jarndyce mildly.

"'May be so, sir: may be so,' returned Gridley almost fiercely. 'I don't want to argue with ladies and gentlemen. I've had enough of arguing to last one man his lifetime.'

"'You have sufficient reason, I dare say,' observed Mr. Jarndyce, 'for being chafed and irritated.'

"'There again!' exclaimed the man, becoming violently angry. 'I'm of a quarrelsome temper. I'm irascible. I'm not polite!'

"'Not very, I think.'

"'Sir,' said Gridley, going up to him as if he

meant to strike him, 'do you know any thing of Courts of Equity?'

"'Perhaps I do, to my sorrow.'

"'To your sorrow?' said the man, pausing in his wrath. 'If so, I beg your pardon. I'm not polite, I know. I beg your pardon! Sir,' with renewed violence, 'I have been dragged for five and twenty years over burning iron, and I have lost the habit of treading upon velvet. Go into the Court of Chancery yonder, and ask what is one of the standing jokes that brighten up their business sometimes, and they will tell you that the best joke they have is the man from Shropshire. I,' he said, beating one hand on the other passionately, 'am the man from Shropshire.'

"'I believe I and my family have also had the honor of furnishing some entertainment in the same grave place,' said Mr. Jarndyce composedly. 'You may have heard my name, — Jarndyce.'

"'Mr. Jarndyce,' said Gridley, 'you bear your wrong more quietly than I can bear mine. More than that, I tell you, and I tell this young gentleman and these young ladies, if they are friends of yours, that if I took my wrongs in any other way, I should be driven mad! It is only by resenting them, and by revenging them in my mind, and by angrily demanding the justice I never get, that I am able to keep my wits together. It is only that,' he said, speaking in a homely, rustic way, and with great vehemence.

"'You may tell me that I over-excite myself. I answer that's in my nature to do it under wrong, and I must do it. There's nothing between doing it, and sinking into the smiling state of the poor little madwoman that haunts the court. If I were once to sit down under it, I should become imbecile.'

"The passion and heat in which he was, and the manner in which his face worked, and the violent gestures with which he accompanied what he said, were most painful to see.

"'Mr. Jarndyce,' he continued, 'consider my case. As true as there is a heaven above us, this is my case. I am one of two brothers. My father (a farmer) made a will, and left his farm and stock, and so forth, to my mother for her life. After my mother's death, all was to come to me except a legacy of three hundred pounds that I was then to pay my brother. My mother died. My brother, some time afterwards, claimed his legacy. I and some of my relations said that he had had a part of it already in board and lodging, and some other things. Now mind! That was the question, and nothing else. No one disputed the will; no one disputed any thing, but whether part of that three hundred pounds had been already paid or not. To settle that question, my brother filing a bill, I was obliged to go into this accursed Chancery. I was forced there, because the law forced me, and would let me go nowhere else. *Seventeen* people were made defendants to that simple suit! It first came on after two years.

It was then stopped for another two years, while the master (*may his head rot off!*) inquired whether I was my father's son — about which there was no dispute whatever with any mortal creature. He then found out that there were not defendants enough, — remember, there were *only* seventeen as yet, — but that we must have another who had been left out, and must begin all over again. The costs at that time — before the thing was begun — were three times the legacy. My brother would have given up the legacy, and joyful, to escape more costs. My whole estate left to me in that will of my father's has gone in costs. The suit, still undecided, has fallen into rack and ruin and despair, with every thing else — and here I stand this day. Now, Mr. Jarndyce, in your suit there are thousands and thousands involved where in mine there are hundreds. Is mine less hard to bear, or is it harder to bear, when my whole living was in it, and has been thus shamefully sucked away?'

"Mr. Jarndyce said that he condoled with him with all his heart, and that he set up no monopoly himself in being unjustly treated by this monstrous system.

"'There again!' said Gridley, with no diminution of his rage. 'The system! I am told on all hands, it's the system. I mustn't look to individuals. It's the system. I mustn't go into court, and say, "My Lord, I beg to know this from you: is this right, or wrong? Have you the face to tell me I have received justice, and therefore am dismissed?" My Lord knows nothing of it. He sits there to administer the system. I mustn't go to Mr. Tulkinghorn, the solicitor in Lincoln's Inn Fields, and say to him, when he makes me furious by being so cool and satisfied, — as they all do, for I know they gain by it while I lose, don't I? — I mustn't say to him, "I will have something out of some one for my ruin, by fair means or foul!" *He* is not responsible. It's the system. But, if I do no violence to any of them here, — I may! I don't know what may happen if I am carried beyond myself at last. I will accuse the INDIVIDUAL WORKERS of that system against me, face to face, before the great eternal bar.'

"His passion was fearful. No one could have believed in such rage without seeing it.

"'I have done,' he said, sitting down, and wiping his face. 'Mr. Jarndyce, I have done. I'm violent, I know. I ought to know it. I have been in prison for contempt of court. I have been in this trouble, and that trouble, and shall be again. I'm the man from Shropshire, and sometimes go beyond amusing them — though they have found it amusing, too, to see me committed into custody, and all that. It would be better for me, they tell me, if I restrained myself. I tell them that if I did restrain myself, I should become imbecile. I was a good-enough tempered man once, I believe. People in my part of the country say they remember me so; but now I must have this vent under my sense of injury, or nothing could hold my wits together. "It would be far better for you, Mr. Gridley," the Lord Chancellor told me last week, "not to waste your time here, and to stay usefully employed down in Shropshire." "My Lord, my Lord, I know it would," said I to him, "and it would have been far better for me never to have heard the name of your high office; but, unhappily for me, I can't undo the past, and the past drives me here!" Besides,' he added, breaking fiercely out, 'I'll shame them.' (As if such a thing were possible!) 'If I knew when I was going to die, and could be carried there, and had a voice to speak with, I would die there saying, "You have brought me here, and sent me from here, many and many a time. *Now send me out feet foremost!*"'"

Here is a bird's-eye view of Chancery from a woman's (Miss Esther Summerson) standpoint. She says, —

"When we came to the Court, there was the Lord High Chancellor sitting, in great state and gravity, on the bench; with the mace and seals on a red table before him, and an immense flat nosegay, like a little garden, which scented the whole Court. Below the table, again, was a long row of solicitors, with bundles of papers on the matting at their feet; and then there were the gentlemen of the bar in wigs and gowns, some awake and some asleep, and one talking, and nobody paying much attention to what he said. The Lord Chancellor leaned back in his very easy chair, with his elbows on the cushioned arms, and his forehead resting on his hand; some of those who were present dozed, some read the newspapers, some walked about, or whispered in groups; all seemed perfectly at their ease, by no means in a hurry, very unconcerned, and extremely comfortable.

"To see every thing going on so smoothly, and tc think of the roughness of the suitors' lives and deaths; to see all that full dress and ceremony, and to think of the waste, and want, and beggared misery it represented; to consider, that, while the sickness of hope deferred was raging in so many hearts, this polite show went calmly on from day to day, and year to year, in such good order and composure; to behold the Lord Chancellor, and the whole array of practitioners under him, looking at one another and at the spectators, as if nobody had ever heard that all over England the name in which they were assembled was a bitter jest; was held in universal horror, contempt, and indignation" (thus would the Probate Court in the United States be held if people understood half its rascalities, its shameless crimes, and cruel persecutions); "was known for something so flagrant and bad that little short of a miracle could bring any good out of it to any one who had no experience of it, — that it was at first incredible, and I could not comprehend it. I sat where Richard put me, and tried to listen and look about me; but there seemed to be no reality in the whole scene, except poor little Miss Flite, the madwoman, standing on a bench and nodding at it.

"When we had been there half an hour or so, the case in progress — if I may use a phrase so ridiculous in such a connection — seemed to die out of its own vapidity, without coming or being by anybody expected to come to any result. The Lord Chancellor then threw down a bundle of papers from his desk to the gentleman below him, and somebody said 'JARNDYCE & JARNDYCE.' Upon this there was a buzz, and a laugh, and a general withdrawal of the by-standers, and a bringing in of great heaps and piles and bags and bagsful of papers.

"I think it came on 'for further directions,' about some bill of costs, to the best of my understanding, which was confused enough. I counted twenty-three gentlemen in wigs, who said they were '*in it;*' and none of them appeared to understand it much better than I did. They chatted about it with the Lord Chancellor, and contradicted and explained among themselves, and some of them said it was this way, and some of them said it was that way, and some of them jocosely proposed to read huge volumes of affidavits, and there was more buzzing and laughing, and everybody concerned was in a state of idle entertainment, and nothing could be made of it by anybody. After an hour or so of this, and a good many speeches being begun and cut short, it was '*referred back for the present*,' and the papers were bundled up again, before the clerks had finished bringing them in.

"I glanced at Richard, at the termination of these

hopeless proceedings, and was shocked to see the worn look of his handsome face."

Let us turn from cause to result, as seen and recorded by Esther Summerson: —

"When we arrived at the shooting-gallery, we saw lying upon a plain canvas-covered sofa, the man from Shropshire — dressed much as we had seen him last, but so changed that at first I recognized no likeness in his colorless face to what I recollected. He had been still writing in his hiding-place, and still dwelling on his grievances, hour after hour. A table and some shelves were covered with manuscript papers, and with worn pens, and a medley of such tokens. Touchingly and awfully drawn together, he and the little madwoman were side by side, and, as it were, alone. She sat on a chair holding his hand. His voice had faded, with the old expression of his face, with his strength, with his anger, with his resistance to the wrongs that had at last subdued him. The faintest shadow of an object full of form and color is such a picture of it, as he was of the man from Shropshire whom we had spoken with before.

"He inclined his head to Richard and me, and spoke to my Guardian: 'Mr. Jarndyce, it is very kind of you to come to see me. I'm not long to be seen, I think. I'm very glad to take your hand, sir. You are a good man, superior to injustice, and God knows I honor you.'

"They shook hands earnestly, my Guardian saying some words of comfort to him.

" 'It may seem strange to you, sir,' returned Gridley: 'I should not have liked to see you, if this had been the first time of our meeting. But, you know, I made a fight for it; you know I stood up with my single hand against them all; you know I told them the truth to the last, and told them what they were, and what they had done to me: so I don't mind you seeing me this wreck.'

" 'You have been courageous with them, many and many a time,' observed my Guardian.

" 'Sir, I have been,' with a faint smile. 'I told you what would come of it, when I ceased to be so; and, see here! look at us — look at us!' He drew the hand Miss Flite held through her arm, and brought her something nearer him. 'This ends it. Of all my old associates, of all my old pursuits and hopes, of all the living and the dead world, this one poor soul alone comes natural to me, and I am fit for. There is a tie of many suffering years between us two, and it is the only tie I ever had on earth that Chancery has not broken.'

" 'Accept my blessing, Gridley,' said Miss Flite in tears. 'Accept my blessing!'

" 'I thought boastfully that they could never break my heart, Mr. Jarndyce. I was resolved that they should not. I did believe that I could, and would, charge them with being the mockery they are, until I died of some bodily disorder. But I am worn out. How long I have been wearing out, I don't know; I seem to break down in an hour. I hope they may never come to hear of it. I hope everybody here will lead them to believe that I died defying them consistently and perseveringly, as I did so many years.

"The roof rang with a scream from Miss Flite, which still rings in my ears, as he ceased speaking.

"'Oh, no, Gridley!' she cried, as he fell heavily and calmly back from before her, 'not without my blessing, after so many years!'

"The sun was down, the light had gradually stolen from the roof, and the shadow had crept upward. But to me the shadow of that pair, one living and one dead, fell heavier across Richard's path than the darkness of the darkest night. I thought of him and the beautiful girl whose destiny was locked in his, as they were the first time I saw them, — he so handsome and joyous, she with the firelight dancing through her golden hair. Ah! how changed is that bright vision!

"I visited them every day now in their little dark corner in Symond's Inn. On these occasions I frequently found Richard absent; at other times writing, or reading papers in the Cause. Sometimes I would come upon him lingering at the door of Mr. Vholes's office, — a man so slow, so bloodless and gaunt, I felt whenever I saw them together that Richard was wasting away beneath the eyes of this adviser, and that there was something of the vampire in him. We sat face to face one day at dinner, and I had an opportunity of observing Richard anxiously.

I was not disturbed by Mr. Vholes (who took off his gloves to dine), though he sat opposite to me at the small table; for I doubt, if looking up at all, he once removed his eyes from his client's face. I found Richard thin and languid, slovenly in his dress, abstracted in his manner, forcing his spirits now and then, and at other intervals relapsing into a dull thoughtfulness. About his large bright eyes that used to be so merry there was a wanness and a restlessness that changed them altogether. His lips were dry, and his fingernails were all bitten away. I cannot use the expression that he looked old. There is a ruin of youth which is not like age; and into such a ruin Richard's youth and youthful beauty had all fallen away. He haunted the Court day after day; listlessly sat there the whole day long, when he knew there was no remote chance of his suit being mentioned; and became one of the stock sights of the place. I wonder whether any of the gentlemen remembered him as he was when he first went there."

The curtain rises on the last scene, the last act, in this sad drama, this mocking farce. "When we came to Westminster Hall we found that the day's business was begun. Worse than that, we found such an unusual crowd in the Court of Chancery that it was full to the door, and we could neither see nor hear what was passing within. It appeared to be something droll, for occasionally there was a laugh, and a cry of '*Silence!*' It appeared to be something interesting, for every one was pushing and striving to get nearer. It appeared to be something that made the professional gentlemen very merry; for there were several young counsellors in wigs and whiskers on the outside of the crowd, and when one of them told the others about it, they put their hands in their pockets, and quite doubled themselves up with laughter, and went stamping about the pavement of the hall.

"We asked a gentleman by us, if he knew what case was on? He replied, '*Jarndyce & Jarndyce.*' We asked him if he knew what was doing in it? He said, really, no, he did not, nobody ever did; but, as well as he could make out, it was over. Over for the day? we asked him. 'No,' he made answer: 'over for good.'

"Over for good! When we heard this unaccountable answer we looked at one another, quite lost in amazement. Could it be possible that the Will had set things right at last, and that Richard and Ada were going to be rich? it seemed too good to be true. Alas, it was!

"Our suspense was short; for a break-up took place in the crowd, and the people came streaming out, looking flushed and hot, and bringing a quantity of bad air with them. Still they were all exceedingly amused, and were more like people coming out from a farce or a juggler than from a court of justice. Presently great bundles of papers began to be carried out,—bundles in bags, bundles too large to be got into bags, immense masses of papers of all shapes and no shapes, which the bearers staggered under, and threw down for the time being, anyhow, on the hall pavement, while they went back to bring out more. Even these clerks were laughing. We glanced at these papers, and, seeing Jarndyce & Jarndyce everywhere, asked an official-looking person who was standing in the midst of them, whether the case was over. 'Yes,' he said; 'it was all up with at last,'—and burst out laughing too.

"At this juncture we perceived Mr. Kenge coming out of court with an affable dignity upon him, listening to Mr. Vholes, who was deferential, and carried his own bag. Mr. Vholes was the first to see us.

"'Here is Miss Summerson, sir,' he said, 'and Mr. Allan Woodcourt.'

"'Mr. Kenge,' said Allan, 'do I understand that the whole estate is found to have been absorbed in costs?'

"'Hem! I believe so,' replied Mr. Kenge. 'But you must reflect, Mr. Woodcourt, that on the numerous difficulties, contingencies, masterly fictions, and forms of procedure in this great cause, there has been expended study, ability, eloquence, knowledge, intellect, Mr. Woodcourt, high intellect. For many years the — a — I would say, the flower of the Bar, and the — a — I would presume to add, the matured autumnal fruits of the Woolsack, have been lavished upon Jarndyce & Jarndyce. If the public have the benefit, and if the country have the adornment of this great Grasp, it must be paid for, in money or money's worth, sir.'

"'In case you should be wanting Mr. C——, sir,' said Mr. Vholes, 'you'll find him in court. I left him there resting himself a little. Good-day, sir. Good-day, Miss Summerson.' As he gave me that slowly devouring look of his, while twisting up the strings of his bag, he gave one gasp as if he had swallowed the last morsel of his client, and his black, buttoned-up, unwholesome figure glided away to the low door at the end of the hall.

"Later in the day, when the fog hung like a pall over Chancery Lane and Symond's Inn, we gather in the room where lay the wreck of what had once been the light-hearted Richard Carstone. Allan had found him sitting in a corner of the court, like a stone figure. On being roused, he had broken away, and made as if he would have spoken in a fierce voice to the judge. He was stopped by his mouth being full of blood, and Allan had brought him home.

"'When shall I go from this place to the pleasant country where the old times are, where I shall have strength to tell what Ada has been to me, where I shall be able to recall my many faults and blindnesses, where I shall prepare myself to be a guide to my unborn child?' said Richard. 'When shall I go?'

"'Dear Rick, when you are strong enough,' returned my Guardian.

"'Ada, my darling!'

"He sought to raise himself a little. Allan raised him so that she could hold him on her bosom, which was what he wanted.

"'I have done you many wrongs, my own. I have fallen like a poor stray shadow on your way. I have married you to poverty and trouble; I have scattered your means to the winds. You will forgive me all this, my Ada, before I begin the world?'

"A smile irradiated his countenance as she bent to kiss him. He slowly laid his face down upon her bosom, drew his arms closer round her neck, and with one parting sob began the world — not this world, oh, not this! the world that sets this right."

Push back the dark locks from the white temples — they will never ache again; fold the hands over the still heart — it will never break again; close gently the dull eyes — they will never weep again. All is finished! Ring down the curtain!

I have collected the facts in this chapter to prove that I am not the only one who has used "strong language," and rebelled against a corrupt system, and the corrupt workers in a corrupt system. Would that a hand as powerful as the illustrious dead's, guided by divine inspiration, might brand upon the hearts of lawgivers, with a pen of fire, the black wrong, the cruel injustice, the deep shame, of this frightful system of robbing the widows and plundering the orphans of this our land to satiate the greed of man!

The only difference between Probate and Chancery appears to be this: Probate does not hold on to cases for centuries as Chancery does, because we are a somewhat faster people, and can make way with dead men's estates in a shorter time, but just as certain. The results are identical. Probate is more criminal in its onslaught upon the defenceless than Chancery. It is man against man in the one case, and it is women and children against men and courts in the other. How unequal the strife! Chancery makes no invidious sex-distinction: it seizes — like the many-armed octopus — all within its grasp, and sucks them into its inextricable maelstrom of destruction. But Probate has a more delicate palate: it fattens upon defenceless widows and tender orphans, until there is not skin enough left upon their fleshless bodies to rattle their bones in.

Not till the grave gives up its dead will the crimes perpetrated under probate law and probate protection be brought to light!

CHAPTER XXVIII.

CONCLUDING REMARKS.

Pro aris et foces.

WHAT shall I say in conclusion? How can I sum up in a single chapter the innumerable abominations practised by the Probate Court, and sanctioned by law? It would take a pen plucked from the wing of the destroying angel, and dipped in blood, to adequately describe this probate confiscation business.

Would that I could trace in words of flame, the days, weeks, and years of corroding uncertainty; the cruel loss of property by being prevented from handling it at an advantageous moment; the robbery of the mother, by an iniquitous inquisition, of the control of her offspring; the crime of being plundered of one's substance; the disgrace of poverty, and the frigidity of acquaintances! I cannot mar the holy name of friendship in this connection. Adversity is the crucible in which that most rare element is tried. Nothing but fine gold can withstand the white heat of adversity. Dross is dissipated like chaff before a gale. It is of the value and consistency of thistle-down upon the air, or foam upon the billow. It partakes of the nature of gases — inconstant, intangible, inconsistent, inscrutable. A widow is a target for thieves; particularly when she stands alone, without a muscular protector in the shape of father, brother, or son. She is robbed, under the guise of friendship, by professed friends of her late husband, who have axes to grind. They want a portion, or all there is left, after the insatiable jaws of the Probate Court have relaxed their hold, to sharpen the edges of those useful implements.

I have been robbed of over a thousand dollars in gold, outside of the flaying by the Probate Court and the Gilroy phlebotomizing, since my husband's death; I have been plundered by confidence-operators — sharpers; I have paid debts for bankrupts — where I owed not a farthing; I lost $150 on my letter of credit, $120 mortgage tax, and $100 lent an individual who is under obligations to me that money cannot pay. For every dollar that I have lost in and out of the court, I pray that swift retribution may overtake the thieves.

I wish that every person who makes it a point to steal by borrowing, or any other nefarious device, had just twenty-four hours in which to make restitution; and, if he did not do it in that time, that then and there he might be hung by the neck until dead. From the highest to the lowest, from the big pilferer to the petty sneak-thief, I wish this law was enacted and put into speedy execution.

What a cathartic it would give this nation! It would be worth an ocean of "*gentle aperients*," such as the lax law bestows upon princely thieves, while a lad that steals a loaf of bread, to keep from starving, is sent to jail to be locked up with hardened criminals for days before he comes to trial; and the man who steals a small amount of money, to buy food for his famishing wife and babes, is sent to San Quentin. He did not dip deep enough! One needs to be a princely thief, with kingly attributes, to command universal admiration through all the descending gradations from the pinnacle of unsullied lawn and ermine to the black-hole of scullion and boot-black.

He must make a grand harvest of the substance of widows and orphans, and the poor man's savings that he has laid up with much toil and privation to buy a home for his loved ones. The lower million must sweat to keep the money-autocrat upon the summit of power. The spectacle of the law with bandaged eyes, and limping sadly, where powerful men are concerned, and bitterly vengeful and abnormally energetic when the vulgar culprit is dragged before the judgment-seat, is not at all improving. The unfortunate wretch who has no money to buy indulgences is wrung to the last withers to pay all kinds of taxes to replenish "Uncle Sam's" capacious pockets, which are open to so many unclean fingers. "To him that hath, much shall be given; but from him that hath not, even that which he hath shall be taken away." This may not be a literal quotation. I don't think it is. It would be a mental impossibility to remember gospel-text while probating. This statement seems strangely familiar. If I have made use of it before in these pages, I beg pardon. Still it will bear repetition.

I give the history of my own case, not because it differs materially from thousands of others, not because I expect to recover any of the squandered substance: I give it for a precedent and a warning to others. Although letters of administration were granted in August, the same month that Mr. Stow died, the inventory, strange to relate, was not filed until the 17th of December. What caused the four months delay? What hidden bonanza was unearthed in all those weeks and months, to warrant any such sacrifice of valuable time and money? Would the judge have been as patient with a widow who was acting without bonds? Would he not have been alarmed for the safety of creditors?

Why does a court of justice protect the power obtained from a dying man? Mr. Stow was in a dying condition when he signed the will, and permitted those men to serve as executors. He was not responsible for what he did, as is proven by his having made no provision for the return of his destitute wife, who was seven thousand miles distant at the time, and by his neglecting to give his sister-in-law the smallest token of remembrance: a woman whom he loved so much; with whom he had lived for eight months before his death; whose house for six weeks had been turned into a hospital, filled with business-men, friends, physicians, night-watchers, and nurses; and she herself having had no rest by day or by night during this time. Was Mr. Stow, when in his right mind, a man to forget these things? To this woman he turned in the last mortal agony; upon her lips his last kiss was pressed; his last look was upon her face; within her arms the wave of life made its last ebb, —

"And the spirit leaped forward — whither, none know!"

The will was ready-made for him to sign. It was made for no other purpose than to get control of the property, for it is executed according to the laws of California; and therefore I am neither a gainer nor loser by the instrument, only so far as I am robbed of the power of administration, and all knowledge of its progress.

There never has been a single publication of a statement of affairs, as is required by statute, up to this writing. Is this LAW? Is this JUSTICE?

Men call it justice: I don't. I call it the extract of barbarism, worthy of fiends but not of men. Manhood should hide its face, and civilization stand aghast, at such an outrage upon common decency. This is a widow's protection under statute law, and this is the highway to ruin of dead men's estates. With a living widow there should be no "dead men's estates." We hear nothing about "dead women's estates" — as regards community property — who leave widowers.

What right has a husband's family to property earned by the joint efforts of himself and wife, after his death, even when there are no children? None at all: any more than the wife's family has a right to one-half or two-thirds of the property, where there are no children, after the husband's death. But the childless widow is never permitted to have all the community property, unless the husband has willed it to her. What a shame! He may have desired it, but neglected to make a will to that effect; and then the one-half or two-thirds reverts to people whom she has never seen, or hates, perhaps, because they thought her husband had made a *mésalliance* by marrying her. If the husband should happen to be the "last of the Grogans," this lovely law, in some of the States, still wrests the half or two-thirds of the property from the rightful owner, and gives it to the State. What business has the State with a widow's property, more than it has with a widower's?

Be not deceived: this court strikes at the vitals of every household in the land. A husband conserves and saves every dollar to make a beautiful or comfortable home for his family; but, if death overtake him before his race is run, this competence falls into Probate, and is scattered to the four winds. Therefore, "know all men by these presents," that you *may be* laying up treasures where moth and rust doth corrupt (the Probate Court), and where thieves (its satellites) do break through and steal.

This laying hold of dead men's estates and eating them up piecemeal, while the rightful owners are dying piecemeal, — dying of hope deferred, of energies wasted, days, months, years, of agonized suspense, — "is being ground to bits in a slow mill; is being roasted at a slow fire; is being stung to death by single bees; is being drowned by drops; is growing mad by grains."

Could I in one terse page exhibit all the misery, all the degradation, all the ruin, which the abuse of this so-called court of justice has, in the last century, accumulated upon the defenceless heads of humanity, not all the famed writers of the past, nor the ambitious aspirants of future greatness, would suffice to portray the horrors practised by this monstrous mountain of iniquity, — with its miners and sappers, its deadly shafts and pit-holes, its upper and lower levels of qualified and unqualified torture, — which lifts its head so sullenly, so defiantly. The rich ore (widow's estates) is crushed by the stamps of modern justice; and, when the "clean-up" comes, the legal vultures — from the Lord High Chancellor Judge down to the pot-of-paste poster — swoop down, and gather up the free gold, and leave the worthless tailings for the widows and orphans. *And this is justice!*

As I, day by day for nearly three years, witnessed the deadly evils culminating in this most corrupt and corruptible institution, I resolved that henceforth and forever my occupation should be to eradicate, expose, and destroy, this sum of all human abominations, — this Probate Court system, on its present basis, as regards community property. Extermination is the keynote; for, what help is there, what panacea, what redemption, so long as this thieving court exists? None whatever: and yet we (widows) are *free!* Yes: —

> "We are as free as sorrow is to laugh and talk,
> Free as sick men are to ride and walk."

All I ask is, that widows may be governed by the same laws which govern widowers; no more, no less. The English law, of which ours is a direct outgrowth, is the most oppressive, in its character and practice, upon women, of any laws in the civilized world. And yet in conservative, monarchical England today, women are granted far more privileges than they are in this country, where a hundred years ago we slipped the English yoke of oppressive intolerance. There women vote in municipal elections under the same conditions that men vote; and since 1870 every wife carrying on a separate business from that of her husband is entirely protected in her industry, as much as though she were a spinster instead of a *femme de couvert.* Such laws are protective, and encourage industry. Wedlock should be no more binding upon a woman than upon a man. In many of the Continental countries the wife is as free — as regards her own property and industry — in wedlock, as out of it.

A widow (in some of the States) in Probate — our High Court of Chancery — is treated precisely like a criminal. He is not allowed to testify for his own benefit, because he has broken the law. She is not allowed to testify for her own benefit, because she has lost her protector. She is not allowed to handle the property which she has earned, if her departed lord willed it otherwise. *And this is justice!*

The Stow estate was inventoried at $40,000, beside the $100,000 claim against the Russell & Erwin Manufacturing Company, which had been in litigation for years at the time of my husband's death. In January, 1876, there was a compromise effected for $26,000, and it was then said that there would be immediate distribution of estate. The middle of the following April, Mr. Pringle, the executor's lawyer, said they could not get the money. How marvellously strange! What caused the delay? It is alleged that the principal and added interest on the Ralston, or Bank of California, claim, amounts to over $40,000, and it is running up, each month, a formidable interest, at one per cent.

My husband said, ere I left for Europe, that he owed no man a dollar; and I believe he spoke the truth. And yet I get not a farthing out of the estate, not even the thousands which I lent him out of my separate property. *And this is justice!*

If I had been permitted to administer upon the estate, I should be at least $1,500 richer than I am, —

that is the per cent awarded upon $40,000,—and I think that I could have closed the affairs of the estate in twelve months without any particular strain of mind or muscle; and I also think with a much better showing than there will be when the matter sees the light from the present incumbents. As near as I can judge from the outer-wall of the situation, it stands just where it did a year ago. It is the 3d of April, 1877, at this writing. I do not think that Milton H. Myrick would have suffered me to go forward for nearly three years without publishing any account of my transactions, particularly if some powerful creditor had insisted, time after time, upon having light where all was darkness; and further, if I had been acting without bonds; and further, if the said powerful creditor believed there was a very big fraud being perpetrated by me, and had brought suit to have me deposed. Verily, it hath a dishonest look and a bad odor. A little daylight would improve the situation. Uncover by all means!

I never have been served with a single notice, as the law requires, by the executors or any other parties to this legal farce in many acts. Judge Myrick has repeatedly promised to get my husband's private correspondence and papers, which the executors never had any business with; but it has ended in promises, nothing else. But Milton H. Myrick is a *just* judge!

Mr. Stow told me three or four years ago, that the Russell & Erwin Manufacturing Company had offered to compromise for $40,000, but that he was advised by his lawyers (Messrs. Pringle and Wilson) and a business associate (Mr. Ralston), not to accept the terms. He further said to me, just before I went abroad, that this suit had cost him over $20,000 in gold to carry it on up to that time. If I had been allowed the control of the property which should have been mine at my husband's death, I should have come to terms of settlement at once with this company. At that time they would have been far more favorably inclined, probably, than seventeen months later, with all the accrued costs. But as it was, the suit was kept brewing with two lawyers here on big pay, and one in New York, after Mr. Stow's death, eating up the estate in lawyers' and court fees, and the deadly one per cent interest on admitted claims. This looks to me like maladministration!

There is another suit of $4,166.66 brought against J. D. Culp and the estate of Hoover, which was still in court when I left San Francisco in January, 1877. I thought Mr. Stow befriended Mr. Culp in his hour of need. If so, why is it necessary to sue him to get back borrowed money, or an honest debt of any kind? and why was not this matter attended to immediately after Mr. Stow's death, when it takes so many months to get a suit, however trivial, through the swift-footed courts? As small a debt as that, I should think, were better not paid at all, than to have the interest on admitted claims, in the time consumed for trial, costs of court, lawyers' fees, and travelling expenses from San Francisco to Gilroy, cancel the amount many times over.

Then, again, Maurice Dore and the other executor and Mr. Culp are loving brother officers, and colossal stock-owners, in the "Gilroy Consolidated Tobacco Company." How strange that they should *love* one day, and *fight* the next!

I see not the shadow of a reason, if there had been the smallest desire on the part of the executors, why the estate should not have been closed up within the year. What right had they to allow any creditor to impoverish it by continuing a lawsuit of $100,000, which any one, with half an eye, could have seen at a glance was better to settle at once upon almost any terms? Who has been benefited? Lawyers and courts; while the estate has melted like snow before the sun. *And this is justice!*

Fidelity to the cause of humanity, especially the cause of widows, requires me to make public the facts of this notorious Probate persecution and depletion, in order to have their true legal position known and fully appreciated; and also to show how entirely destitute a widow — without influential male kindred — is of any legal protection except what the will and wishes of the executors secure her — in my case that was none at all; and also to demonstrate the fact that Probate law everywhere, in relation to widows, not only gravitates towards an absolute despotism, but even protects, sustains, and defends a despotism of the most arbitrary and absolute kind. Therefore, in order to have her social position changed legally, the need of this change must first be seen and appreciated by the people, — the voters of the Republic. To correct legal abuses we must begin at the ballot-box. The voice of the people, and the voice of the people alone, will effect the much-needed reform. Legislators will act when the people desire it, but never before. They are the mouthpiece of the people, the echo of the popular voice. Therefore the people must be educated, and demand a change, ere legislators will act in the matter.

The only property which should go into Probate is that of entire orphans, separate estates, and bequests; and these should never be thrown into court unless a fraud was to be perpetrated. I would not permit a farthing of an estate to be sequestered in unconscionable courts if it could be avoided. Friendly adjustment and peaceful arbitration should be exhausted ere it fell into ruinous litigation, with its entail of deferred hopes, squandered time, engendered malice, and all its vast sisterhood of evils.

If forensic squabbles were settled as they were four hundred years ago in Germany, they would not be quite so protracted, and litigants would be the gainers. At that date of the world's history, in courts of justice men fought with their fists, instead of their tongues, to see who should have the decision of the court; and, if the judge's decision was unsatisfactory, then the judge fought with the council. How I should enjoy witnessing such a tussle in the San Francisco Probate

Court! I may live to see it. We've got back the whipping-post. No telling what the next revolution of the wheel will bring forth.

Before the readers of this book condemn, because I have written so bitterly, let them pause and consider what I have suffered at the hands of the law and its manipulators; what a furnace of white heat I have passed through by having my substance stolen from me. If my house is consumed by flames, I call it burning; if my friend accidentally gets under water, and is suffocated, I call it drowning; if I am despoiled of my substance, I call it stealing. You may indulge in a more refined *sobriquet:* I don't. These law-protected thieves have reduced me to the condition of a beggar and an emigrant — with all its attendant horrors; they have made out my husband a PAUPER — when he died a rich man. I marvel that a man of his personal pride can rest in his grave under such a vile stigma. I should think he would rise up in his cerements, and lay his cold hands, in a withering blight, upon their guilty heads.

Against the combined power of executors, creditors, lawyers, judges, and courts, I cry out. This adamantine combination is what causes the financial and moral ruin of so many widows and orphans. These human vultures are leagued together to get every farthing they can lay hold of. I cannot express my loathing of such criminal proceedings and practices in words that convey half I feel upon this subject. I hate them with a perfect hatred; and pray for more height, and depth, and length, and breadth of capacity, with which to hate them. I hurl against them the anathemas of outraged womanhood; the scorn of a soul too white to take a bribe; the groans of the millions that they have scorched with the fires of ruin, and blasted with the simoom of despair.

Tamerlane asked for one hundred and sixty thousand skulls, with which to build a pyramid to his honor. He got the skulls, and built the pyramid but, if the bones of all those who have fallen a prey to Probate confiscation could be piled up, they would make a monster pyramid. Talk not of Waterloo and Austerlitz: they were not fields of blood compared with this great Golgotha.

Upon the Probate altar, smeared with blood and tears, burn day by day the fortunes and hopes of widows and orphans, — a ghastly holocaust, — and, when they are allowed to gather up the fragments, the flame is spent — there remains nothing but ashes. I have endeavored, in these pages, to spread before my readers the cruelty, the woes, the terrors, the anguish, the perdition, of this evil, hoping thereby to rouse them to a true sense of the unspeakable injustice of the Probate Court.

My prayer is, that for the bitter drops moneyed-might, sex-might, and law-might press into my cup, I may have strength to drink them to the dregs, — without flinching, — and then have strength enough remaining to hurl the empty cup, with my fiercest denunciation and deathless defiance, into the face of such shameless injustice. And I further pray, morning, noon, and night, to Christ, who hung upon the cross to atone for the sins of a lost world, that he will bring swift retribution upon the heads of all those who directly or indirectly rob the widow and the orphan. My curse — *a widow's curse* — is upon them. May poverty and pestilence overtake them; may their dreams be haunted with the glare of dead men's eyes, and the icy touch of dead men's fingers, whose widows and orphans they have plundered or debauched; may their days on earth be short, and filled with all disaster; and when death clutches them with too firm a grasp to be shaken off, and they are compelled to leave their ill-gotten spoils, may they have a *scorcher* prepared for them down below, with the ghosts of avenging widows to pile on the fagots, and heap up the brimstone!

REVIEWS BY THE PRESS

EXTRACTS

FROM

REVIEWS BY THE PRESS

["Evening Post," San Francisco.]

WITH the keenness of a cimeter blade Mrs. Stow dissects the incongruities and useless formalities that for centuries have cumbered the practice of courts, and many of which have no further reason for their existence than that the dust of ages has sanctified them. Her experience but confirms the oft-repeated maxim that "*law is a dear luxury*." She certainly makes a strong *prima facie* case of personal disappointment, delay, and mental suffering. And who shall say that even as the private wrongs of an oppressed subject, when told in the public market-place, have formed the battle-cry of revolution that has overturned reigning dynasties, the recital of her story may not reach the popular heart, and, by enlisting sympathy, result in more discriminating legislation?

["Daily Examiner," San Francisco.]

Mrs. Stow makes a savage attack on the present Probate Court system, which may be entirely justifiable; but with the wrongs of the lady author it is not our purpose now to deal. From the manifestations of intellectual vigor disclosed in the volume, we are inclined to believe that she can well maintain her own rights, or avenge her own wrongs. She has undertaken — as it appears from a circular — to raise, by subscription, the net proceeds of lectures, readings, and the sale of her books, "*Probate Confiscation*" and "*Little Etta's Frontier Life*," the sum of $25,000 to establish HORTICULTURAL COLLEGES FOR WOMEN. She hopes to secure that amount by the spring of 1880; at which time, if her expectations are realized, she intends to establish the initial school. She is most anxious to open up this beautiful branch of industry in the United States to women. She found, while travelling in Europe in 1874, that it was largely in their hands, both on the Continent and in the United Kingdom, particularly floriculture. It is in all its varied departments an avocation admirably fitted to women. There is perfect harmony between it and them. It is healthful and remunerative.

The undertaking in which this energetic and talented lady has engaged is a most deserving one, and we wish her eminent success in her efforts to ameliorate the present condition of her sex.

["Sunday Chronicle," San Francisco.]

Mrs. Stow makes an indignant protest against the probate laws of the State. Her book contains an account of the death of her husband, her efforts to obtain her allowance, her conversations with lawyers, and her many grievances and privations. The style of the work is entertaining, and it affords considerable lively reading.

["Morning Call," San Francisco.]

The book is of more than ordinary merit.

["Daily News," Oakland, Cal.]

"*Probate Confiscation*" is the title of a work laid upon our table by the author, Mrs. J. W. Stow. No man was more widely known, or more highly spoken of, than her husband; and the announcement of his death caused universal sorrow. It was believed by all his friends that he had a very valuable estate; but the report of the executors to the probate judge discloses the fact that he was insolvent. His widow, in trying to save something for herself from the estate, has been initiated into the wonderful mysteries of the Probate Court. She gives her opinions boldly, and without mincing her words, of the disgrace to the present age of such a corrupt system. Her arguments in behalf of a change in the probate laws will be hard to answer, and should be read by all. Her treatment has been simply outrageous, and done under the color of law makes it harder to bear. We hope she will succeed in so changing the laws that are made to protect widows and orphans, that no such case as she portrays will ever be heard of in the State again. To get an estate to administer upon is equal to a bonanza. We say to all, Read this book, and learn what probate confiscation means.

["Evening Express," Los Angeles, Cal.]

Mrs. Stow addresses herself mainly to the operation of the law in regard to widows, and cites instances where the whole substance of estates has been swallowed up by post-mortem litigation, and where the red-tape circumlocution, tedious delays, and extraordinary expenses, have left nothing for the support of the widow and orphans. Everybody who is at all conversant with the machinery of our Probate Courts knows that they are cumbersome and exhaustive, and that great wrongs are inflicted on survivors by the slow process of winding up the estates of deceased persons. It would be to the credit of the State if California should reform the abuses complained of; and if Mrs. Stow can, in her crusade, contribute to this reformation, she will have the good wishes of all right-thinking people.

["New North-West," Portland, Or.]

Probate Confiscation, as the title indicates, shows up in scathing terms the property laws of California, and the gross injustice to which they subject woman. Women who wish to understand what every woman should understand — the laws that most nearly concern their personal interest — should have a copy of this book.

["The Daily Bee," Sacramento, March 31, 1877.]

New York journals of a recent date give some notable instances of the outrageous manner in which the estates of deceased persons are not unfrequently plundered and squandered under the present probate system, and the families of the deceased wantonly robbed by harpies acting under the authority and cognizance of probate courts and probate laws. A man named Taylor died, leaving property worth over two millions of dollars, with liabilities amounting to about a quarter of a million of dollars. In less than five years the executors and other harpies, including a goodly number of the legal fraternity, made away with every dollar of the assets, and the wardrobe of the widow — which was very valuable — was sold at sheriff's sale, to satisfy an execution for money loaned her to supply her necessities while the legal hyenas were robbing her under cover of law. Another man died, leaving property worth half a million, with scarcely any incumbrance, also a widow and children. The other day, after a lapse of about two years, the executor presented his accounts to the court, showing that he had managed his opportunities for stealing under the forms of law so well that only $180 was left to be distributed among the heirs. The abuses practised under the probate system of New York are liable to be practised in California, because the systems of the two States are practically identical. In fact, the system in all the States is nearly identical, and seems to have been framed with the express purpose of promoting litigation, and enabling parties to become rich by plundering the dead, and impoverishing the living.

In this State, a few years ago, a Mrs. J. W. Stow, as many others have been, was made the victim of unjust probate laws. Being a woman of pluck, energy, business capacity, and intelligence, she commenced a vigorous war upon the present pernicious system. She laid before the Legislature of this State a bill having for its object a law providing, that, upon the death of the husband or wife, one-half of the entire community property — without administration — belongs to the surviving husband or wife, together with the home and all pertaining thereto, and the other half to their children, the issue of their marriage; but if there are no children the entire property belongs to the survivor; also, that the survivor shall have the sole management, care, control, and disposition of said community property, as a surviving partner has the sole power to settle the affairs of a co-partnership at the death of one of the partners. In furtherance of her ideas she presented an address to the Legislature, and also published a book upon the subject. The volume which is now before us is filled with powerful arguments in support of her views, and seems to thoroughly demonstrate the correctness of her position. We understand that she is about issuing from the press of Boston a new and revised edition of the valuable work. If by her efforts she succeeds in obtaining a much-needed reform of the probate laws of the land, Mrs. Stow will achieve a greater good for man and woman than has been or is proposed to be achieved by any of the army of social and political reformers now displaying their banners in the field of progress and advancement.

["Boston Daily Globe."]

"Probate Confiscation" is an earnest protest against the present system of law by which the administration of dead men's estates is made fruitful in injury to widows and fatherless children entitled to the property. The narration of the author's personal experience gives interest and emphasis to the recital of these defects in the probate law; and it will be impossible to read her story without sympathizing with her efforts to ameliorate the condition of women who are thus left at the mercy of its apparently inequitable provision. Incidently, the whole system of marriage is considered in its bearings upon women, both in regard to their property and their feelings. The right to vote is also earnestly maintained, and the exposition of the condition of the sex under present social and legal relations is vividly portrayed. It is not surprising, perhaps, in view of the author's experience, that her book is so full of passionate protests against abuses. Its graphic record of personal wrongs is well calculated to excite public interest, which its very vehemence will tend to intensify.

["Evening Transcript," Boston.]

It is a comfort in these days, when there is so much that is commonplace and tedious in the line of literary issues, to meet with something which bears evidence of having been written with a purpose, whose words come hot from the heart, as it were, and retain their heat after being placed on paper. Such a book is "Probate Confiscation," whose author, Mrs. J. W. Stow, is well known to many of our best citizens. She was the wife of Joseph W. Stow, a wealthy resident of San Francisco, who died while she was on a visit abroad. On her return she found herself literally penniless. The estate had gone into the hands of lawyers and executors, and her separate property was tangled up with it. The Probate Court after a long time granted her a small sum of money, to be paid monthly for a single year. Although Mr. Stow was supposed to be very wealthy, his estate was declared insolvent: Mrs. Stow believed differently. Her treatment, and the treatment of other widows, by the Probate Court, roused her indignation; and in the present work she has shown the weak points of probate law, and the rank injustice which is often done to those who are left, like herself, dependent upon its provisions. Many readers of the book will undoubtedly condemn it for its scathing language, and the relentless manner in which she pillories lawyers and judges, dishonest executors and creditors, in its pages. But one can hardly wonder at these characteristics of her work, after hearing her story. She feels that her rights as a woman and wife were outraged, and that it was done under cover and protection of law.

["Boston Herald."]

"Probate Confiscation," by Mrs. J. W. Stow of San Francisco, is the title of a handsome volume which has been written with the noble purpose of bringing prominently before the public the unjust laws which govern women. The author has had, judging from her story, a hard and bitter experience in the Probate Court of San Francisco; and the injustice which she has experienced has prompted her to expose the faults of a system by which she has been grievously wronged. The book is sold only by the author, price $2; and orders addressed to Mrs. J. W. Stow, New-York City, or to her printers, Rand, Avery, & Co., Boston, Mass., will be promptly answered.

["The Commonwealth," Boston.]

Mrs. Stow writes with an energy and indignation, pouring out a lava-flood of denunciation, sarcasm, and reproach, upon the Probate-Court officials, the lawyers in its interest, and other participants, as they came to her knowledge in San Francisco, where her husband's affairs had to pass in review after his decease. Mrs. Stow seems to compass, with a woman's intuition, all the difficulties which surround one of her sex without money or friends, caused by such a dilemma as that of suddenly losing a husband and fortune. She was made to bitterly feel her humiliation in claiming what belonged to her. She was badgered, condemned, harassed, put off, seeing her husband s estate diminishing and fritted away, until her soul overrun in this scathing exposure of ill-treatment. Those who think women have no reason to claim a share in the government should read such a work as "Probate Confiscation." They will get new light, and begin to feel that they have indeed some interest in the proper making and execution of the laws.

["Daily Evening Traveller," Boston.]

"Probate Confiscation; Unjust Laws which Govern Woman," is a volume evidently from the pen of an aroused woman, — a woman who feels that an outrage, or a series of outrages, has been committed upon her. She is to be feared, and, moreover, to be respected, like the woman of the poem who was spurned. The author, Mrs. J. W. Stow, has taken an advanced station as a lecturer upon social topics, mainly connected with the unjust and restrictive laws concerning property-holding. She is bitterly in earnest, and feels equally strongly the wrongs done her own sex and herself. Individual injustice, of course, caused the book's conception, and is the guiding principle which makes the lady's life-work as is set forth. The volume is crammed full of truth, and, to a just man, altogether unpalatable truth. In her preface, the author gives the reasons for her entering upon the war against the injustice of probate laws in this country, especially in California, where her personal grievances were experienced. She points out that the widow is protected by the law less than most criminals; that courts of justice, as far as widows are concerned, are worse than the "circumlocution-office;" that the judges, lawyers, and executors are more than often only the "Barnacles" who live on the plunder or "expenses" which are wrung out of the widow and the fatherless. Widows are treated as rebels are in time of rebellion. Confiscation is often the lot of both. The running account of her own trials and troubles after the death of her husband, the natural and passionately indignant comments on the manner in which she was treated, citation of like examples of unjust legislation, and depiction of the manner in which a woman is too frequently treated in court and in public, make up the volume's contents. We imagine that a quieter temper, less open and avowed and hearty indignation, would have given the work more influence in some places and upon some minds; but Mrs. Stow's writings are marked by so much honesty and so much vigor, that a jesuitical or politic course would seem unnatural. She goes to the root of matters, as far as her experience shows her the way; and when she has a hard name to call she does not mince matters, but "speaks right out." The work is an engine, an instrument in a crusade which the author has undertaken, — a war which she opens single-handed, but in which she is sure to be soon surrounded with earnest followers. The volume deserves to be read; for it touches upon subjects which ought to lie close to the heart of every father and mother, every husband and wife, in the land. No loving father wishes to leave his children unprovided for and homeless; no loving husband, his wife to be worried to death in the courts, appealing and begging for what no one, not even judges, denies to be her honest right. It has been a pleasure to read a book with such snap and point to it, and all who take it up will probably agree with us.

["Daily Post," Boston.]

Mrs. J. W. Stow of San Francisco, Cal., has written and published a work on probate law, which should be carefully read, for it touches upon a vital question, — the rights of the widow and the fatherless. The *exposé* of iniquities practised under cover of law is vividly portrayed in the pages of "Probate Confiscation." Mrs. Stow proposes to visit every State in the Union, with the determination to enlighten public opinion upon the necessity of a revision of the entire probate system, as far as it relates to widows' estates left by their deceased husbands. Whatever good she may be able to accomplish, in her warfare against injustice, will be a godsend to those who would otherwise suffer under probate absorption, as she has suffered.

["Woman's Journal," Boston, Mass.]

The book is an indignant protest against, and exposure of, the Probate-Court system, and of the special court through which Mrs. Stow herself suffered gross injustice and wrong. The volume is almost fierce in its delineations and execrations of the probate system. The work has a decided value over and above the personal case of Mrs. Stow, which it details, because it calls attention to a great system of wrong which exists in every State, and which cannot bear the light of day. If every wronged widow had the ability to write a book, and give all the facts to the public, and the means to publish it, the very exposure would go far to correct existing abuses. Mrs. Stow has done a good service in this direction. The book should be widely read.

["Eastern Argus," Portland, Me.]

Among the many books that are written to please and entertain, with occasionally one to instruct, it is pleasant to find one written with a purpose by one who has suffered oppression and wrong, whose whole nature cries out against it, and who takes this method of righting what seems to her to be a wholly iniquitous and outrageous condition of things. Such a book is "Probate Confiscation." Some people may find fault with it, for the radical style in which it is written; but the work has the merit of frankness and sincere conviction, and of going directly to the point. It should be read to be appreciated.

["Portland Daily Advertiser," Me.]

Mrs. J. W. Stow of San Francisco has written and published a book entitled "Probate Confiscation," in which she brings forward and holds up to view the mischievous features of the system of law, by which the settling, by the Probate Court, of dead men's estates, is made to result in unnecessary hardship and wrong to those most interested, — the widow and children. Mrs. Stow had a bitter probate experience, which set her to thinking. She found plenty of other women suffering in the same way. She found that while a man losing his wife is allowed to manage the ruins of his home, with his and her property and children, as suits him best, — is not dragged through the Probate Courts, not obliged to see his property filched from him by any process of law, — at the same time a woman losing her husband loses also every thing; control of her home, property, children, — even of her unborn child, if her husband chooses to appoint a guardian for it in advance, — and is left quite at the mercy of strangers, who are either coldly indifferent or selfishly interested. She found, too, that, where there are half-orphans, it is only in case of maternal rights that an overwhelming anxiety seizes upon legislators. They take precautions for the children against the mother, which are not considered necessary against the father.

Mrs. Stow believes that marriage should be an equal civil contract, and equally binding on both parties; that the common property should belong as much to the one as the other; that a man should deal as honestly and openly with his wife as with his business partner; and that there can never be true harmony or friendship between husband and wife, so long as one is made by law dependent on the whim of the other in life and after death. Many a woman has found the rule of a living master hard enough to bear, even though a living master may be softened by the humility, tenderness, and faithfulness of his subject. But harder still, in many unvoiced instances, has she found the reign of a dead ruler, whom no tears nor prayers nor deserving can win or conciliate, or prevail upon. To impress these things on the public mind, to draw attention to these and kindred hardships under which women suffer under the law, Mrs. Stow has written her book, and inaugurated a single-handed crusade against a sex-despotism, which is deserving all praise. May a merited success crown her efforts!

["The Daily Patriot," Concord, N.H.]

"Probate Confiscation" is a book written with a purpose, as its title would indicate, by one who has suffered oppression and wrong, and who, having failed to receive redress in the courts, has appealed to the public, hoping to effect a reform which will enable others who may be similarly situated to escape her sad experience. She claims that the laws affecting the family relations should be as familiar to every one as household words; that an unjustifiable ignorance is the cause of the present legal status of wives and widows. Her lively book will certainly awaken thought and discussion upon the subject. She makes a stirring appeal for the protection of the widow and the fatherless; and all right-minded people must sympathize with her earnest effort in their behalf. The book is sold only by subscription, and by the author herself. Mrs. Stow comes to us as a brave, courageous woman of high respectability, and will be cordially welcomed by every true friend of the sex.

["Free Press and Times," Burlington, Vt.]

Mrs. J. W. Stow, author of "Probate Confiscation," has undertaken to procure a change of the probate laws of every State in the Union, and of the laws affecting the property of women generally. Her book is written with a very free pen, and is typographically a very handsome volume. She is canvassing for it in person; her object being not only to support herself, but to procure a fund for establishing horticultural colleges for women. The list of subscribers to her work contains the names of many distinguished philanthropists, literary gentlemen, legislators, and private citizens, in other States; and she will doubtless add many to the number in Vermont.

["Hartford Daily Courant," Conn.]

Mrs. J. W. Stow of San Francisco, Cal., has written and published a book on the inequalities of probate law

Her purpose is, broadly, to improve the condition of woman in respect to property rights; and in this she will have the sympathy of all right-minded men. When a man and woman together accumulate property, he by labor outdoors and she by equally necessary labor and care of house and family, there is no reason why the wife should not have an equal voice in disposing of it. The agitation of the whole subject is of great importance; and one who brings hidden truths to light should be sustained and encouraged in the laudable effort. Mrs. Stow has also another object. She hopes, from the sale of her lively book, subscriptions, and donations, to raise money to establish colleges of horticulture for women. Both are praiseworthy, — one to give women more protection in law, the other to give them a new and congenial employment.

["Evening Post," Hartford, Conn.]

Mrs. Stow appears in defence of a grand principle. "Probate Confiscation" is a work of merit and value, and it has an important mission in the world.

["Daily Journal," Providence, R.I.]

We have received from the author, Mrs. J. W. Stow, "Probate Confiscation," second edition, revised and enlarged. It is a book which claims careful consideration. If Mrs. Stow writes in strong, plain language, she seems to be justified by her fruitless efforts to obtain, under the sanction of the laws, that portion of her husband's estate which belonged to her at the time of her marriage, and that fair and equitable allotment in the distribution of his separate property which should belong to her after his death. Her case is certainly a hard one; and her book clearly demonstrates, that, in the present administration of justice, woman has not always an equitable share. If the laws are founded in charity as well as wisdom, their execution should be made to agree with individual as well as public rights.

["The Providence Press," R.I.]

Mrs. Stow is the widow of a San Francisco gentleman of wealth, who, while upon his death-bed and in the absence of his wife in Europe, made disposition of the joint property of both. *Prima facie* it was an unjust will, and such as Mr. Stow in health, and surrounded by his family, would not have made. Through great trials and perplexities the widow arrived at her home in San Francisco, to find her affairs in the hands of the Probate Court, with executors inimical to her interests. The court knew no mercy; it only knew *law;* and the widow was forced by the injustice which she suffered to examine the whole subject of estates and probates from both a legal and equitable view. Mrs. Stow is smart enough to do the whole subject justice, fearless enough to tell the whole truth, and has suffered enough to make her arraignment of the laws and processes of probate stinging and terrible. It is one of the severest arraignments we ever read.

We have long been of the opinion that this whole chain of laws and processes for the settlement of estates of deceased persons is a relic of barbarism; that it had its source in the theocratic government of Judaism, which denied woman — mothers, sisters, wives, and daughters — all rights except the mere right to live without being murdered. While the progress of society has been marked in many respects, and woman in the social sphere has arisen to her proper dignity and crowning, yet in legal rights she has advanced but little. The laws are against her; and there *is* force in the argument that it is because she has no voice in the making of laws to which she must submit, and by which she is often abused and oppressed. If women could assist in the making of the probate laws, especially, there would be less suffering of widows, less separation of families, and less of unwelcome guardianship of orphans whose mothers are by nature and the laws of God their natural guardians. The law stands, in many cases, for the rankest injustice. At the death of a husband, the joint family property is ruled, controlled, taxed, wasted, and made a legal plaything for courts and interested parties to deplete "according to law." The probate business, and the law which governs it in our own State, need revision badly. If Mrs. Stow can awaken an interest in this subject by her book, we bid her God speed.

DEC. 19, 1877.

AN ACT

FOR

THE PROTECTION OF WIDOWS,

AND

COMPARATIVE LAW.

BY MRS. J. W. STOW.

SECTION 1. That, in all marriages hereafter contracted, life and property shall enter into the union, unless the latter is protected by special contract; and the joint estate thus formed, together with the added accumulations during wedlock, shall be known as common property. Separate estates protected by ante-nuptial contracts, legacies, gifts, and bequests, shall constitute the private property of each, which shall be exempt from the debts, crimes, or torts of the other.

SECT. 2. At the death of either husband or wife, the survivor shall actually own — after the payment of all debts — half of the common property, and enjoy the use of the other half during life, unless a re-marriage takes place. In that event the estate shall be divided, one-half going to the children, or other heirs-at-law where there are no children, unless otherwise ordained by the testator. No testament placed over the common property, by the deceased, shall take effect until after the death of the surviving partner, if he or she remain single.

SECT. 3. All debts or claims against the joint estate shall be settled by the survivor, subject to the same law which regulates a copartnership existing between two persons when one of them dies.

SECT. 4. Fathers and mothers shall have equal rights of succession to the property of their own unmarried children who die intestate.

SECT. 5. Only in case of separation shall each claim all of his or her separate property and an equal share of the joint estate accumulated during wedlock.

SECT. 6. The survivor shall have the sole guardianship of his or her own children.

SECT. 7. A homestead not exceeding the value of a thousand dollars, created from the unembarrassed common fund, shall belong to the survivor, exempt from all claims made by creditors, with the exception of a mortgagee.

I MAINTAIN that women earn money in wedlock. No city husband would like to exchange his position as the "money-getter" for the never-ending cares of the household. Placing the wife in the light of a companion, or superintendent only, still, I say, she earns money in excess of her board and clothes. It is an absurd idea that a wife is supported by the husband. His feeding and clothing her is but a fraction of what is hers by right. I cannot find a lady companion, who is my peer in education and social position, who will perform her duties faithfully for simply her board and clothes; and that is all a wife gets. True, a widow gets a miserable third; but every wife is not sure of being a widow. Numbers of noble men say to me, "I have willed every thing to my wife. If she does not do right by her children, who will?" And when I say, "But if she dies first she cannot will away any of the property which she has helped to earn, — a pewter spoon nor an iron toasting-fork," — they answer, "I know it; and it is a legal outrage that she is thus deprived of her rights."

The wife of a farmer works harder, and many more hours, than he does; and she makes the butter and cheese, and raises the poultry, which brings in the ready money; and yet at his death she has, by law, only the *use* of a starvation third of the farm. She cannot sell it, and make herself comfortable in her old age. To be sure, her husband, Smith, may will her the use of the entire farm if she does not marry Jones; but if she does (Smith detests Jones) she shall be cut off with nothing, for in that case she forfeits her "thirds." This is a wise law, made by wise men, for the "*protection*" of unwise women. Then, as superintendent of the household: I know men-superintendents who get all the way from two hundred to two thousand dollars a month for services not half as onerous as a wife's often are. Her duties are priceless. No money value can be set upon them. Therefore, I say, she ought to have the conceded right to devise half of the estate gathered during coverture, this testament to take effect at the re-marriage or death of her widower. This is simple, even-handed justice. The home and property should no more be broken up when a husband dies out of it than when a wife dies out of it. The loss of the husband and father is grief enough without the added loss of home and fortune.

But it is said, "If a wife is to legally own half of

the accumulations of wedlock, there will have to be an appraisement of property before marriage." True; and a wiser thing could not happen. This would give lovers pause, who frantically fall in love one day, marry the next, and divorce the day after. A financial deception on either side is a mighty love-cooler. An ante-nuptial inventory would save a world of heart-burnings and divorce-suits; for "Look before you leap" is not proverbial of the youthful American in the first — or second, as to that matter — gush of the divine afflatus. Such a law would give to wives a feeling of security which is above price.

It is, or should be, a very humiliating thing to a woman who has earned all the way from fifty to five hundred dollars a month, by her ability, talents, or accomplishments, to find after marriage that she is leading the life of a pauper, as the law has it, in being "*supported*" by her husband, and that she has to beg for every thing she has like a mendicant. Any system that should place a man, arrived at the maturity of his bodily and mental powers, in such a state of subjection, and should bind him, moreover, to hard labor for a mere maintenance, would be reckoned a monstrous tyranny.

What is the origin of this subjection, this labor without pay? In what soil is hidden the root of this flourishing tree? If we search with the lighted candle of truth, we shall find it in the substratum of barbarism; in the ownership of wives; in might, not right; in the power of the strong over the weak.

Going back to the earliest twilight of human society, we find that wives were first won by capture, and subjugated with a bludgeon. They were then simply beasts of burden to their masters; and, as prisoners of war, women were held as slaves until ransomed, or wived, — which was but another form of slavery. Then came the period of purchase, when fathers knocked down their daughters — and their wives too, if they could find purchasers — to the highest bidder. A man in purchasing a woman for a wife knew that he was acquiring a creature far more valuable, in a material sense, than an ordinary slave. Still he grumbled angrily at the social innovation which wrested from him his natural title to any woman whom he was strong enough to seize and keep. The symbol of the husband's domestic rule was a shoe; and, in token of the transfer of authority over the bride, it was customary for the father to present the groom with that ensign of power, on the receipt of which he became the absolute owner of the woman he had wed. She was as much his property as his dog or his horse. No one can fail to see the appropriateness of the symbol, when used to mark the transfer of degrading power over a human creature. The covering of the foot was the instrument with which a victor demonstrated the subjugation of a fallen foe.

Leading on came the era of infantile wedlock, when babes and sucklings were mated in the cradle, ringed in the nursery, and brought to the church-porch with lollipops in their mouths. And the worst feature of all this was, that when they had grown up into men and women they were powerless to free themselves from these frightful bonds. Both Church and State, in the quintessence of all wisdom, protected, or refused to annul, these disastrous nuptials; thus obliging the participants to dwell together in perpetual discord (for they were rarely well mated), or to drag out a miserable life of celibacy.

In feudal England women were condemned to the perpetual tutelage of parents, husband, or guardian. A sex created to labor and obey were never supposed to have attained the age of reason and experience. They were classed with children, criminals, and idiots, before the law then, as they are to-day. The old common law gave the husband a right to govern the wife with stripes and imprisonment, while the civil law permitted him to beat her with a stick the size and thickness of his thumb.

Investigators who have studied that vaunted period called "the age of chivalry," in the court-records and law-books, tell us that respect for woman is a thing of which those records show no trace. In the age of chivalry the widow and the fatherless were regarded by lords, knights, and parsons as legitimate objects of plunder; and woe to the widow who prosecuted the murderers of her husband or the ravagers of her estate! The homage which the law paid to women consisted in burning them alive for the offences which brought upon men the painless death of hanging.

Tracing carefully this slowly-ascending scale, we arrive at "The Mayflower," and note its curious official record, which forcibly illustrates the value set upon women by the Pilgrim Fathers. In this record we find so many men, fifty adults, eighteen of whom are marked with a star. Those stars represent the women, our foremothers; and, in spite of the meagre record, they proved themselves stars of the first magnitude. But the first mention of women is made in connection with clean shirts for men. The witty chronicler — brevity being the soul of wit — saith, "And the women went on shore to wash, of which there was much need."

Mind you, this was after the ship had cast anchor in the harbor-bay. Not a word is spoken about their kindly ministrations during the tempest-tossed voyage: which, to my way of thinking, was an unpardonable oversight; for of all domesticated animals man is the most exacting, unreasonable, and unmanageable, when suffering from sea-sickness.

Up to a comparatively recent date, the common law has been the governing principle of all English-speaking peoples. All statutory law is imperfect and complicated, being made up of patchwork and shreds, oftentimes by culpably ignorant legislators, whose energies would have been better conserved in making bricks instead of laws.

To fortify my position, I will quote from Gov Hubbard's "message" to the Legislature of Connecticut in 1877. He says, "The old common law assumed the subjugation of the wife, and stripped her of the better part of her rights of person, and nearly all her rights of property. It is a matter of astonishment, that Christian nations should have been willing, for eighteen centuries, to hold the mothers of their race in a condition of legal servitude. It has been the scandal of jurisprudence. The property-relations of husband and wife do not to-day rest on any just or harmonious system. Not only has the husband absolute disposal of all his own property, freed from all dower-rights, but he is practically the owner during coverture of all his wife's estate not specially limited to her separate use; and, after her death, has, in every case, a life-use in all her personal, and, in most cases, in all her real property, by a title which the wife, no matter what may have been his ill-deserts, is powerless to impair or defeat: whereas, on the other hand, the wife has, during her husband's life, no more power of her own right to sell, convey, or manage her own estate, than if she were a lunatic or slave; and, in case of his death, has a life-use in only one third part of the real estate of which he dies possessed, and no indefensible title whatever in any of his personal estate. As a consequence, a husband may strip his wife, by mere voluntary disposition to strangers, of all claim on his estate after his death, and thus add beggary to widowhood."

Stirred up by the governor's message to a partial sense of the injustice to wives, the Connecticut Legislature passed an "act" for the protection of the separate property and the earnings (outside of the domestic relations) of the wife, before the close of the session. But this "act" does not protect the wife's *earnings* in any true sense; for whatever she earns in the service of the husband belongs to him absolutely. Few wives earn money other than as the servant of the husband. A slave's services no more belong to his master than a wife's do to her husband, in all labor pertaining to the household. She marries at maturity, and spends the prime of her life in accumulating a fortune in which she owns not a farthing legally if the husband survives her. At the risk of life and health, she bears his children. Over those children she has no legal control. The father's power is as absolute as though she were dead. She works more hours a day than the hired servant; and, were that labor recompensed as the labor of single women is recompensed, it would insure her a handsome support for her old age. Yet the law offers her no pretence, even, of such a recompense; forgetting the old maxim, that "the laborer is worthy of his hire." There is not a State in the Union where a woman, as wife, earns money in the domestic service of her own household. What a shame! This is an unpruned, vigorous branch of the old common law. Get out the pruning-hook of progress, and lop it off. It has outlived its day. Away with it!

In Continental Europe the hideous barbarity of the old common law has long since disappeared. In the

Northern countries, — Iceland and Denmark, Norway and Sweden, — it never had any lasting power. They were less affected by Roman or canon law than either Germany or France; and owing to an immobility of customs, which seems inherent in the North, their laws have undergone no considerable change since the tenth century. It is refreshing to observe, that, at a very early period in the North, the position of woman conformed in more than one relation to many of the requirements of modern reformers. She had a legal right to her own person and property; while in Scotland, in the last quarter of the nineteenth century, it is the *first* principle of law, that a married woman has no existence therein. In regard to survivorship, there was no aristocracy of sex. A widow became the sole manager of the community-property, and guardian of the children.

A German wife, under the most usual marriage-law, — the community system, where life and property both enter into the union, — has equal rights with her husband over the property of both, irrespective of its nature; and she is nearly equal with him as regards succession. At the death of either, the survivor succeeds to half the common fund, and has the use of the other half for life. In every way a German wife enjoys a much greater equality in *property rights* with her husband than a wife does in England or in the United States. The old feudal preference for males has been nearly obliterated, excepting in the noble and peasant lines, where it still gives a *couleur de rose* to legal transactions.

Under the Roman dotal system, as it exists in Germany, at marriage each makes the other a bridal gift, from his or her property, known as dowry and nuptial donation. In case of neglect or desertion, the wife can demand maintenance from both; and, if the husband becomes bankrupt, she is still entitled to both, free from all claims made by creditors. How much more humane this law is than one that permits real or *imaginary* creditors to swoop down like vultures, and carry off every thing in their legal talons, while the widow and babes are left to starve, or become objects of charity, as the probate system permits them to do, under certain conditions, in this our beloved land of freedom, progress, and enlightenment!

In France a husband can will but half of the legal community; and in case of separation the wife's claim on the general fund is superior to that of any mortgagee or creditor made subsequent to the marriage, for she has what is called a legal *hypothique* thereon. The funeral expenses she may incur for her husband are at the charge of his heirs, while *he* cannot charge the common fund. This rule is of Roman origin, where husbands are not bound to mourn for their wives. The reason for the French custom probably is, that mourning is less expensive to husbands than to wives; for, whilst a widower need only mourn for his wife six months, a widow must mourn for her husband thirteen and a half.

As widow, a French mother has full control of her

children's education: she alone can oppose or consent to their marriage; she has the use of their property, and can appoint them a guardian by will. A father cannot deprive a mother of the guardianship of her children. Compare this with our law, where a mother can in no case appoint a guardian by will, when the father is living; and where she can only act as guardian, if the husband has appointed no other, and she continues unmarried.

Here are the views of Col. T. W. Higginson on this subject, taken from "The Woman's Journal" of Nov. 24, 1877: "A Rhode-Island lady came to me in great indignation, the other day, asking if it was true, that, under Rhode-Island laws, a husband might by his last will bequeath his child away from its mother, so that she might, if the guardian chose, never see it again. I replied that it was undoubtedly true, and that such was the law in most of the States of the Union.

"'But,' she said, 'it is an outrage. The husband may have been one of the worst men in the world; he may have persecuted his wife and children; he may have made the will in a moment of anger, and have neglected to alter it. At any rate, he is dead, and the mother is living. The guardian whom he appointed may turn out a very malicious man, and may take pleasure in torturing the mother; or he may bring up the children in a way their mother thinks ruinous for them. Why do not all the mothers cry out against such a law?'

"'I wish they would,' I said. 'I have been trying a good many years to make them even understand what the law is; but they do not. People who do not vote pay no attention to the laws until they suffer from them.'" The actual text of the law is as follows: —

"Every person authorized to make a will, except married women, shall have a right to appoint by his will a guardian or guardians for his children during their minority" (Gen. Statutes R. I., chap. 154, § 1).

There is not associated with this, in the statutes, the slightest clause in favor of the mother, nor any thing which could limit the power of the guardian in respect to her, although he could in certain extreme cases be removed by the court, and another guardian appointed. There is not a line of positive law to protect her. Now, in a case of absolute wrong, a single sentence of law is worth all the chivalrous courtesy this side of the middle ages.

It is idle to say that such laws are not executed. They are executed. I have had letters, too agonizing to print, expressing the sufferings of mothers under laws like these. There lies before me a letter — not from Rhode Island — written by a widowed mother who suffers daily tortures, even while in possession of her child, at the knowledge that it is not legally hers, but held only by the permission of the guardian appointed under her husband's will. "I beg you," she says, "to take this will to the hill-top, and urge law-makers in our next Legislature to free the State record from the shameful story, that no mother can control her child unless it is born out of wedlock."

"From the moment," she says, "when the will was read to me, I have made no effort to set it aside. I wait till God reveals his plans, so far as my own condition is concerned. But out of my keen comprehension of this great wrong, notwithstanding my submission for myself, my whole soul is stirred, — for my child, who is a little woman; for all women, — that the laws may be changed which subject a true woman, a devoted wife, a faithful mother, to such mental agonies as I have endured, and shall endure till I die."

In a later letter she says, "I now have his [the guardian's] solemn promise that he will not remove her from my control. To some extent, my sufferings are allayed; and yet never, till she arrives at the age of twenty-one, shall I fully trust the word of her father's blood. I wish that mothers who dwell in sheltered and happy homes would try to bring to their minds the condition of a mother whose possession of her only child rests upon the 'promise' of a comparative stranger. We should then get beyond the meaningless cry, 'I have all the rights I want,' if mothers could only remember that among these rights, in most States of the Union, the right of a widowed mother to her child is not included."

How different all this is in France, and other Continental countries, where fathers and mothers share that control over their children which the law of force once assigned to the fathers alone; and which, alas! is still extant in both England and America. There are cases in this enlightened Christian federation, where widows are treated, under the cover of law, far more rigorously than criminals are. At the death of their husbands they are stripped of their fortune and the guardianship of their children; and yet this nation boasts of its civilization.

There is one point of law in which the French Code, and those that have been modelled upon it, stand in marked superiority to the laws of other countries that are still enamoured of traditional inequalities. This is in respect to *wills* and *succession*. All difference of privilege between the sexes was destroyed by the Revolution, and by its best fruit, the Code Napoléon.

In England a wife is still practically unable to make a will; and in this country, as we have shown, she cannot legally will away a hair-pin nor a tooth-pick unless she has purchased them with separate estate, or with money earned outside of the domestic relations. But it is expressly laid down in the Code, that a wife can make a will *without* the authorization of the husband; and, in case of intestate succession, there is no difference between sons and daughters, or between paternal and maternal ascendants.

Compare this with our law in some of the States, where, if an unmarried child dies intestate, his or her property ascends to its father; and if he be dead, then it goes in equal shares to its mother, brothers, and sisters. She who has borne and reared the child has a fraction with the *other* children. This equitable law ought to court and wed a widow's SUBLIME THIRDS!

The Italian Code follows closely those principles of natural justice which were the offspring of the French Revolution, and the glory of its Code. An Italian wife is an independent woman in a business point of view. She can validly make creditors and contracts on her own account, independent of judicial or marital control; and, with regard to survivorship, there remains no stigma of sex distinction in the Italian Code.

The present legal status of women in Italy is most encouraging; for, before the Code was made, they occupied generally in the peninsula a very low position. But, now that the legal cerements are cast off, a new life of useful activity invites them onward.

"The best criterion of the condition of nations is their written laws."

Thus we find that Continental countries enjoying the highest civilization have erased from their laws the rude relics of antiquity, and adjusted the legal status of wives and widows in regard to property, so it compares favorably with the general enlightenment of the age, leaving England and the United States far behind in this respect. For the condition of women in English law is worse than it is in any other portion of Europe; while with us, whether legally or socially, there is one law for men, and another for women. The principles of law are the same in the two countries, and thus they will remain until men have the courage to arraign all effete customs and hereditary barbarisms at the bar of liberty.

The legal inferiority of women does not result from any law of nature, or from any inherent necessity of things: it is simply a legislative creation, and capable, therefore, of legislative alteration. For the disabilities of one country are restricted or absent in another; and the comparison of different countries gives us not only a practical ideal for the possible range of our reforms, but a refuge as well from those taunts of Utopianism which are often so potent a weapon in the hands of the indifferent or uninstructed.

In the States that were first settled by Continental immigration, we find a much larger liberality accorded to wives and widows, in property rights, under the law. A California widow gets – if it is not stolen from her by executors and courts — half of the property both real and personal where there are children; and where there are none she becomes the first heir of the husband's estate, and gets another fourth, that is, if he died intestate. And the same equality of rights in the common property is maintained in some of the Western States. A widow is not turned out of doors at the end of forty days on a starvation "*third.*" Still there is no intrinsic justice here; for, if a wife dies, she cannot devise a sixpence out of her half that will stand the white-heat of the crucible of law made by chivalric man for her protection. In the State of Louisiana, there is a just and equal rule of succession between husband and wife; the fundamental idea being that of the settlement of the affairs of a business firm upon the death of one of the partners. The capital originally contributed to the general stock by the respective parties goes back to the one, or the heirs of the one, from whence it came. Unless otherwise provided by agreement before marriage, the husband has no preference over the wife in the remainder of the estate, called the *acquests*, and consisting of property acquired during the marriage from the earnings of the joint labor or capital of husband and wife. This property is treated as the profits of a partnership between equals, and not, as at common law, as the sole estate of a male superior. We look in vain through the various tinkering statutes of States settled from Anglo-Saxon sources to find any such fair and frank recognition of the wife's equal services with the husband in accumulating an estate.

At the death of a husband, he can by will place executors over the entire estate gathered in wedlock. If he desires it, these executors can act without bonds. This of itself is a crime of the first magnitude; for it corrupts society. Some men cannot bear temptations. How many thieves in high places could trace their initiation to the threshold of dead men's estates if they chose to do so! How often the latent spark of dishonesty is kindled into a flame, when the opportunity is offered, the invitation given, to rob the widow and the fatherless! Partners in business will be honest with each other — sometimes; but how is it when one of them dies? One example shall answer this question, although thousands could be added to it.

A California gentleman, possessed of a large fortune, on the eve of a business visit to Mexico, made his two partners the executors of his will without bonds. Several months later, news came that the man had been shot as a spy. It was during some intestine outbreak in that chaotic country. Then the probating commenced, and continued until his family were utterly beggared. Suddenly, without an instant's warning, he, the dead man, — his mausoleum had been a prison, — shot like a comet athwart the path of his dear bondless partners and bosom-friends! There was consternation, some hurried explanations, and then a great *hush;* for it was in the upper stratum of society. But the penniless widow blossomed into a millionnaire's wife; "*and all the world wondered!*"

Kind husbands make their wives the sole executors of their wills without bonds, and create them guardians of their children. *Create a mother the guardian of her offspring!* WHAT A CREATION! The six-days' creation, rib and all, could not hold a candle to it. But this is no excuse for the cruel and unjust law which wrests these natural God-given rights from a mother who has been cursed all her life by an unkind husband. Laws should be protective and general, not optional and exceptional.

During the present year (1877) I have visited the leading cities in every State in New England, and talked with thousands of people upon the subject of "Probate Confiscation" and the inequalities of the laws generally. Everywhere from Maine to Rhode Island I met brave, just men who sympathized with me in my work. Everywhere, even in Boston, I met men who said, "Our laws are perfect as regards property. Women are treated far more liberally than men are," &c. I believe they are honest in their convictions, and that from their stand-point all looks fair. Still, although they have fashioned women's legal garment so deftly, so cunningly, she can exclaim with Paulus Emilius, who, being asked why he put away his wife for no visible reason, replied, "This shoo" (holding out his foot) "is a neat shoo, a new shoo; and yet none of you know where it *wrings* me."

A wife to-day, in every State in the Union, if she owns no separate property, and earns none outside of the domestic relation, is in the same financial condition that the captured or purchased wives were in the dark ages; that is, if the husband survives her. Widowhood is her only reprieve. If she has labored five years or forty, if she has borne one child or a dozen, if the property accumulated during coverture be of the value of two dollars or of two millions, it is all the same. At her death she cannot will away a farthing of it, nor make a lawful distribution of personal apparel or jewels; she cannot place a guardian over her minor children. Is a slave required to do more for his master without pay than all good wives — and the majority of them are good — do for their husbands and families without pay? A wife works all her life for board and clothes. This is the only kind of an apprenticeship which lasts a lifetime.

In speaking of this injustice to a prominent lawyer of Boston, he exclaimed, "A wife earns no money: she is supported by the husband. What does a wife want to will away a third of her husband's estate for? What does it matter to a *dead* woman what becomes of her thirds?" — "*Much*," I replied, — "just as much as a husband cares about willing away his *two* thirds. She is just as anxious about the welfare of her children, and would like to secure her thirds for their benefit." — "But she has no right to do that," he continued: "she has been *supported*. She has spent the money the husband has earned, wisely or unwisely, — most likely the latter in the majority of cases; for women don't know the value of money. I earn the money, and my wife spends it." — "Have you children, servants, and an establishment, sir?" I questioned. "Yes." — "Is there no labor in the oversight of all this, and no extra danger and suffering for the wife and mother, sick-nurse, and housekeeper, that you, the husband, father, and money-getter, escape? Would you exchange places with this '*supported*' woman?" His reply was, "The subject is interminable, madam, and my time presses."

This is a leonine partnership, where the wife dies first, in which the husband has all the profits, and she has none. Unless *he* desires it, nothing goes to her children as long as he lives. He can squander the property, or give or will it all away from them. They have no legal right to restrain him. This is absolutism. This is a king and subject. A wife and mother, with her hand upon the helm of the household, with its developing children and crude servants and the claims of society, is a general in the field, as regards care, responsibility, and danger; while the husband is a private in the ranks in comparison with her duties, with his profession and business hours, his trained clerks or posse of workmen, who are not "*givin' warnin'*" every other day in the seven.

One of the black points of law in this republic is that a married woman who owns no separate estate is legally a *pauper*. A pauper earns nothing; and at his death he has nothing to bequeath, because he has been supported. Their financial condition before the law is identical.

A husband can, in many of the States, by deed and other legal contrivances for the benefit of men and the financial depletion of women, make way with all the marriage property as effectively as though he were a bachelor, instead of a husband and father; for no law interferes with parental or paternal estates and authority. It is only in case of maternal rights that an overwhelming anxiety seizes upon legislators. They take precautions for the children against the mother, which are not considered necessary against the father. This is a cruel and invidious distinction; for the whole animal kingdom bears evidence that a mother is the more tender and self-sacrificing parent.

The wife should have entire control of her own person, joint authority with her husband over the children they nurture and over the property they accumulate. There is no reason why the wife should not have that legal interest both in the control and in the proceeds of the marriage partnership to which her unremitting toil entitles her. Even in those classes where the wife's burden is lighter, it is unwise to lessen her interest. Were the husband obliged to yield to the wife the confidence of a real partnership, there would be fewer cases of thoughtless extravagance on one side, and of selfish personal expenditure on the other. In no other business firm is a single partner given absolute control of the common property; and, considering also its additional bond of affection, that feature of the marriage partnership must be as unnecessary as it is unnatural.

Never will marriage rest upon a firm basis until both parties to the contract are equally independent. Independence will produce a superior type of wifehood and motherhood and womanhood, and divorce-suits will lessen in proportion.

"With most women the natural dependence of

minority is continued by want of suitable employ ment till marriage. Then the great majority of our married women become something more than self-supporting: they contribute their full share to the maintenance of a family, and to the accumulation of an estate. A few of the class which society has relieved of all domestic service, without substituting any worthy employment in its place, are justly chargeable with frivolity, extravagance, and incompetency. It is chiefly from observation of this class that conservative writers draw their hasty conclusion of woman's *natural* dependence: but the mass of our married women are of no such stamp; and, in general, the wife labors as hard as, and more continuously than, the husband. It is a notorious fact, that she is frequently broken down by hard labor; he, seldom. On what principle, then, is she deprived of full legal equality with her husband? The just rule of all free society recognizes independence as the reward of self-support; but no sooner has woman, by her services as wife, earned her freedom, than the law steps in, and rewards her with servitude. Then dependence has its unavoidable effect upon her. The natural capacities of the young wife, who is often the superior of her husband in intellect and culture, never develop. As responsibilities increase, his judgment strengthens, and his views widen. Her acquirements, on the other hand, wither from disuse, her judgment is weakened, and her views are narrowed by ceaseless attendance to a routine of petty detail, and by habits of reliance on the worldly wisdom of her spouse and on the spiritual wisdom of her pastor. She inconsiderately adopts and intensifies her husband's political and social hatreds; and, as the married life progresses, the legal inferiority grows into a real inferiority. In cases of peculiar hardship, the wife's temper dulls into that of a drudge, or sharpens into that of a scold: she submits servilely, or revolts noisily and unreasonably, after the manner of all subjects under all despotic rule. Thus, independence makes the man; dependence, the woman; and the result is charged upon Nature!

"The married woman of property has that property reserved from marital authority, but receives no further relief. The married woman who has no property remains bound, as of old, to labor for her husband for board wages. If the marriage venture is successful, she is secured no share in *his* earnings; but, if unsuccessful, she endures an equal share of *his* poverty; and, should he die, she will be confined in the poor-house, in some States (Connecticut for one), if she fails to support *his* children."

"But," cry the startled conservatives, "make marriage a copartnership, and that bars a husband from devising his estate." Ah, no! not his *half* of it. His will, the same as the will of his wife, will take effect at the re-marriage or death of the survivor. During this interim the executors could act as trustees in protecting the property from being squandered. If this law works well in Louisiana, why should it not work well in all the States? If it has not caused "ruin and disaster" there, why should it cause "ruin and disaster" here?"

As a stepping-stone to this grand result I offer the following petition: "That, until this law shall take effect, every widow may have the *legal* right to act as one of the executors of the husband's will, if she desires to do so, and is not barred by legal disqualifications." The law protects one-third or one-half of the property to her: now let it go a step farther, and protect her in having the careful supervision of that "third" or "half;" and let no woman have the shamefacedness to plead *ignorance* as a disqualification.

If women knew with what utter contempt men looked upon ignorance, in them, of the ordinary concerns of every-day life, they would study day and night until they mastered the more important details of what affects them so vitally. Said a man to me in Hartford, Conn., "Make women more responsible? No! The most of them are fools in business. My life is tormented out of me by questions of stupid women about matters that an ordinary child ten years old ought to comprehend at a glance."

"Lack of responsibility is just what is the matter," I replied. "That develops self-respect, self-poise, and self-reliance. It is one of the very best intellectual tonics. Men keep women in leading-strings, and then growl when they have to be led. O man, consistent man! how long will it be before the scales drop from your eyes?

To the Honorable Senate and House of Representatives of the Commonwealth of Massachusetts in General Court assembled.

The petition of the undersigned citizens of Massachusetts respectfully represents, That widows are in all common cases entitled to a proportionately large share of the property left by their deceased husbands, and, where strangers are appointed executors of their husbands' wills, often experience serious inconvenience from delay and expense in obtaining what the law gives them.

Therefore your petitioners pray, that, to remedy this grievous hardship, you will enact that every widow, who has any legal interest in the property of her deceased husband who has left a will, shall be an executor of said will, if she desires to accept an executorship, jointly with any executor or executors named therein who act as such, with the same powers and rights, and on the same terms, as are provided by said will, and the law for any other executor or executors named in the will.

This enactment shall not bar the judge of probate from appointing some person, when he deems it expedient, to serve with her in the settlement of an intestate estate, or when an executor named in the will declines to act in that capacity.

Wm. T. Bowditch.
Micah Dyer, Jun.
Thomas Russell.
G. A. Somerby.
Stillman B. Allen.
Chas. P. Curtis.
Stephen M. Allen.
Augustus Russ.
Samuel E. Sewell.
Nath. J. Bradlee.
A. A. Ranney.
Wm. A. Simmonds.
James Sturgis.
John W. Candler.
Otis Clapp.
Rufus S. Frost.
E. R. Mudge.
Charles Francis Adams.
Franklin Haven.
Chas. C. Barry.
Wm. Perkins.
Waldo Higginson.
Marshall P. Wilder.
Chas. G. Davis.
Fenno Tudor, widow.
L. Maria Child.
Sarah S. Russell.
Mary Mann.[1]
Sarah H. Mills.
Harriet M. Emerson.
Mary C. Ames.[2]
Jacob Edwards.
Isaac Fenno.
Geo. C. Richardson.
Chas. A. B. Shepard.
John A. Burnham.
D. R. Whitney.
R. Waldo Emerson.
Wm. Lloyd Garrison.
Rev. Minot J. Savage.
Rev. A. A. Miner.
Henry W. Longfellow.
Henry I. Bowditch, M.D.
S. Cabot, M.D.
James L. Little.
Rev. R. Laird Collier.
Amos A. Lawrence.
E. L. Barney.
Rev. James Freeman Clarke.

[1] Widow of Horace Mann.
[2] Widow of Isaac Ames, late Probate Judge of Suffolk County.

MEMORIAL

IN SUPPORT OF

A BILL FOR THE PROTECTION OF WIDOWS.

Mr. Chairman, and Honorable Gentlemen of the Probate and Chancery Committee.

As men of intelligence, you cannot be ignorant of the fact that the laws affecting the rights of widows are far from just; that the controlling power over the financial community of interest, existing between husband and wife, is vested solely in the husband; that in law there is no money value attached to a woman's services as wife; that, as widow, she has no control over the property which she has helped to earn, save what is delegated by husband or court.

This is a grievous hardship: therefore I pray that a widow, when not legally disqualified, may be one of the executors of the joint estate accumulated during coverture, whenever she desires to exercise the trust. This change involves no special departure from the present order of things: for every husband has the right to appoint his wife the executor of his will; and, if he dies without making a will, the Judge of Probate enjoys the same privilege. But in no case is the widow allowed an individual voice upon this important subject which affects her so vitally. She occupies the position of a child or an imbecile. Her lips are closed. She is set aside by a legal enactment that refuses to acknowledge that a woman who enters upon a career as wife — leaving, perhaps, a remunerative occupation — earns money in that capacity.

"The assumption, that women earn no money in wedlock, is extremely vicious; because it is based on the common-law theory of dependence. If property were largely hereditary in this country, as it is in England, it would be different; but it is not: therefore the simple right of the wife to her separate estate is far from just; for the accumulations of wedlock are still based upon the common law of dependence, instead of upon equity law, with its underlying principles of *independence*."

Marriage is often a business venture with men. It is not always love alone that lures them on to perpetrate the deed; and, when they claim that wives should be contented and satisfied with the love of their husbands, — taking that uncertain quantity in payment for services well and faithfully rendered as wife, mother, companion, sick-nurse, and housekeeper, — they do not understand the situation.

When I hire a man-servant or a maid-servant, I do not accept or reject their services on the strength of their affectional natures, but on their ability to labor. And a man, in seeking a helpmate, often exercises a like care. Said a gentleman to me who had travelled widely, seen much of society, and sown his "wild oats" broadcast, "When I marry, I shall look out for a fine woman, — I mean by that a fine animal, — the same as I would were I purchasing a thorough-bred dog, or horse, or bullock. I shall take good care that no impure blood is mingled with mine in the veins of my children. None of your tendrils for me, *if you please*. They are well enough under gaslight; but, if reverses should overtake me, I want a wife that can put her shoulder to the wheel without flinching."

This man spoke honestly and openly the real sentiments of a large number of marrying men. They do not admit it, perhaps, because they have not analyzed their feelings upon the subject. I am not complaining of this. It is right that both should contribute toward the material wealth of the household. But supposing, Mr. Chairman, that the wife performs no manual labor: what then? If there is no money value in the society and companionship of a wife, then the law is inconsistent; for it is upon this supposition that it allows the husband heavy "vindictive" damages in compensation for his wife's society, should a third party entice her away from him. Is it usual for single women of culture and refinement to serve as companions for simply their board and clothes? That is all a wife gets for her services, unless she is widowed. And then a wife-companion bears children at the risk of her life, and oftentimes at the ruin of her health. This duty, like love, is priceless. I know of a case where a bachelor offered a woman whom he admired twenty-five thousand dollars if she would bear him a child. But it was declined; not on account of losing caste, for she was a woman of the world, the same as he was a man of the world, — they stood on the same plane, — but because she would not risk her life and health, and endure the pain, for that sum of money.

It is not fashion and frivolity alone which create a distaste for child-bearing. Love of life and health, and a dread of physical suffering, is by far the greater obstacle. I believe that every true woman — I speak from experience — likes to wear the matchless crown of motherhood. She may not desire to have a large family of children; deeming it wiser to add to the world's population a less number, but of a superior quality, and thus develop a nobler type of manhood.

Some people claim that because this law, which puts all power in the hands of the husband, is more than a thousand years old, that it should not be changed; that it should be regarded with a sort of filial piety, and clung to like some rich acquisition which no one has a right to touch. To them antiquity is synonymous with wisdom, and every improvement is a dangerous innovation. If laws, like wine and men, improved with age, there might be some sense in clinging to them; but they do not. It is a degradation to be governed by laws which were made during the middle ages, — a period of ignorance, ferocity, and licentiousness; a period when injuries were unredressed, crime unpunished, and superstition unrebuked. There can be no stronger evidence against a law than its age and antiquity. Laws should keep step, by constant revision, with the march of the centuries. Woman's social and intellectual progress has outstripped her legal progress: therefore much that pertains to her best good is out of balance. The trinity must walk hand in hand, if the real welfare of mankind would be conserved.

The inconsistency of a law which gives with one hand and withholds with the other must be seen at a glance. It gives a widow the third of an estate, but allows a husband to appoint executors who have the absolute control of this third; and the daily records of the press of the country reveal how that trust is often betrayed by embezzlement and larceny, because the hands which carry off the plunder are law-hidden. This state of things corrupts society; for it is a tacit invitation to steal, especially when executors are appointed to serve without bonds, as they often are. There are thousands of thieves in high places who can trace their first downward step to the settlement of dead men's estates. In their initiation in wrong-doing they betrayed the confidence reposed in them, committed fraud upon the living, dishonored the memory of the dead, and paved the way for their own destruction.

You may claim, gentlemen, that, in case of malfeasance, a widow has legal redress. Ah, yes! she has in one sense; but litigation is an expensive luxury, and she has no money perhaps to prove that the executors are derelict in duty. It is an inside view which discloses the situation; and that is seldom accorded her. Not until lawyers, courts, and judges are omniscient, can they know what is being done for the best interest of an estate during the progress of its settlement. The actors alone are behind the scenes. The court is the audience. What I ask for the widow is, that she may be an actor instead of a spectator; for it is a stanch old maxim, that, if one would be well served, he must serve himself.

A widow with executor guardians over her property walks the earth with the ever-conscious weight of a dead hand upon her, which is stronger and more potent than her living will. If she offends the all-powerful executors, she may be kept upon the rack of suspense for weeks, months, and years, beyond the allotted time for the settlement of the estate. This is cruelty to animals, and should come under the statutory laws created for the protection of the *lower* order.

The law as it now stands protects the widow in her thirds. It is arbitrary on this point. Why not go one step farther, and give her the right to have the careful supervision of these thirds? The benefit resulting from such a law would be incalculable. You may say that few are qualified to perform the trust. True, undoubtedly, in some cases; but the right to exercise a dormant faculty develops that faculty. Responsibility is one of the greatest educators. Self-reliance and self-government are the spring and source of all real progress. If wives knew that this right could not be wrested from them, they would make themselves intelligent upon the subject. They would keep abreast with financial affairs, and shape their expenditures accordingly, thereby averting many a failure, and by their ready aid and counsel bridge over many a disastrous business chasm. The timely advice of a wife has saved many a man from ruin. What business firm would expect to prosper if the head partner refused to counsel with his co-laborer, but allowed him to spend all the money he could get, not knowing a thing about the strength of the bank-account or the success of the enterprise? Would such an establishment prosper? No! And, what is more, no one would expect it to prosper. It would be the laughing-stock of the community where it was located. And yet this is precisely the condition of the marriage firm to-day; and, when disaster overtakes it, the blame is too often attached to the innocent.

One gentleman when asked to sign the petition said, "If you secure the widow an executorship, why not do the same by the children and *other* heirs?" — "For this reason," I replied: "the widow-mother, in the most of cases, has richly earned her thirds, and therefore should not be kept on the same plane with her children. The child earns its father, on an average, far less than it costs him, from the time of its birth till it arrives at majority. Such is not the case with the wife. Most women marry at maturity, and spend the prime of their lives in the service of their husbands. They often work more hours a day than the hired servant; and, were that labor recompensed as the labor of women other than wives is recompensed, it would secure them a handsome support for their declining years. But the law offers a wife no such recompense; for whatever she earns in the service of the husband belongs to him absolutely. Is this just? Should not all persons be protected in their industry?

"Why a fortune built up by the joint effort of two persons should be held, in law, to belong exclusively to one of them, is beyond my powers of comprehension, unless the enactment is grounded solely on the survival of the strongest.

"Then, again, the widow is a legal heir to the estate, while the children are not, (what a law which allows a father by devisement to beggar his offspring!) and she should not be classed with other heirs who have contributed nothing towards the acquirement of the property. Her superior claim is but a just recognition of services rendered."

Many prominent lawyers have said to me, "We always advise men, who consult us upon the subject, to appoint their wives their executors, and also advise widows to serve as administrators." Men in the profession understand the value of the position.

So long as the law invites a husband to set aside his wife like an imbecile, so long will she be treated like a child, under the cover of "protection." It is a mistaken idea, that society will not prosper unless one half of its adult population is watched over and protected by the other half, at nearly every turn in life. Self-protection is pure gold, whilst restrictive protective law, as all history demonstrates, is pure dross.

What have I sought to prove? This much: That the law, as it now stands, is unjust; that it is unnatural; that it is inconsistent; that it fosters ignorance; that it invites to plunder; that it corrupts society; that it needs revision.

Do I expect this bill, for the protection of widows, to pass? Certainly I do; for between the extremes of conservatism and radicalism there is a class, by no means small, of the alert and the sagacious, who respond quickly and heartily to the progress of events. They accept what has been accomplished, turn their backs to the past, and are ready to go forward with the new tasks which are pressing upon them. They are the leaven that quickens the whole mass; and to this element, feeling secure with the radicals, I appeal. If they support the bill, its provisions must be adopted, and become a law of Massachusetts. A noble precedent! to be quickly followed by the other States in New England, and elsewhere throughout the Republic.

Very respectfully submitted to the generous consideration of this honorable committee by

MRS. J. W. STOW,
SAN FRANCISCO, CAL.

STATE HOUSE, BOSTON, Feb. 6, 1878.

The passage of the bill was most earnestly and ably urged by Senator Joseph S. Ropes, who took charge of it, Hon. Samuel E. Sewall, William Lloyd Garrison, and others; but it did not pass, for this reason: the great mass of the people have not thought upon the subject, and discussed its merits. Public sentiment must be aroused, ere legislators will act.

APPENDIX.

THE STOW BILL,

ENTITLED

"AN ACT FOR THE PROTECTION OF WIDOWS."

SECTION 1. When a man dies leaving a last will and testament wherein he has appointed executors to the exclusion of his widow, then, in all such cases, the surrogate of the county, wherein said will shall be probated, shall, on application of the widow of the deceased, grant and issue letters testamentary, to said widow, if she is legally competent and not otherwise objectionable, in the same manner as though she had been named in the will, she to be vested with the same powers and bound by the same obligations under said will as they are, and such widow shall have the sole guardianship of the persons of her minor children, she being in every respect qualified and approved by the proper court having jurisdiction.

SECTION 2. After the payment of all debts, and the proper charges against the estate, one-third of the *personal* property left by a deceased husband, shall, in all cases, belong to his widow absolutely.

PETITION IN SUPPORT OF THE BILL.

To the Honorable Senate and Assembly:

The petition of the undersigned citizens of the State of New York, respectfully represents: That a widow is entitled to a proportionately large share of the property left by her deceased husband, and that where men are appointed, to her exclusion, executors of his last will and testament, she often experiences serious inconveniences from delay and expense in obtaining what the law allows her. Therefore, your petitioners pray, that as a simple act of justice, you will enact that no last will and testament made by a deceased husband shall bar the right of his widow, when she is legally competent and not otherwise objectionable, from having an active voice in the settlement of the estate; that she, upon application to the surrogate of the county wherein the last will and testament of her deceased husband is probated, may have letters testamentary granted and issued to her, if she is legally competent and not otherwise objectionable, in the same manner as the executors named therein, and that in every respect she be vested with the same powers and bound by the same obligations as they are; and that such widow shall have the sole guardianship of the persons of her minor children, she being in every respect qualified and approved by the court having proper jurisdiction. And your petitioners further pray that after the payment of all debts and proper charges against the estate, one-third of all the *personal* property left by a deceased husband shall, in all cases, belong to his widow absolutely.

GEORGE WILLIAM CURTIS,
HENRY W. BELLOWS,
J. S. SHULTZ,
HENRY BERGH,
A. V. STOUT,
WM. A. HALL,
PETER COOPER,
O. B. FROTHINGHAM,
JAMES W. SIMONTON,
OSWALD OTTENDORFER,
B. F. TRACY,
A. A. REDFIELD,
T. W. HOLCOMB,
M. V. MCDANIEL,
A. P. VAN GIESEN,
S. L. CALDWELL,
J. BACKUS,
CYRUS MACY,
DANIEL W. GUERNSEY,
C. SWAN,
JAMES MAKIN,
JOHN F. SMYTH,
HENRY L. LAMB,
JAMES MCWADE,
A. VAN ALLEN,
H. R. PIERSON,
W. C. LITTLE,
DAVID A. THOMPSON,
THURLOW WEED BARNES,
JOHN E. BRADLEY,
A. B. PRATT,
S. J. BANCROFT,
W. S. PADDOCK,
V. P. HINMAN,
F. C. CALLICUT,
E. NEWCOMB,
DAVID A. THOMPSON,
MARTIN D. CONWAY,
JAMES A. MCKOWAN,
ANSON J. UPSON,
HENRY DARLING,
R. M. TOWNSEND,
ROBT. H. MCLELLAN,
HARVEY J. KING,
M. T. CLOUGH,
WILLIAM KEMP,
CHARLES I. BAKER,
C. L. ALDEN,
J. M. LANDON,
E. F. BULLARD,
R. A. PARMENTER,
H. W. DAY,
C. C. PARMELEE,
A. E. POWERS,
DANIEL D. BUCKLIN, M.D.,
H. B. NIMS & CO.,
GEO. C. BALDWIN,
W. E. KISSELBURGH,
THOMAS COLEMAN,
R. M. HASBROUCK,
CHARLOTTE FOWLER WELLS,
LAURA CARTER HOLLOWAY,
CLEMENCE S. LOZIER, M.D.,
E. B. WHITNEY,
JOSEPHINE SHAW LOWELL,
JULIA A. RAY,
HELEN W. WEBSTER, M.D.,
M. M. EASTMAN,
ANNIE C. HOWLAND, M.D.,
BETSY HART,
LEWIA C. SMITH,
HELEN MILLER,
LAURA G. SHEARMAN,
ELIZABETH CLIFTON,
MARIA M. WELCH,
AMMI CUTTER,
ELIZABETH L. LEWIS,
ZEBULON FERRIS,
JAMES FRAZE GLUCK,
W. R. CURTIS,
ALBERT JONES,
W. C. BRYANT,
JAMES B. & H. B. GREEN,
O. H. MARSHALL,
J. W. TYLER,
DAVID GREY,
THAD. C. DAVIS,
SHELDEN PEASE,
DAVID F. DAY,
A. G. RICE,
L. VAN BOKKELAN,
THEO. F. ROCHESTER, M.D.,
S. SCHEW,
WM. EDWARD FOSTER,
J. C. HARRISON,
GEO. W. TIFFT,
W. D. SHUART,
H. R. SELDEN,
W. MARTIN JONES,
J. SULLIVAN,
SETH H. TERRY,
D. L. CRITTENDEN,
CHAS. E. FITCH,
JAMES B. SHAW,
FRANCIS S. REW,
HARMON C. RIGGS,
WM. CORNING,
D. W. POWERS,
JAMES VICK,
M. B. ANDERSON,
HIRAM SIBLEY,
E. O. HAVEN,
NELSON MILLARD,
MOSES SUMNER,
CARROL E. SMITH,
H. RIEGEL,
CHAS. E. IDE,
W. P. GOODELLE,
GEO. N. KENNEDY,
JOHN L. KING.

THE WIDOW'S PORTION.

Chapter 470, Laws of New York.

An Act to amend section nine, title three, chapter six, part two of the Revised Statutes.

Passed May 18, 1874; three-fifths being present.

The people of the State of New York, represented in Senate and Assembly, do enact as follows:

Section 1. Section nine, title third, chapter six, part two of the Revised Statutes is hereby amended so as to read as follows:

§ 9. Where a man having a family shall die, leaving a widow or a minor child or children, the following articles shall not be deemed assets, but shall be included and stated in the inventory of the estate, without being appraised:

1. All spinning-wheels, weaving-looms, one knitting-machine, one sewing-machine, and stoves put up or kept for use by his family.

2. The family Bible, family pictures and school-books, used by or in the family of such deceased person, and books not exceeding in value fifty dollars, which were kept and used as part of the family library, before the decease of such person.

3. All sheep to the number of ten, with their fleeces, and the yarn and cloth manufactured from the same, one cow, two swine, and the pork of such swine, and necessary food for such swine, sheep or cow for sixty days, and all necessary provisions and fuel for such widow, or child, or children, for sixty days, after the death of such deceased person.

4. All necessary wearing apparel, beds, bedsteads and bedding, necessary cooking utensils, the clothing of the family, the clothes of the widow and her ornaments proper for her station; one table, six chairs, twelve knives and forks, six plates, twelve tea-cups and saucers, one sugar-dish, one milk-pot, one tea-pot and twelve spoons, and also other household furniture, which shall not exceed one hundred and fifty dollars in value.

Sec. 4. When a man having a family shall die, leaving a widow or minor child or children, there shall be inventoried by the appraisors and set apart for the use of such widow or for the use of such widow and child or children, or for the use of such child or children, in the manner now prescribed by the ninth Section of Title third, Chapter sixth of Part second of the Revised Statutes, necessary household provisions or other personal property in the discretion of said appraisors, to the value of not exceeding one hundred and fifty dollars, in addition to the articles of personal property now exempt from appraisal by said Section.—1842, Chap. 157, Sec. 2.

Section 1. Every father, whether of full age or a minor, of a child likely to be born, or of any living child under the age of twenty-one years and unmarried, may, by his deed or last will duly executed, dispose of the custody and tuition of such child during its minority, or for any less time, to any person or persons in possession or remainder.—(Sixth edition Revised Statutes, 1875, Vol. 3, page 167.)

Women in America

FROM COLONIAL TIMES TO THE 20TH CENTURY

An Arno Press Collection

Andrews, John B. and W. D. P. Bliss. **History of Women in Trade Unions** (*Report on Conditions of Woman and Child Wage-Earners in the United States,* Vol. X; 61st Congress, 2nd Session, Senate Document No. 645). 1911

Anthony, Susan B. **An Account of the Proceedings on the Trial of Susan B. Anthony, on the Charge of Illegal Voting at the Presidential Election in November, 1872,** and on the Trial of Beverly W. Jones, Edwin T. Marsh and William B. Hall, the Inspectors of Election by Whom her Vote was Received. 1874

The Autobiography of a Happy Woman. 1915

Ayer, Harriet Hubbard. **Harriet Hubbard Ayer's Book:** A Complete and Authentic Treatise on the Laws of Health and Beauty. 1902

Barrett, Kate Waller. **Some Practical Suggestions on the Conduct of a Rescue Home.** *Including* **Life of Dr. Kate Waller Barrett** (Reprinted from *Fifty Years' Work With Girls* by Otto Wilson). [1903]

Bates, Mrs. D. B. **Incidents on Land and Water;** Or, Four Years on the Pacific Coast. 1858

Blumenthal, Walter Hart. **Women Camp Followers of the American Revolution.** 1952

Boothe, Viva B., editor. **Women in the Modern World** (*The Annals of the American Academy of Political and Social Science,* Vol. CXLIII, May 1929). 1929

Bowne, Eliza Southgate. **A Girl's Life Eighty Years Ago:** Selections from the Letters of Eliza Southgate Bowne. 1888

Brooks, Geraldine. **Dames and Daughters of Colonial Days.** 1900

Carola Woerishoffer: Her Life and Work. 1912

Clement, J[esse], editor. **Noble Deeds of American Women;** With Biographical Sketches of Some of the More Prominent. 1851

Crow, Martha Foote. **The American Country Girl.** 1915

De Leon, T[homas] C. **Belles, Beaux and Brains of the 60's.** 1909

de Wolfe, Elsie (Lady Mendl). **After All.** 1935

Dix, Dorothy (Elizabeth Meriwether Gilmer). **How to Win and Hold a Husband.** 1939

Donovan, Frances R. **The Saleslady.** 1929

Donovan, Frances R. **The Schoolma'am.** 1938

Donovan, Frances R. **The Woman Who Waits.** 1920

Eagle, Mary Kavanaugh Oldham, editor. **The Congress of Women,** Held in the Woman's Building, World's Columbian Exposition, Chicago, U.S.A., 1893. 1894

Ellet, Elizabeth F. **The Eminent and Heroic Women of America.** 1873

Ellis, Anne. **The Life of an Ordinary Woman.** 1929

[Farrar, Eliza W. R.] **The Young Lady's Friend.** By a Lady. 1836

Filene, Catherine, editor. **Careers for Women.** 1920

Finley, Ruth E. **The Lady of Godey's:** Sarah Josepha Hale. 1931

Fragments of Autobiography. 1974

Frost, John. **Pioneer Mothers of the West;** Or, Daring and Heroic Deeds of American Women. 1869

[Gilman], Charlotte Perkins Stetson. **In This Our World.** 1899

Goldberg, Jacob A. and Rosamond W. Goldberg. **Girls on the City Streets:** A Study of 1400 Cases of Rape. 1935

Grace H. Dodge: Her Life and Work. 1974

Greenbie, Marjorie Barstow. **My Dear Lady:** The Story of Anna Ella Carroll, the "Great Unrecognized Member of Lincoln's Cabinet." 1940

Hourwich, Andria Taylor and Gladys L. Palmer, editors. **I Am a Woman Worker:** A Scrapbook of Autobiographies. 1936

Howe, M[ark] A. De Wolfe. **Memories of a Hostess:** A Chronicle of Friendships Drawn Chiefly from the Diaries of Mrs. James T. Fields. 1922

Irwin, Inez Haynes. **Angels and Amazons:** A Hundred Years of American Women. 1934

Laughlin, Clara E. **The Work-a-Day Girl:** A Study of Some Present-Day Conditions. 1913

Lewis, Dio. **Our Girls.** 1871

Liberating the Home. 1974

Livermore, Mary A. **The Story of My Life;** Or, The Sunshine and Shadow of Seventy Years . . . To Which is Added Six of Her Most Popular Lectures. 1899

Lives to Remember. 1974

Lobsenz, Johanna. **The Older Woman in Industry.** 1929

MacLean, Annie Marion. **Wage-Earning Women.** 1910

Meginness, John F. **Biography of Frances Slocum, the Lost Sister of Wyoming:** A Complete Narrative of her Captivity of Wanderings Among the Indians. 1891

Nathan, Maud. **Once Upon a Time and Today.** 1933

[Packard, Elizabeth Parsons Ware]. **Great Disclosure of Spiritual Wickedness!!** In High Places. With an Appeal to the Government to Protect the Inalienable Rights of Married Women. 1865

Parsons, Alice Beal. **Woman's Dilemma.** 1926

Parton, James, et al. **Eminent Women of the Age:** Being Narratives of the Lives and Deeds of the Most Prominent Women of the Present Generation. 1869

Paton, Lucy Allen. **Elizabeth Cary Agassiz:** A Biography. 1919

Rayne, M[artha] L[ouise]. **What Can a Woman Do;** Or, Her Position in the Business and Literary World. 1893

Richmond, Mary E. and Fred S. Hall. **A Study of Nine Hundred and Eighty-Five Widows Known to Certain Charity Organization Societies in 1910.** 1913

Ross, Ishbel. **Ladies of the Press:** The Story of Women in Journalism by an Insider. 1936

Sex and Equality. 1974

Snyder, Charles McCool. **Dr. Mary Walker:** The Little Lady in Pants. 1962

Stow, Mrs. J. W. **Probate Confiscation:** Unjust Laws Which Govern Woman. 1878

Sumner, Helen L. **History of Women in Industry in the United**

States (*Report on Conditions of Woman and Child Wage-Earners in the United States,* Vol. IX; 61st Congress, 2nd Session, Senate Document No. 645). 1910

[Vorse, Mary H.] **Autobiography of an Elderly Woman.** 1911

Washburn, Charles. **Come into My Parlor:** A Biography of the Aristocratic Everleigh Sisters of Chicago. 1936

Women of Lowell. 1974

Woolson, Abba Gould. **Dress-Reform:** A Series of Lectures Delivered in Boston on Dress as it Affects the Health of Women. 1874

Working Girls of Cincinnati. 1974